Politics, Social Change, and Economic Restructuring in Latin America

Politics, Social Change, and Economic Restructuring in Latin America

Edited by
William C. Smith and
Roberto Patricio Korzeniewicz

The mission of the North-South Center is to promote better relations and serve as a catalyst for change among the United States, Canada, and the nations of Latin America and the Caribbean by advancing knowledge and understanding of the major political, social, economic, and cultural issues affecting the nations and peoples of the Western Hemisphere.

Permission to reprint a revised version of the following article has been granted by Blackwell Publishers, Oxford, England:

Portes, Alejandro, and José Itzigsohn. 1994. "The Party or the Grassroots: A Comparative Analysis of Urban Political Participation in the Caribbean Basin." In *The International Journal of Urban and Regional Research* 18 (3), 491-508.

To order or to return books, contact Lynne Rienner Publishers, Inc., 1800 30th Street, Suite 314, Boulder, CO 80301-1026, 303-444-6684, fax 303-444-0824.

Library of Congress Cataloging-in-Publication Data
Politics, social change, and economic restructuring in Latin America / edited by William C. Smith and Roberto Patricio Korzeniewicz.
     p. cm.
Includes bibliographical references (p.) and index.
ISBN 1-57454-018-1 (alk. paper: pbk.)
     1. Structural adjustment (Economic policy)--Social aspects--Latin America. 2. Economic stabilization--Social aspects--Latin America. 3. Social change--Latin America. 4. Social movements--Latin America. 5. Political participation--Latin America. I. Smith, William C., 1946- . II. Korzeniewicz, Robert Patricio.
HC125.P658 1997   97-19640
338.98—dc21   CIP

Printed in the United States of America, EB/NC
02 01 00 99 98 97 9 8 7 6 5 4 3 2

Contents

Part III. Comparative Case Studies

Part IV. Social Change and the World Economy

Acknowledgments

Social, economic, and political practices and institutional arrangements in Latin America are undergoing a profound transformation. Orthodox stabilization and structural adjustment programs are dismantling the postwar system of state regulation of the economy at a vertiginous pace. Many academics and policymakers applaud these market-oriented reforms as paving the way for the emergence of a new, more dynamic model of development. In contrast, critics question not only if these market reforms are really compatible with democratic governance but also the capacity of neoliberalism to achieve sustained growth with minimally acceptable levels of social equity.

Searching for some clarity on these issues brought to mind *The Great Transformation*, Karl Polanyi's magisterial study on an earlier period of unfettered capitalism. In view of their magnitude and possible consequences, to what extent are changes underway in Latin America comparable to the momentous transformations that gave rise to the vision of self-regulating markets analyzed by Polanyi? If this analogy has any validity, could it be possible that the *endiosamiento* of the market will prove transitory, with the free markets of the 1990s eventually giving way to new social and political practices and institutional arrangements? What arrangements have the potential of being more responsive to the imperatives of democratic governance and more responsive to demands for the amelioration of the poverty and inequalities plaguing Latin America?

To explore these issues, we challenged a group of social scientists whose work we admire to think creatively about processes of social and political change under market-oriented restructuring. We met for two days of intense debate during a symposium held in April 1994 at the University of Maryland's College Park campus. The labor of subsequent revision, translations, and editing offered further opportunities to share ideas and cement friendships. We thank our colleagues for their patience in seeing their contributions to print.

On behalf of all the contributors to this volume, we wish to express our great appreciation to those who made this project possible. For the necessary financial support, we owe special thanks to the North-South Center, especially to Ambler H. Moss, Jr., Robin Rosenberg, and Jeff Stark. In later stages of the project, the involvement of the Center's editorial and publications staff, especially Jayne Weisblatt, Kathy Hamman, Mary Mapes, and Susan Kay Holler, was essential to the preparation of the manuscript for publication. We also gratefully acknowledge the support we received from

Saúl Sosnowski and the Latin American Studies Center and from the Department of Sociology at the University of Maryland at College Park. The collaboration of our graduate students was fundamental to the project's success. At the University of Miami's Graduate School of International Studies, Eric Bridoux, Mariela Córdoba, Julie Diehl, Vanessa Gray, María Eugenia Mujica, Holly Peirce, and Dori Powell labored long and hard to see this volume to publication. At the University of Maryland, invaluable help was provided by Darrin Helssel, Timothy Patrick Moran, Mitali Sen, and Eva Vilarrubi. To María de Lourdes, Nancy, Gabriela Lucía, Adrian, and Gabriel, we are grateful for their patience and unflagging support.

William C. Smith
Roberto Patricio Korzeniewicz
Coral Gables and College Park
February 25, 1997

Contributors

ALVARO DÍAZ is a sociologist and economist currently directing the Executive Secretariat of Science and Technology at the Chilean Ministry of Economy. He has written extensively on the restructuring of the Latin American working class and the relationships among economic and social transformation, entrepreneurial organization, and political identity. He is the author (with Javier Martínez) of *Chile: The Great Transformation* (1996).

DIANE E. DAVIS is Associate Professor of Sociology and Historical Studies at the Graduate Faculty of Political and Social Science at the New School for Social Research. She has published widely in academic journals and is the author of *Urban Leviathan: Mexico City in the Twentieth Century* (1994). She is the coeditor of *Political Power and Social Theory,* published at the Center for Studies of Social Change at the New School.

LILIANA R. GOLDÍN is Associate Professor of Anthropology at the State University of New York at Albany. She has published widely in such journals as *Human Organization, Journal of Quantitative Anthropology, Ethnology, Comparative Studies in Society and History,* and *Economic Development and Cultural Change.* Her current research on economic and cultural change in predominantly Mayan townships in Guatemala focuses on questions such as the strategies employed to cope with land scarcity.

JOSÉ ITZIGSOHN is Assistant Professor of Sociology at Brown University. He has recently published papers on remittances and development, grassroots political participation, and urbanization in the Caribbean in *Social Forces, International Journal of Urban and Regional Research,* and *Latin American Research Review.* His current research focuses on the rise of ethnic economies in the United States and the informal economy in Latin America.

ELIZABETH JELIN is a sociologist and senior researcher with CONICET and the Instituto de Investigaciones Sociales at the Universidad de Buenos Aires in Argentina. She is the author of dozens of articles and several books, including *¿Ante, de, en, y?: Mujeres, derechos humanos* (1993) and *Vida cotidiana y control institucional en la Argentina de los noventa* (1986). She has edited several volumes, including *Family, Household, and Gender Relations in Latin America* (1991), *Women and Social Change in Latin America* (1990), and (with Eric Hershberg) *Constructing Democracy: Human Rights, Citizenship, and Society in Latin America* (1996).

ROBERTO PATRICIO KORZENIEWICZ is Assistant Professor of Sociology at the University of Maryland in College Park. He is the editor (with William C. Smith) of *Latin America in the World-Economy* (1996). His articles on labor, commodity chains, and inequality have appeared in the *American Journal of Sociology, Sociological Forum, Review, Latin American Research Review, Hispanic American Historical Review, Revista Mexicana de Sociología, Desarrollo Económico, Bulletin of Latin American Studies*, and *Political Power and Social Theory*. He is currently completing a book on labor, gender, and political identity in Argentina.

ALEJANDRO PORTES is Professor of Sociology at Princeton University after many years as Chair of Sociology and John Dewey Professor of Sociology and International Relations at Johns Hopkins University. During 1997 he is Emilio Barcardí Professor of Cuban Studies at the University of Miami. He is the author of many books, including *Labor, Class, and the International System* (with John Walton, 1981), *Latin Journey: Cuban and Mexican Immigrants in the United States* (with Robert L. Bach, 1985), *Immigrant America: A Portrait* (with Rubén G. Rumbaut, 1990), *City on the Edge: The Transformation of Miami* (with Alex Stepick, 1993). He also is the editor of numerous volumes, including *The Informal Economy: Studies in Advanced and Less Developed Countries* (with Manuel Castells and Lauren A. Benton, 1989) and *Comparative National Development: Society and Economy in the New Global Order* (with A. Douglas Kincaid, 1995), *The Sociology of Immigration* (1995), and *The Second Generation* (1996).

IAN ROXBOROUGH is Professor of Sociology at the State University of New York at Stonybrook. He previously taught political sociology at the London School of Economics. He has published widely in academic journals in the United States, Europe, and Latin America and is the author of *Unions and Politics in Mexico: The Case of the Automobile Industry* (1984) and *Theories of Underdevelopment* (1979), and (with Philip O'Brien and Jackie Roddick) *Chile: State and Revolution* (1977) and editor (with Leslie Bethell) of *Latin America Between the Second World War and the Cold War, 1944-1948* (1992).

WILLIAM C. SMITH is Professor of Political Science at the Graduate School of International Studies of the University of Miami. He is the author of *Authoritarianism and the Crisis of the Argentine Political Economy* (1989) and is the editor of several volumes, including (with Carlos H. Acuña and Eduardo A. Gamarra) *Latin American Political Economy in the Age of Neoliberal Reform* (1994) and *Democracy, Markets, and Structural Reform in Latin America* (1994), *Security, Democracy, and Development in U.S.-Latin American Relations* (with Lars Schoultz and Augusto Varas, 1994), and (with Roberto Patricio Korzeniewicz) *Latin America in the World-Economy* (1996). His articles on Latin American political economy have appeared in the *Revista Mexicana de Sociología, Desarrollo Económico, Dados, Journal of Interamerican Studies and World Affairs, Studies in Comparative International Development*, and *Political Power and Social Theory*.

JUAN CARLOS TORRE is a political scientist and senior researcher at the Instituto Torcuato Di Tella in Buenos Aires, Argentina. He has published widely on working class politics and the politics of economic reform in such journals as *Desarrollo Económico, Journal of Democracy,* and *Problems d'Amerique Latine.* He is the author of several books, including *Los sindicatos en el gobierno. Argentina 1973-1976* (1983) and *La vieja guardia sindical y Perón: Sobre los orígenes del peronismo* (1990). He is the editor of *Desarrollo Económico* published by the Instituto de Desarrollo Económico y Social in Buenos Aires.

SERGIO ZERMEÑO is Professor of Sociology and senior researcher at the Instituto de Investigaciones Sociales at the Universidad Nacional Autónoma de México (UNAM) in Mexico City. He is the author of numerous articles and several books, including *México, una democracia utópica: El movimiento estudiantil del 68* (1978) and *Imperialismo y desarrollo capitalista tardio: Una crítica al concepto de dependencia* (1979), and is the editor (with Jesús Aurelio Cueva Díaz) of *Movimientos sociales en México durante la década de los 80* (1990).

Part I.

Theoretical and Historical Perspectives

Chapter 1

Latin America and the Second Great Transformation

William C. Smith and
Roberto Patricio Korzeniewicz

Introduction

S ocial, economic, and political practices and institutional arrangements in
Latin America are undergoing a profound transformation. Orthodox
stabilization and structural adjustment programs are dismantling the postwar
system of state regulation of the economy at a vertiginous pace.[1] Advocates
of neoliberal, market-oriented reform, dominating academic and policy
debates, argue that extending the reach of markets and shifting responsibility
for the allocation of resources away from state elites is essential to the creation
of a new framework for growth and development based upon enhanced
economic efficiency and greater international competitiveness (Edwards
1995). In pursuit of this goal, state enterprises are being privatized, markets
are being deregulated, and domestic and transnational firms and financial
institutions are acquiring greater power over processes of capital accumulation, developing new networks linking production and market niches within
global commodity chains.[2]

Simultaneously, the democratic transitions in the 1980s and early 1990s
are contributing to the emergence of a new and distinct, although still
inchoate, matrix of political dynamics and modes of organization (Smith,
Acuña, and Gamarra 1994a; Oxhorn and Ducatenzeiler forthcoming; Oxhorn
and Starr forthcoming). Various observers note that some of the most
influential forces of the past, such as trade unions or the military, are
experiencing a significant erosion of their power (Drake 1996, Acuña and
Smith 1995). Others call attention to emerging actors such as new urban and
rural social movements and non-governmental organizations (NGOs) that are
vibrantly raising their voices on behalf of the interests of subaltern classes long
excluded and marginalized from national politics (Escobar and Alvarez 1992,
Levine 1992, Castañeda 1993, Foweraker 1995, Chalmers et al. 1996, Jelin and
Hershberg 1996). Concomitantly, political parties and parliamentary institutions are struggling with only modest success to expand their roles in weakly

or informally institutionalized polyarchies (Mainwaring and Scully 1995, O'Donnell 1994a and 1996) characterized by the aggrandizement of executive power and the emergence of *sui generis* neopopulist leadership styles by elected presidents (Roberts 1995).

A great deal of theoretical and careful empirical research will be required before the full implications of the deep changes sketched here with such telegraphic brevity can be assessed with any degree of precision. Nevertheless, the changes already visible in Latin America are of sufficient magnitude, scope, and consequence to merit comparison with the "Great Transformation" described a little over 40 years ago by Karl Polanyi (1957). According to this influential analysis, the sweeping changes in the sociopolitical landscape of world capitalism in the nineteenth and early twentieth centuries generated a powerful and seductive vision of a self-regulated economy "directed by market prices and nothing but market prices" (Polanyi 1957, 43).[3] As Polanyi perceived, however, the wrenching social changes that undergirded this powerful vision also conjured into being social practices and anti-systemic movements that led to the eventual demise of the self-regulating market economy. New institutional arrangements and forms of state regulation and democratic class compromise — as embodied in the "Keynesian" formulas of core countries and the statist and populist strategies pursued in the Latin American semiperiphery — subsequently emerged to replace the self-regulating market.

With Polanyi's analysis in mind, future social scientists possibly may interpret the last years of the twentieth century in Latin America as another Great Transformation, one that may open developmental paths foreshadowing new, and as yet embryonic, modes of social and political regulation of the market economy. From the perspective of the *longue dureé*, therefore, the current celebration of the market and the "end of history" heralded by some academics and public and private sector policymakers may prove quite transitory, notwithstanding the fundamental significance of the market and the apparent hegemony of its politics, culture, and values in a moment of fundamental historical rupture.

Although heated debate will continue, academic scholarship on Latin America focusing on the political economy of democratic transitions (Haggard and Kaufman 1995), the main features of the "new economic model" in Latin America (Bulmer-Thomas 1996), and the status of democratic governance (Mainwaring, O'Donnell, and Valenzuela 1992; Domínguez and Lowenthal 1996; Linz and Stepan 1996; Agüero and Stark 1997) is now quite abundant. Much less theoretical and empirical work has been done on the political sociology of market-oriented economic restructuring. Hoping to address such issues, this volume seeks to shift the terms of the conversation somewhat by venturing some innovative perspectives regarding the rapid reconfiguration of Latin American civil society. A brief overview of the most salient recent trends in the Latin American macroeconomy dealing with inflation, growth, finance, employment, wages, poverty, and inequality will provide useful context for this discussion.

Recent Trends in Economy and Society

Opinions differ considering the extent to which orthodox stabilization and the projects of market-oriented restructuring associated with the so-called "Washington Consensus" (Williamson 1990a and b, 1994, and 1996; Bresser Pereira, Maravall, and Przeworski 1993; Smith, Acuña, and Gamarra 1994a; Edwards 1995; Stewart 1996) have provided a sound basis for future economic growth and development.[4] For example, optimists highlight the fact that orthodox stabilization programs have succeeded in taming the high inflation and, in some cases, hyperinflation that plagued the region in the 1980s. Table 1 chronicles the macroeconomic instability of the early 1990s, when annual inflation still raged at 888 percent in 1993 and 337 percent in 1994, before declining sharply to 26 percent in 1995 and about 20 percent in

Table 1.
Inflation Rates, 1980-1996
Variations in Consumer Price Indexes[a]

| | Annual Average Rate of Inflation | | Annual Variations | | | | | | |
	1980-1984	1985-1989	1990	1991	1992	1993	1994	1995	1996[b]
Argentina	222.8	444.4	1,343.9	84.0	17.5	7.4	3.9	1.6	0.4
Bolivia	195.6	268.8	18.0	14.5	10.5	9.3	8.5	12.6	9.7
Brazil	121.8	383.3	1,584.6	475.8	1,149.1	2,489.1	929.3	22.0	10.6
Chile	22.1	20.2	27.3	18.7	12.7	12.2	8.9	8.2	6.6
Colombia	22.8	24.0	32.4	26.8	25.1	22.6	22.6	19.5	21.9
Costa Rica	35.5	16.2	27.3	25.3	17.0	9.0	19.9	22.6	14.0
Ecuador	24.4	41.5	49.5	49.0	60.2	31.0	25.4	22.8	26.2
El Salvador	13.7	23.2	19.3	9.8	20.0	12.1	8.9	11.4	7.2
Guatemala	5.7	17.0	59.6	10.2	14.2	11.6	11.6	8.6	10.4
Honduras	9.8	4.9	36.4	21.4	6.5	13.0	28.9	26.8	26.0
Mexico	53.7	77.3	29.9	18.9	11.9	8.0	7.1	52.1	27.8
Nicaragua	30.1	1,674.4	13,490.2	775.4	3.5	19.5	12.5	11.1	9.2
Panama	5.7	0.4	0.8	1.1	1.6	0.9	1.4	0.8	1.0
Paraguay	15.3	25.5	44.1	11.8	17.8	20.4	18.3	10.5	8.8
Peru	82.7	371.8	7,649.6	139.2	56.7	39.5	15.4	10.2	11.9
Uruguay	43.3	70.8	129.0	81.3	59.0	52.9	44.1	35.4	25.5
Venezuela	13.0	30.6	36.5	31.0	31.9	45.9	70.8	56.6	109.2

Source: CEPAL 1996, Table A.3.

a = Excluding Cuba and the Dominican Republic and covering the year from December - December, unless otherwise indicated.

b = Statistics corresponding to the variation of prices within the last months ending in November 1996.

1996. Venezuela stands out, in this context, for its persistently high inflation, with prices in 1996 rising more than 100 percent. Still many countries, including, significantly, Brazil, held inflation to 10 percent or less in 1996, with prices rising less than 1 percent in Argentina.

Likewise, some optimistic analysts have interpreted the gradual convergence of the region's economies toward moderate rates of growth in the mid-1990s as a validation of the priority given to macroeconomic stabilization. In effect, economic growth in Latin America during the 1980s had averaged only a meager 1.1 percent a year. In the first half of the 1990s, the trajectory of economic expansion subsequently resumed at a moderate annual pace of 3.2 percent. Control over inflation and resumed moderate growth went hand-in-hand with greater discipline in managing public sector fiscal deficits and some movement toward equilibrium in external accounts.

Supporters of the new economic model point out that despite frequent problems associated with overvalued currencies and attendant difficulties in maintaining export competitiveness, growth was made possible in this context by dismantling the protectionist barriers associated with the previous phase of import-substitution, thereby allowing exports to become the principal stimulus to expansion (as the volume of exports grew at practically triple the rate of increase in GDP as a whole). Defenders of globalization also highlight the importance of greater access to international financing as a second factor responsible for the resumption of moderate growth. They point out that the net outflow of capital in the amount of nearly $200 billion in the 1980s began to reverse in 1991, leading in the first six years of the current decade to a net inflow of external capital of $104 billion. These capital flows primarily have gone to Argentina, Brazil, Chile, and Peru in an effort by foreign asset holders (including those Latin Americans responsible for massive capital flight in the 1980s) to reap the benefits of the privatization programs carried out by many governments. Foreign investment, together with rising medium- and long-term indebtedness, has modified the composition of capital flows and somewhat reduced the region's reliance on highly volatile speculative flows of short-term "hot money". These large capital flows ($50 billion in 1996) have been necessary to compensate for the region's current account deficit (approximately 2 percent of regional GDP at mid-decade) associated with rapid trade liberalization. Data on capital flows for individual countries are presented in Table 2.

Concomitantly, the region's total external debt increased from $220.4 billion in 1980, to $444 billion in 1990, to $607.2 billion in 1996. Still, as the defenders of the negotiations that led to the rescheduling of the region's external obligations will point out, service on this increased debt had declined steadily, equaling 14.5 percent of total regional exports in 1996, down significantly from a peak of nearly 35 percent in 1985.

Critics of these developments express greater reservations. For example, data compiled by the Economic Commission on Latin America and the Caribbean (ECLAC) reveal that despite resumed growth, per capita GDP has risen only 1.4 percent annually in the 1990s, meaning that average per capita incomes remain below the 1980 levels, before the explosion of the debt crisis.

Table 2.
Net Transfer of Resources of Selected Countries[a]
(Millions of dollars and percentages)

	Net Transfer of Resources						Ratio of the Export of Goods and Services					
	1991	1992	1993	1994	1995	1996[b]	1991	1992	1993	1994	1995	1996[b]
Latin America	3,460.0	26,640.0	31,362.0	8,367.0	18,452.0	12,030.0	2.2	15.7	17.1	3.9	7.2	4.2
Argentina	-1,573.0	6,258.0	8,953.0	7,458.0	-592.0	2,700.0	-10.9	42.5	57.3	40.3	-2.5	10.0
Bolivia	7.0	218.0	393.0	45.0	196.0	655.0	0.1	27.0	44.3	3.8	15.8	49.6
Brazil	-8,570.0	584.0	-1,633.0	-723.0	19,951.0	15,500.0	-24.5	1.5	-3.7	-1.5	37.9	28.2
Chile	-872.0	1,186.0	763.0	1,813.0	-850.0	1,885.0	-7.8	9.5	6.5	12.5	-4.4	10.1
Colombia	-2,676.0	-1,648.0	783.0	1,299.0	2,135.0	1,820.0	-29.4	-17.8	7.9	10.9	15.5	12.5
Costa Rica	341.0	355.0	335.0	191.0	203.0	-120.0	15.6	13.8	11.5	5.8	5.2	-3.0
Ecuador	-515.0	-897.0	-74.0	-81.0	-602.0	-1,695.0	-15.1	-24.7	-2.0	-1.8	-11.5	-29.7
El Salvador	22.0	191.0	118.0	36.0	252.0	160.0	2.5	19.5	10.5	2.3	11.4	6.9
Guatemala	638.0	507.0	685.0	500.0	257.0	370.0	37.8	26.9	33.7	22.0	9.1	12.5
Honduras	79.0	162.0	-47.0	90.0	-3.0	80.0	7.8	15.5	-4.4	7.6	-0.2	4.9
Mexico	14,777.0	16,406.0	18,427.0	-1,808.0	-1,271.0	-11,410.0	28.7	29.6	30.0	-2.5	-1.4	-10.7
Nicaragua	-249.0	340.0	136.0	344.0	351.0	445.0	-73.6	109.6	37.0	76.0	54.2	57.8
Paraguay	617.0	225.0	566.0	1,070.0	1,114.0	430.0	30.5	11.8	20.2	31.3	25.5	10.5
Peru	905.0	1,146.0	1,386.0	3,877.0	3,339.0	3,930.0	21.2	25.3	31.3	67.8	49.0	53.1
Uruguay	-162.0	7.0	230.0	439.0	348.0	540.0	-7.4	0.3	8.3	13.5	10.6	15.4
Venezuela	311.0	1,158.0	134.0	-5,610.0	-5,907.0	-2,890.0	1.9	7.5	0.8	-31.7	-29.0	-11.9

Source: CEPAL 1996, Table A.15.

a = The net transfer of resources is equivalent to the net increase of capital (not including freestanding capital), less the wages contained in "Rent" (net payment of utilities and interests). The negative quantities indicate a resource transfer from the exterior.

b = Preliminary estimates.

This general pattern of moderate growth should not obscure the considerable diversity portrayed in Table 3. At one end of the spectrum, Chile has continued to be characterized by extremely high rates of economic growth, and a similar, if less dynamic, pattern has characterized Colombia. At the other end of the spectrum, a considerably slower pace of economic growth has characterized cases such as Brazil, Mexico, and Bolivia. The most striking pattern of change has characterized countries such as Argentina and Peru, where the profound instability of the 1980s was followed by a spurt of extremely rapid growth. However, Argentina and Mexico, together with Venezuela, serve as cautionary tales. The Mexican financial debacle in 1994

Table 3.
Evolution of Gross Domestic Product, 1990-1996
(Percentages based on values at 1990 prices)

		Annual Rates of Variation						Cum. Var.		Per Capita Cum. Var.	
	1990	1991	1992	1993	1994	1995	1996	1981-1990	1991-1996	1981-1990	1991-1996
Latin America	-0.3	3.4	2.7	3.8	5.3	0.3	3.4	1.1	3.2	-0.9	1.4
Oil-exporting Countries											
Bolivia	4.6	5.3	1.6	4.2	4.8	3.7	4.0	0.2	4.0	-1.9	1.5
Colombia	3.8	1.6	4.0	5.1	6.3	5.7	3.5	3.7	4.4	1.6	2.4
Ecuador	0.3	5.3	3.7	2.5	4.7	2.7	2.0	1.4	3.4	-1.1	1.2
Mexico	5.2	4.3	3.7	1.9	4.6	-6.6	4.5	1.9	2.0	-0.2	0.2
Peru	-5.4	2.8	-0.9	5.8	13.9	7.7	2.0	-1.2	5.1	-3.3	3.3
Venezuela	7.0	9.7	6.1	0.7	-25.0	2.3	-1.5	-0.7	2.4	-3.2	0.1
Non-oil-exporting Countries											
Argentina	-0.1	9.5	8.4	5.3	6.7	-4.6	3.5	-0.3	4.7	-1.8	3.3
Brazil	-4.7	0.1	-1.1	4.4	5.7	3.9	3.0	1.3	2.7	-0.7	1.2
Chile	3.3	7.1	10.5	6.0	4.1	8.2	6.5	3.0	7.0	1.3	5.3
Paraguay	3.0	2.4	1.6	4.1	2.9	4.5	2.0	3.0	2.9	0.0	0.2
Uruguay	0.6	3.2	7.8	3.3	6.9	-2.8	5.0	0.0	3.8	-0.6	3.2
Central American Common Market											
Costa Rica	3.5	2.1	7.3	6.0	4.4	2.3	0.5	2.2	3.7	0.6	1.3
El Salvador	4.8	3.6	7.5	7.4	6.0	6.1	3.5	-0.4	5.6	-1.4	3.2
Guatemala	3.0	3.7	4.9	4.0	0.1	5.0	3.0	0.9	4.1	-2.0	1.2
Honduras	-0.8	2.0	6.3	7.0	-1.3	3.2	3.5	2.4	3.4	-0.8	0.4
Nicaragua	0.0	-0.3	0.9	-0.4	4.0	0.7	5.5	-1.5	2.4	-0.8	0.4
Non-Central American Common Market											
Panama	8.0	8.1	7.5	3.8	3.8	1.9	2.0	1.6	4.5	-0.5	2.6

Source: CEPAL 1996, Table A.1.

and 1995, the collateral recessionary effects of the *tequilazo* in Argentina, and Venezuela's erratic performance all demonstrate the region's continuing vulnerability to the vagaries of international financial flows mentioned above. These events also underscore the possibility that major crises may still occur. Latin America clearly continues to be vulnerable to the risk of a rise in interest rates and a future tightening in international liquidity.

Opinions are also likely to vary as to the social consequences of economic restructuring. Supporters of market-oriented reforms often point to the example of Chile. As indicated in this volume in the chapters by Alzaro Díaz (see also Martínez and Díaz 1996) and Roberto Patricio Korzeniewicz, Chile over the last decade has experienced uninterrupted economic growth (at an average annual rate of over 6 percent), and since 1982-1983, economic restructuring has been accompanied by rising wages and a reduction of unemployment and poverty levels. Thus, in the early 1980s, urban unemployment rates in Chile hovered around 20 percent. Subsequently, high rates of economic growth over the late 1980s and early 1990s were accompanied by a substantial reduction in rates of urban unemployment, to less than 5 percent by 1993. In addition, the workforce as a whole has begun to grow more rapidly in Chile as women and youth are incorporated into the labor market. Accompanying the drop in unemployment, real wages have increased steadily since 1987.

A more critical evaluation points out that the Chilean model is difficult to replicate elsewhere in the region. Argentina has shown among the fastest rates of economic growth in recent years, but rather than declining, urban unemployment has reached the highest levels since the 1930s, and the only sources of employment that have shown some growth are in non-wage jobs and the service sector. The recovery of urban employment also has been slow in Brazil, Ecuador, Mexico, Panama, Paraguay, Peru, and Uruguay. In fact, CEPAL (1996) indicates in its recent preliminary balance that urban unemployment rates in 1996 were the highest in the decade, as shown in Table 4.

Reflecting similar cyclical and structural dynamics, most countries in the region also have experienced falling real wages, as depicted in Table 5 on page 9. For Latin America as a whole, the late 1980s and early 1990s were characterized by "a widening wage differential between white-collar and blue-collar workers, which has exacerbated the feeling that the recovery has hardly improved the welfare of those at the lower end of the wage scale" (IDB 1992, 19). Generalizing about regional trends, several recent studies of labor force participation indicate that employment has become increasingly precarious and less subject to regulation by state agencies or organized labor (Tardanico and Menjivar Larín 1997). With the exception of Chile, where labor market reforms and rapid economic growth have led to substantial increases in the relative importance of formal employment, most other Latin American countries have been characterized by greater informality in employment and a deterioration in the relative bargaining power of workers in formal activities.

Concomitant with these general trends of rising unemployment and falling wages, available data and studies, such as those reviewed in this

Table 4.
Urban Unemployment: 1980-1996
(Average Annual Rates)

	1980	1985	1990	1991	1992	1993	1994	1995	1996[a]
Regional Average	6.2	7.3	5.8	5.8	6.3	6.3	6.4	7.3	7.7
Argentina (Urban total)	2.6	6.1	7.5	6.5	7.0	9.6	11.5	17.5	17.2
Bolivia (Department capitals)	—	5.8	7.3	5.8	5.4	5.8	3.1	3.6	3.5
Brazil (Six Metropolitan areas)	6.3	5.3	4.3	4.8	5.8	5.0	5.1	4.6	5.7[b]
Chile[c] (Metropolitan region)	11.7	17.2	6.5	9.3	7.0	6.2	8.3	7.4	7.2[d]
Colombia[e] (Seven Metropolitan areas)	10.0	13.9	10.5	10.2	10.2	8.6	8.9	8.9	11.4[f]
Costa Rica (Urban total)	6.0	6.7	5.4	6.0	4.3	4.0	4.3	5.7	—
Ecuador[e] (Urban total)	5.7	10.4	6.1	8.5	8.9	8.9	7.8	7.7	—
El Salvador (Urban total)	—	—	10.0	7.9	8.2	8.1	7.0	7.0	7.5[g]
Guatemala (National total)	2.2	12.1	6.5	6.4	5.7	5.5	5.2	4.3	—
Honduras (Urban total)	8.8	11.7	7.8	7.4	6.0	7.1	4.0	6.0	6.3
Mexico (Urban total)	4.5	4.4	2.7	2.7	2.8	3.4	3.7	6.3	5.7[b]
Nicaragua (National total)	—	3.2	11.1	14.2	17.8	21.8	20.7	18.2	16.1
Panama[e] (Metropolitan region)	9.9	15.6	20.0	19.3	17.5	15.6	16.0	16.2	16.4
Paraguay[h] (Metropolitan Asunción)	4.1	5.2	6.6	5.1	5.3	5.1	4.4	5.3	—
Peru[i] (Metropolitan Lima)	7.1	10.1	8.3	5.9	9.4	9.9	8.8	8.8	8.7
Uruguay (Montevideo)	7.4	13.1	9.2	8.9	9.0	8.4	9.2	10.8	12.6[d]
Venezuela (Urban total)	6.6	14.3	11.0	10.1	8.1	6.8	8.9	10.9	11.9[g]

Source: CEPAL 1996, Table A.4.

a = Preliminary figures.

b = Corresponds to January - October.

c = From 1991, the data correspond to a new sample.

d = Corresponds to January - September.

e = Includes hidden unemployment.

f = Corresponds to the March, June, and October averages.

g = Corresponds to the first semester.

h = From 1994, the figures correspond to the entire metropolitan area.

i = The data from 1995 and 1996 come from a new survey and refer to the first semester of each year.

Table 5.
Average Real Wages, 1980-1996, for Selected Countries

	1980	1985	1990	1991	1992	1993	1994	1995	1996[a]
	Average Annual Indexes (1990=100)								
Argentina[b]	130.0	135.7	100.0	101.3	102.7	101.3	102.0	100.9	100.8
Bolivia[c]	—	64.9	100.0	93.4	97.1	103.6	111.8	113.5	113.5
Brazil[d]									
Rio de Janeiro	94.0	98.2	100.0	79.3	79.5	85.7	87.1	91.8	105.7
São Paulo	88.6	93.8	100.0	88.3	85.0	94.6	98.0	102.0	108.4
Chile[e]	95.4	89.3	100.0	104.9	109.6	113.5	118.8	123.6	128.9
Colombia[f]	85.0	97.4	100.0	97.4	98.6	103.2	104.1	105.5	107.7
Costa Rica[g]	115.8	106.8	100.0	95.4	99.3	109.5	113.6	111.4	—
Mexico[h]	128.3	97.4	100.0	106.5	114.3	124.5	129.1	111.5	98.8
Peru[i]	309.3	250.2	100.0	115.2	111.1	110.2	127.4	116.7	112.6
Uruguay[j]	108.5	95.5	100.0	103.8	106.1	111.2	112.2	109.0	109.8

Source: CEPAL 1996, Table A.5.

a = Preliminary data.

b = Manufacturing industry. 1996: January - September average.

c = Private sector in La Paz. 1996: Averages from March, June, and September.

d = Workers protected by social and labor legislation. 1996: January - October averages.

e = Until April 1993, non-agricultural salaried. Since May 1993, index of wages. 1996: January - October averages. Until April 1993, non-agricultural salaried. Since May 1993, index of general average hourly wages. 1996: January - October averages.

f = Workers in manufacturing industry. 1996: January - August averages.

g = Average declared wages for workers enrolled in social security system.

h = Manufacturing industry. 1996: January - September averages.

i = Private-sector workers in metropolitan Lima. 1996: March - June averages.

j = Average non-agricultural wages. 1996: January - September averages.

volume by Korzeniewicz, indicate that the incidence of poverty grew throughout the region in the 1980s. For example, between 1980 and 1985, the incidence of poverty among households in Latin America increased from 33 percent to 39 percent (Bonilla 1990, 215). In Argentina and Chile, according to CEPAL (1992, 6), there was a doubling of the population lacking sufficient income to meet basic needs. Furthermore, the available evidence suggests a rapid increase in the incidence of poverty during recessionary periods but a slow reduction of poverty during periods of economic growth (CEPAL 1992, 5; Altimir 1994 and 1996). Yet, despite the recovery of the 1990s, poverty has remained alarmingly high. As the Inter-American Development Bank notes,

> ...there is evidence that the living conditions of a vast segment of the population have worsened, and every day more people are finding it increasingly difficult to meet their basic needs. Although the problem of poverty is not new to the region, stemming as it does from structural rather than cyclical causes, its persistence and spread are having an adverse effect on sustainable economic growth and the stability of democracy (IDB 1993, 16).[5]

Even more than poverty, general trends of income inequality are difficult to identify, as the available data are limited to a few years, and the interpretation of these data is problematic (see, for example, the relevant discussions in the chapters by Torre and Korzeniewicz). As suggested by Carlos Acuña and William C. Smith (1994, 24), "How should one analyze statements affirming the 'regressive redistribution of income,' when in some cases this signified a decline in the relative income of the popular sectors combined with an increase in their absolute income levels (as in Brazil), while in others it meant both relative and absolute declines in the incomes of workers and the popular sectors (as in Argentina)?"

Despite the limitations in available information, it is clear that economic restructuring and structural adjustment programs have had a profound impact on existing social arrangements. The following section discusses the character of these changes in practices and institutional arrangements.

Comparing Great Transformations

The extent of current changes in the organization of commodity chains evokes what Polanyi labelled the great transformation experienced by the world economy in the nineteenth century. Now as then, the widespread introduction of *laissez-faire* policies has served to promote new levels of integration of production networks on a global scale. Careful observers of Latin America in the late nineteenth century would find a similarly intense process of globalization. Then, as today, working people in the region found themselves in the midst of dramatically new circumstances, as the forces shaping local wages and employment levels were altered by unprecedented global flows of people and capital.

For many, the global transformation of commodity chains has entailed new opportunities. This is illustrated in Chapter 6 of this volume by social anthropologist Liliana Goldin, who highlights the opportunities generated in Latin America's rural sector by the implementation of adjustment policies. Her microanalysis of a small Maya Indian community in the western highlands of Guatemala points out that even under general conditions of malnutrition, environmental degradation, and rural unrest with high levels of political repression, peasants have not lost agency, and even with limited resources, some have been able to take advantage of the market opportunities created by market-oriented reform. Emphasizing that the interaction of local and global changes has led to growing rural differentiation, Goldin also provides important insights to some of the accompanying cultural transformations undergone by the peasantry.

What becomes readily apparent as well is that the transition entails the erosion of agency in other areas. Thus, in Chapter 7 of this volume, sociologist Sergio Zermeño examines Mexican politics, asking where have the social movements gone. Departing from an analysis of several possible future scenarios, Zermeño depicts contemporary Mexico in terms of the radical dismantling of the collective actors of civil society that were forged through the urbanization and industrialization of the country in the postwar era.

Zermeño criticizes the obliteration of identities, spaces of communicative interaction, and the shrinkage of the public sphere. He argues that this process creates not only atomized individualistic consumers, but simultaneously undermines cultural traditions and promotes the massification of poverty, thereby creating the conditions for a resurgence of personalized leadership.

Zermeño argues that "many Mexicos" are emerging from economic crisis, demographic transformations, and globalization. These many Mexicos range from the modernity of the North American Free Trade Agreement (NAFTA), to the indigenous uprising in Chiapas, to the El Barzon movement that has gained notoriety in the wake of the recent financial meltdown. On a pessimistic note, Zermeño concludes that although weakened intermediate actors and the lack of a secure social order are the result of Mexico's longstanding vicious cycles of a strong state and a weak civil society, they are now assuming new and more perverse forms.

In Chapter 3, sociologist and economist Alvaro Díaz tackles the double-edged thrust of contemporary reforms. On the one hand, restructuring exhibits a destructive face, as reflected in processes of social disarticulation, erosion of traditional forms of identity, anomie, and a declining capacity for collective action on the part of affected groups and classes. On the other hand, Díaz indicates that there also exists a less visible process of social (re)articulation constituting new collective actors, ranging from new entrepreneurs and economic conglomerates to new forms of labor, novel forms of social organization, and new sectors representing a middle class.

The contrasts between the diagnoses put forth by Zermeño and Díaz are discussed by sociologist Juan Carlos Torre in Chapter 2. Torre points out that present discrepancies in the analyses of the consequences of market reforms might reflect the particular vantage points of Zermeño and Díaz. Thus, "Zermeño writes from the perspective of a country still in the throes of the difficult and traumatic adjustment to market reforms," while "Díaz, in contrast, writes from the perspective of a country in which the process of social and economic transformation began at an earlier date and has been carried out more thoroughly." As a process of transition, with considerable diversity in both the pace of reforms and the resiliency of institutional legacies, the precise contours of future arrangements might be hard to establish by "historians of the present."

Historians of the past, however, might notice that similar transformations were experienced by social movements throughout the region in the late nineteenth century. Then, new patterns of accumulation went hand-in-hand with the gradual emergence of labor movements that were to become (in the twentieth century) key national political actors. The emergence of such a political actor was accompanied by the displacement of other political and social forces. For example, local manufacturers and craft workers experienced the intense competition of factory-made products (sometimes imported from industrial nations, but often produced in the growing urban areas of Latin America itself). Toward the end of the nineteenth century, while the urban labor movement faced the promise of future growth and considerable empowerment, workers and independent producers in much of the country-side faced the uncertainty that characterizes unemployment induced by technological innovation.

Clearly, new and old social movements face new patterns of political rule. The restructuring of the economy, together with the political transition toward more competitive and participatory politics, is sometimes interpreted erroneously as signifying an across-the-board retreat of state power. However, a smaller state can be weaker (control fewer resources, lose entrepreneurial functions, and so on) but simultaneously stronger, more autonomous, more coherent, and more effective in regulating macroeconomic and microeconomic behaviors (see Huber 1995). From this perspective, as in the nineteenth century, the hegemony of liberal strategies does not necessarily imply a weaker state. True, some forms of state regulation have appeared to wither away. The collision between mobile capital and the globalization of production, on the one hand, and national and local actors in Latin America, on the other, appears to have resulted in a sharp erosion of the capacity of national states to manage major macroeconomic variables (Mahon 1996, Keohane and Milner 1996). A more nuanced understanding of the recasting of political power, however, calls attention to new patterns in the relation between political rule and accumulation. From this point of view, the boundaries of political rule and regulation become redefined, as traditional political institutions at the national level increasingly negotiate and coordinate their operations with new agencies of political regulation functioning at a supranational level.

Again, it is useful to compare these transformations to those taking place in the region during the late nineteenth century. Then, new forms of political regulation were emerging at the level of the national state, but these state apparatuses appeared as rather incipient in both the magnitude of their effective operation and the actual extent of their reach. In many instances, even the relative monopoly of national armies over the means of violence was still under challenge, and political rule often depended on the maintenance of fragile agreements between national leaders and regional elites. Furthermore, for much of the population living in rural areas (the majority of the population in most Latin American countries at the turn of the century), the authority of local leaders was of much greater consequence than the diffused rule of the national state. During this period of transition, then, established forms of political rule (such as those enforced by local leaders and caudillos) co-existed uneasily with the new forms of political rule developing at the level of the national state.

These new political arrangements often appear primarily to reflect initiatives imposed from above. From this point of view, although neo-utilitarian prescriptions call for rolling back the state and weakening governmental mechanisms of macroeconomic regulation (Bierstekker 1990 and 1995, Evans 1995), growing globalization and international competition have compelled state elites to augment their power capabilities to impose a market-driven model of accumulation. Market-friendly growth strategies premised on greater economic orthodoxy are likely to require not less but greater concentration of administrative power and more autonomy, particularly from specific entrepreneurial and trade union interests. Similarly, greater ortho-doxy may imply not less but more effective coordination and regulation of the private sector (such as overseeing of the stock and financial markets, broadening the tax base, upgrading the skills of workers, promoting competi-tiveness and technological innovation, correcting market failures in environ-mental protection, and so on). The performance imperatives of contested markets (especially labor and financial markets) thus give rise to *sui generis* combinations of intra-firm coordination through hierarchy and innovations in the ways state agencies administer third-party enforcement of effective regulations and legal norms guaranteeing private property (Bowles and Gintis 1993, Acuña and Smith 1994, Bradford 1994, Díaz 1996, Berensztein 1996).

Markets, in this sense, continue to require extensive regulation for their very survival. Consequently, while obeying their own separate dynamics, the logic of accumulation and the logic of rule remain deeply and inextricably intertwined. Seen from this perspective, the recasting of relations between the state and the market is a manifestation of a fundamental redrawing of the existing boundaries between politics and economics and between the public and the private.

But today's uneasy alliances between national rulers and supranational agencies of regulation are actually whipsawed between the growing hege-mony of markets, as reinforced by the exigencies of the world economy, and the intensification of pressures for redistribution and the alleviation of poverty brought not only by new possibilities for popular participation but also by the expansion of citizenship rights in the context of competitive politics and the logic of procedural democracy. While supranational agencies such as the World Bank often have been perceived as operating to impose policies geared to promote efficiency and capital accumulation, such organizations are also searching for policy strategies that can ensure the success of economic restructuring by establishing minimum standards of social welfare. In search-ing for these strategies, these supranational agencies often have developed a close relationship with non-governmental organizations in peripheral and semiperipheral countries (in fact, many NGOs often have developed a closer working relationship with such supranational agencies than with national political authorities).

Here again, there are interesting parallels with the transformations of the nineteenth century. While 19th-century labor movements often found their identity in opposition to existing political arrangements, the practice of negotiation often led trade unions and their leaders to enter into close cooperation with political authorities. This meant that political arrangements and property rights throughout the region often were designed directly to reflect the influence of such negotiations. More importantly, however, a considerable measure of the very political legitimacy of the national state developed precisely in relation to the existence of labor as an (actual or potential) political force.

In this regard, sociologist Ian Roxborough uses Chapter 4 in this volume to identify several paradoxical consequences of neoliberal reforms. Going somewhat against the grain of most critics of structural adjustment, Roxborough notes that even in cases of rigorous application of market-driven policies, there are trends toward the strengthening of certain forms of political organization in civil society, as well as toward an increasingly tight integration of parts of civil society and the state, even while the state is under pressure to curtail its role in the economy. In fact, according to Roxborough, active social movements might not be a necessary component of a thriving democracy, for "it might well be that a high-quality democracy has a fairly low level of political mobilization. Politics in a high-quality democracy may, sometimes, be quite institutionalized and a little dull."

From a different perspective, Argentine sociologist Elizabeth Jelin, in Chapter 5, observes that the return to democracy in the 1980s implied a reinvigoration of political parties and a renewed commitment to institution-building, a trend that emphasized the construction of institutions within the political system, guided by the logic of governability. However, this effort often clashes with the less institutionalized collective means of expressing old and new social demands and even with the more participatory pressures in the process of democratization. While neoliberalism and the logic of the market are seen by some as implying greater individualism and "growing apathy and the loosening of social ties," Jelin points out that in today's market economies, "in fact, the logic of social interests is even more visible, more transparent than in the past." Based upon this point of departure, Jelin examines the conditions that facilitate or constrain social movements and the formation of new collective identities in the context of the limits placed by "democratization-with-adjustment" and the contradictory pressures of global-ization and localization. Jelin concludes with provocative speculations about the medium-term future of social movements, highlighting the dual role of social actors as collective systems of reciprocal recognition with important cultural and symbolic components, while also serving as non-party political intermediaries linking the demands of unarticulated voices to the public sphere and to state institutions.

The character of new political arrangements invites the attention of the last two chapters in this volume's third section. In Chapter 8, sociologist Diane Davis argues that scant attention has been paid to political parties in the current transition, except to hold them responsible for macroeconomic populism and the economic bottlenecks and political crises that spur the support of social movements for democracy and markets in the first place. This is a mistake, in her view, because parties, by mediating between the state and civil society in the context of economic restructuring, are key actors in the politics of the popular sectors in emerging democracies. Davis conducts a detailed comparative analysis of the interaction of social movements with two very different types of political parties — the Mexican Institutional Revolution-ary Party (Partido Revolucionario Institucional - PRI) and the Brazilian Workers Party (Partido dos Trabalhadores - PT) — in order to critique the common assumption that parties and social movements have contradictory objectives, or that party dynamics work to fragment or undermine social movements, thus impeding democratization.

Chapter 9 of this volume, by sociologists Alejandro Portes and José Itzigsohn, provides a rich empirical analysis focusing on five capital cities in the Caribbean Basin in order to examine the patterns of political participation and attitudes toward different forms of participation of urban low-income groups. They examine the extent of actual community grassroots participation as well as attitudes toward participation through social movements or through traditional political parties. Portes and Itzigsohn highlight the significance of variations in political systems and state policies in promoting or deactivating popular mobilization. Their principal contribution is to identify both individual-level and national-level variables embedded in the political system as determinants of differences in participation and sympathy for community-based organizations.

Conclusion

Whether or not these *laissez-faire* projects ultimately succeed, the current transformation of institutional arrangements in Latin America will have enduring consequences. As a moment of transition, the precise character of these new institutional arrangements is difficult to ascertain. As indicated by political scientist Juan Carlos Torre in Chapter 2, one must be mindful of the difficulties of the "historian of the present" and consider that precipitous judgments "may condemn our work to the same destiny as previous interpretations — the charitable twilight of the libraries." At the very least, however, the conversations engaged by the contributors to this volume serve to raise important areas for further inquiry.

While considerable effort has been made to assess the social consequences of economic restructuring and structural adjustment, more theoretical and empirical work is needed to elucidate the emerging tripartite relationship among (NSMs) new social movements, non-governmental organizations, and national and transnational political agencies. How does this relationship serve to recast the boundaries of political regulation? How and to what extent are these new practices and institutional arrangements likely to incorporate old and new concerns regarding social equity, citizenship, and democracy? Responses to these questions are constrained in familiar ways by the boundaries of academic discourse. The questions themselves, however, help identify the contours of a social and political terrain that subsequent research should strive to delineate with greater specificity.

Notes

1. See Cavarozzi 1992 and 1994 for pioneering analyses of the rise and decline of the state-centric matrix. Also see the essays in Smith, Acuña, and Gamarra 1994a and 1994b and Korzeniewicz and Smith 1996.

2. Global commodity chains are networks of households, enterprises, and states that serve to articulate production, distribution, and consumption as world-economic processes. Within these networks, the ability of individuals and organizations to appropriate wealth is unevenly distributed (Wallerstein 1983; Hopkins and Wallerstein 1986; see, also, the essays in Gereffi and Korzeniewicz 1994 and Korzeniewicz and Smith 1996). Within these networks, production processes and commodities exhibit "production cycles," "starting off as core products and eventually becoming peripheral products" (Wallerstein 1983, 36; see also Arrighi and Drangel 1986; Arrighi 1991 and 1994). This interpretation shares similarities with Joseph Schumpeter (1934 and 1942), for whom innovative processes were at the root of the "creative destruction" that characterizes capitalism as a system. More recently, this focus on innovation (rather than industrialization) as the basis for comparative advantages in the world economy has been at the fore of influential studies on economic organization (Vernon 1979, Porter 1985 and 1990).

3. Karl Polanyi argued that in all modes of social organization prior to the nineteenth century, human interactions (such as economic transactions) had been regulated through customary moral arrangements, maintaining economies "submerged in... social relationships" (1957, 46). The Great Transformation of the nineteenth century involved the construction of a self-regulated market, with transactions becoming "directed by market prices and nothing but market prices" (1957, 43), and where "social relations are embedded in the economic system" (1957, 57). This self-regulating market revolved around three principal commodities (labor, land, and money), which were entirely fictitious in that "[n]one of them is produced for sale" (1957, 72). The use of these resources as commodities "subordinate[d] the substance of society itself to the laws of the market" (1957, 71).

4. Unless specifically noted, all statistical data cited in this section are taken from CEPAL 1996.

5. The IDB has attempted to follow up on this recognition of the mounting social costs and potential destabilizing consequences with initiatives focused on "strengthening civil society." A document circulated at a 1994 IDB conference on this topic recognized that something more than market reforms may be required to "...ensure that all social strata share more fully in the benefits of growth.... The persistence of poverty and of other factors of economic exclusion ... calls for a more comprehensive approach to development that, while stimulating economic reforms, will promote internal socioeconomic integration, modernization of the State, and consolidation of democratic institutions" (IDB 1994).

References

Acuña, Carlos H., and William C. Smith. 1994. "The Political Economy of Structural Adjustment: The Logic of Support and Opposition to Neoliberal Reform." In *Latin American Political Economy in the Age of Neoliberal Reform: Theoretical and Comparative Perspectives for the 1990s*, eds. William C. Smith, Carlos H. Acuña, and Eduardo A. Gamarra. Coral Gables, Fla.: University of Miami North-South Center.

Acuña, Carlos, and William C. Smith. 1995. "The Politics of 'Military Economics' in the Southern Cone: Comparative Perspectives on Democracy and Arms Production in Argentina, Brazil and Chile." *Political Power and Social Theory* 9: 121-157.

Agüero, Felipe, and Jeffrey Stark. Forthcoming 1997. *Fault Lines of Democratic Governance in the Americas*. Coral Gables, Fla.: North-South Center Press at the University of Miami.

Altimir, Oscar. 1994. "Income Distribution and Poverty through Crisis and Adjustment." *CEPAL Review* 52.

Altimir, Oscar. 1996. "Economic Development and Social Equity: A Latin American Perspective." *Journal of Interamerican Studies and World Affairs.* 38(2/3).

Arrighi, Giovanni. 1991. "World Income Inequalities and the Future of Socialism." *New Left Review* 189: 39-65.

Arrighi, Giovanni. 1994. *The Long Twentieth Century: Money, Power, and the Origins of Our Times*. London: Verso.

Arrighi, Giovanni, and Jessica Drangel. 1986. "The Stratification of the World-Economy: An Exploration of the Semiperipheral Zone." *Review* 10: 9-74.

Berensztein, Sergio. 1996. "Rebuilding State Capacity in Contemporary Latin America: The Politics of Taxation in Argentina and Mexico." In *Latin America in the World-Economy*, eds. Roberto Patricio Korzeniewicz and William C. Smith. Westport, Conn.: Praeger.

Bierstekker, Thomas J. 1990. "Reducing the Role of the State in the Economy: A Conceptual Exploration of IMF and World Bank Prescriptions." *International Studies Quarterly* 34: 477-492.

Bierstekker, Thomas J. 1995. "The 'Triumph' of Liberal Economic Ideas in the Developing World." In *Global Change, Regional Response: The New International Context of Development*, ed. Barbara Stallings. Cambridge: Cambridge University Press.

Bonilla, Elssy. 1990. "Working Women in Latin America." In *Economic and Social Progress in Latin America: 1990 Report*. Washington, D.C.: Interamerican Development Report.

Bowles, Samuel, and Herbert Gintis. 1993. "The Revenge of Homo Economicus: Contested Exchange and the Revival of Political Economy." *The Journal of Economic Perspectives* 7 (1): 83-102.

Bradford, Colin I., Jr., ed. 1994. "Redefining the Role of the State: Political Processes, State Capacity and the New Agenda in Latin America." In *Redefining the State in Latin America*, ed. Colin I. Bradford, Jr. Paris: Organization for Economic Cooperation and Development (OECD).

Bresser Pereira, Luiz Carlos, José María Maravall, and Adam Przeworski. 1993. *Economic Reforms in New Democracies: A Social-Democratic Approach.* New York: Cambridge University Press.

Bulmer-Thomas, Victor, ed. 1996. *The New Economic Model in Latin America and its Impact on Income Distribution and Poverty.* New York: St. Martin's Press.

Castañeda, Jorge G. 1993. *Utopia Unarmed: The Latin American Left After the Cold War.* New York: Alfred A. Knopf.

Cavarozzi, Marcelo. 1992. "Beyond Democratic Transitions in Latin America." *Journal of Latin American Studies* 24: 665-684.

Cavarozzi, Marcelo. 1994. "Politics: A Key for the Long Term in Latin America." In *Latin American Political Economy in the Age of Neoliberal Reform: Theoretical and Comparative Perspectives for the 1990s*, eds. William C. Smith, Carlos H. Acuña, and Eduardo A. Gamarra. Coral Gables, Fla.: University of Miami North-South Center.

CEPAL (Comisión Económica para América Latina y el Caribe). 1992. *El perfil de la pobreza en América Latina a comienzos de los años 90.* Santiago: Naciones Unidas.

CEPAL (Comisión Económica para América Latina y el Caribe). 1996. *Balance preliminar de la economía de América Latina y el Caribe 1996.* Santiago: Naciones Unidas.

Chalmers, Douglas A., et al. 1996. *The New Politics of Inequality in Latin America: Rethinking Participation and Representation.* New York: Oxford University Press.

Díaz, Alvaro. 1996. "Economic Dynamism and Institutional Rigidity in Chile: Risks and Opportunities at the Turn of the Twentieth Century." In *Latin America in the World-Economy*, eds. Roberto Patricio Korzeniewicz and William C. Smith. Westport, Conn.: Praeger.

Domínguez, Jorge I., and Abraham F. Lowenthal. 1996. *Constructing Democratic Governance: South America in the 1990s.* Baltimore, Md.: The Johns Hopkins University Press.

Drake, Paul. 1996. *Labor Movements and Dictatorships: The Southern Cone in Comparative Perspectives.* Baltimore, Md.: The Johns Hopkins University Press.

Edwards, Sebastian. 1995. *Crisis and Reform in Latin America: From Despair to Hope.* New York: World Bank/Oxford University Press.

Escobar, Arturo, and Sonia E. Alvarez, eds. 1992. *The Making of Social Movements in Latin America: Identity, Strategy, and Democracy.* Boulder, Colo.: Westview Press.

Evans, Peter. 1995. *Embedded Autonomy: States and Industrial Transformation.* Princeton, N.J.: Princeton University Press.

Foweraker, Joe. 1995. *Theorizing Social Movements.* London: Pluto Press.

Gereffi, Gary, and Miguel Korzeniewicz, eds. 1994. *Commodity Chains and Global Capitalism.* Westport, Conn.: Greenwood Press.

Haggard, Stephan, and Robert R. Kaufman. 1995. *The Political Economy of Democratic Transitions.* Princeton, N.J.: Princeton University Press.

Hopkins, Terence K., and Immanuel Wallerstein. 1986. "Commodity Chains in the World-Economy prior to 1800." *Review* 10: 157-170.

Huber, Evelyne. 1995. "Assessing State Strength." In *Latin America in Comparative Perspective: New Approaches to Methods and Analysis*, ed. Peter H. Smith. Boulder, Colo.: Westview Press.

IDB (Inter-American Development Bank). 1992. *Social and Economic Progress in Latin America*. Washington, D.C.: IDB.

IDB (Inter-American Development Bank). 1993. *Social and Economic Progress in Latin America*. Washington, D.C.: IDB.

IDB (Inter-American Development Bank). 1994. "Toward an Inter-American Bank (IDB) Strategy for Strengthening Civil Society." Executive Summary circulated at the Conference on Strengthening Civil Society, Washington, D.C., September.

Jelin, Elizabeth, and Eric Hershberg, eds. 1996. *Constructing Democracy: Human Rights, Citizenship, and Society in Latin America*. Boulder, Colo.: Westview Press.

Keohane, Robert O., and Helen V. Milner, eds. 1996. *Internationalization and Domestic Politics*. New York: Cambridge University Press.

Kincaid, A. Douglas, and Eduardo A. Gamarra. 1996. "Disorderly Democracy: Redefining Public Security in Latin America." In *Latin America in the World-Economy*, eds. Roberto Patricio Korzeniewicz and William C. Smith. Westport, Conn.: Praeger.

Korzeniewicz, Roberto Patricio, and William C. Smith. 1996. "A Great Transformation?" In *Latin America in the World-Economy*, eds. Roberto Patricio Korzeniewicz and William C. Smith. Westport, Conn.: Praeger.

Levine, Daniel H. 1992. *Popular Voices in Latin American Catholicism*. Princeton, N.J.: Princeton University Press.

Linz, Juan J., and Alfred Stepan. 1996. *Problems of Democratic Transition and Consolidation: Southern Europe, South America, and Post-Communist Europe*. Baltimore, Md.: The Johns Hopkins University Press.

Mahon, James E., Jr. 1996. *Mobile Capital and Latin American Development*. University Park: Pennsylvania State University Press.

Mainwaring, Scott, and Timothy R. Scully, eds. 1995. *Building Democratic Institutions: Party Systems in Latin America*. Stanford, Calif.: Stanford University Press.

Mainwaring, Scott, Guillermo O'Donnell, and J. Samuel Valenzuela, eds. 1992. *Issues in Democratic Consolidation: The New South American Democracies in Comparative Perspective*. Notre Dame, Ind.: University of Notre Dame Press.

Martínez, Javier, and Alvaro Díaz. 1996. *Chile: The Great Transformation*. Washington, D.C.: The Brookings Institution/United Nations Research Institute for Social Development.

O'Donnell, Guillermo. 1994a. "Delegative Democracy." *Journal of Democracy* 5 (January): 55-69.

O'Donnell, Guillermo. 1994b. "On the State, Democratization and Some Conceptual Problems (A Latin American View with Glances at some Post-Communist Societies). In *Latin American Political Economy in the Age of Neoliberal Reform: Theoretical and Comparative Perspectives for the 1990s*. eds. William C. Smith, Carlos H. Acuña, and Eduardo A. Gamarra. Coral Gables, Fla.: University of Miami North-South Center.

O'Donnell, Guillermo. 1996. "Illusions about Consolidation." *Journal of Democracy* 7 (April): 34-51.

Oxhorn, Philip D., and Graciela Ducatenzeiler, eds. Forthcoming. *What Kind of Democracy? What Kind of Market? Latin America in the Age of Neoliberalism*. University Park: Pennsylvania State University Press.

Oxhorn, Philip D., and Pamela Starr, eds. Forthcoming. *The Political Limits to Economic Reform: Economic Change and Democratic Consolidation in Latin America*. Boulder, Colo.: Lynne Rienner.

Polanyi, Karl. 1957. *The Great Transformation: The Political and Economic Origins of Our Time.* Boston: Beacon Press.

Porter, Michael. 1985. *Competitive Advantage: Creating and Sustaining Superior Performance.* New York: The Free Press.

Porter, Michael. 1990. *The Competitive Advantage of Nations.* New York: The Free Press.

Przeworski, Adam. 1985. *Capitalism and Social Democracy.* Cambridge: Cambridge University Press.

Przeworski, Adam. 1990. *The State and the Economy under Capitalism.* New York: Academic Publishers.

Roberts, Kenneth M. 1995. "Neoliberalism and the Transformation of Populism in Latin America: The Peruvian Case." *World Politics* 48: 82-116.

Schumpeter, Joseph A. 1934. *The Theory of Economic Development.* Cambridge, Mass.: Harvard University Press.

Schumpeter, Joseph A. 1942. *Capitalism, Socialism and Democracy.* New York: Harper & Row.

Smith, William C., Carlos H. Acuña, and Eduardo A. Gamarra, eds. 1994a. *Latin American Political Economy in the Age of Neoliberal Reform: Theoretical and Comparative Perspectives for the 1990s.* Coral Gables, Fla.: University of Miami North-South Center.

Smith, William C., Carlos H. Acuña, and Eduardo A. Gamarra, eds. 1994b. *Democracy, Markets, and Structural Reform in Latin America: Argentina, Bolivia, Brazil, Chile, and Mexico.* Coral Gables, Fla.: University of Miami North-South Center.

Stewart, Frances. 1996. "John Williamson and the Washington Consensus." Paper presented to a conference on "Development Thinking and Practice" organized by the Inter-American Development Bank, Washington, D.C., September 3-5.

Tardanico, Richard, and Rafael Menjívar Larín. Forthcoming 1997. "Restructuring, Employment, and Social Inequality: Comparative Urban Latin American Patterns." In *Global Restructuring, Employment Transformations, and Social Inequality in Urban Latin America,* eds. Richard Tardanico and Rafael Menjívar Larín. Coral Gables, Fla.: North-South Center Press at the University of Miami.

Vernon, Raymond. 1979. "The Product Cycle Hypothesis in a New International Environment." *Oxford Bulletin of Economics and Statistics* 41: 255-267.

Wade, Robert. 1990. *Governing the Market: Economic Theory and the Role of Government in East Asian Industrialization.* Princeton, N.J.: Princeton University Press.

Wallerstein, Immanuel. 1983. *Historical Capitalism.* London: Verso.

Williamson, John, ed. 1990a. *The Progress of Policy Reform in Latin America.* Washington, D.C.: Institute for International Economics.

Williamson, John, ed. 1990b. *Latin American Adjustment: How Much Has Happened?* Washington, D.C.: Institute for International Economics.

Williamson, John, ed. 1994. *The Political Economy of Policy Reform.* Washington, D.C.: Institute for International Economics.

Williamson, John. 1996. "The Washington Consensus Revisited." Paper presented to a conference on "Development Thinking and Practice" organized by the Inter-American Development Bank. Washington, D.C., September 3-5.

Chapter 2

The Politics of Transformation in Historical Perspective

Juan Carlos Torre

Introduction

As if they were historians of the present, sociologists practice a difficult art; they sometimes lack the distance necessary to evaluate the magnitude and direction of the changes that take place before their eyes. In such circumstances, a retrospective view of the literature produced can yield disturbing conclusions regarding one's capacity to know and to understand: The force with which present events enter the perception of those who try to register and interpret them usually produces hasty judgments that often do not stand up to a second reading. This is especially true when the aim is to follow closely the changes of contemporary Latin America.

Throughout this century, the countries of the region evolved through processes that were anything but gradual and endogenously directed. This period illustrates well the characteristics peculiar to the great historic changes occurring in Latin America. As market reform policies unfold, one may also observe the influence of external shocks, the systemic character of change, and the leading role played by state elites. The simultaneous presence of all these features within the space of a few years has given rise to a period of extraordinary policymaking, the observation of which is difficult to resist because the transformations set in motion seem to signal the beginning of a new era.

From this standpoint, a development pattern more centered on the market and more open to the world's trade and finance relations is emerging in Latin America. Yet, more precisely, what does this dawning economic and social order herald? Compelled by reasons of their own, there are many who claim to know and, on the basis of the data available today, foresee a future for Latin America that is somber for some and more promising for others. Lacking the perspective possible only with the passage of time, the assessments of these historians of the present have a strongly idiosyncratic flavor; they reflect, more than is expected in all social analyses, either their own experiences or their own preferences.

Capturing and evaluating the societal transformations at the moment they are taking place is a frustrating, yet familiar, experience. To illustrate this point, consider what occurred in Latin America in the time between the postwar period and the outbreak of the petroleum crisis in the early 1970s. During those years, the region's political and intellectual elites, overwhelmed by the burden of protracted structural problems, did not always perceive that their countries were in the midst of an expansive process that stimulated growth and broadened the capacity for social integration. In the social sciences, that perception advanced only through strong controversy. Fernando H. Cardoso, in association with Enzo Faletto (1969), made it clear that toward the end of the 1960s, Latin American countries were developing in spite of, or thanks to, their relations of dependence.

Cardoso's questioning of the stagnation thesis then in vogue — condensed in the formula "the development of underdevelopment" coined by André Gunder Frank (1967) — gathered its strength from a personal experience that was not his alone, namely the formidable transformation then under way in Brazil. Very soon others, traveling along the path blazed by Cardoso, also were able to discern what was happening in their own countries and to discover, in retrospect, a process of ongoing development. The course of this discovery was completed later when Norbert García and Víctor Tokman (1985) demonstrated that Latin America's rate of growth during the period from 1950 to 1980 was considerably higher than that of the United States during its own earlier period of "take-off."[1]

The acknowledgment that Latin American economies were expanding did not mean, however, a full reconciliation with the transformations taking place at the time. Thus, although willing to admit that growth existed, many intellectuals hurried to add that it was a growth pattern that deprived wide segments of the population of the benefits of modernization. The void left by the demise of the stagnation thesis was filled by a new perspective focusing on the exclusionary nature of development. In its popularized version, this latter thesis was no more a faithful description of reality than the first, although this only would be recognized after the foreign debt crisis of the 1980s had taken its toll on the Latin American economies.

The sharp decline of social indicators in the 1980s cast a more benevolent light on the period that was so abruptly interrupted; thus, it was verified that different measurements of welfare had registered gradual and sustained improvement between 1950 and 1980. The scope of that progress — achieved with no significant change in the unequal distribution of income — can, of course, be a matter for analysis and debate, which, to be productive, should be based on a strategy of comparative analysis. Yet existing surveys are unequivocal in revealing that during those 30 years, the capacity for social integration of Latin American countries was more dynamic than the thesis of exclusionary development led one to believe (Altimir 1981).

There are many obstacles that hinder the possibility of being truly contemporary and, therefore, able to perceive correctly the historical process under way. This is a complex matter that cannot be treated here with the attention it deserves.[2] It is mentioned here only to call attention to some of the problems that surface when assessing the politics of transformation in Latin America. Increased awareness of these problems counsels against rash judgments that may condemn today's work to the same destiny as previous interpretations — the charitable twilight of the libraries.

Assessing the Social Impact of Structural Reforms

An example of these difficulties concerns the social correlates of market reforms. With currently available information, this issue is not easy to address. The welfare implications of the new development pattern can, at most, only be estimated tentatively. Latin America has not accumulated the requisite 12- to 15-years' experience with neoliberal economic reforms required to give firm answers regarding these social impacts.

Latin America's first reaction to the external shocks caused by the abrupt cessation of external financing at the beginning of the 1980s was a succession of attempts at adjustment. The novelty of these adjustment policies lay, above all, in their magnitude. Yet, in general, in common with other adjustment experiences of the past, they did not alter the main economic institutions already in place. It was only later, and as a second reaction to persistent macroeconomic imbalances, that a variety of structural reform packages began to be implemented.

In assessing the social impact of structural reforms, one stumbles not only upon the novelty of these reforms (as they became widespread only toward the end of the 1980s) but also upon the fact that the consequences of *adjustment* and neoliberal *structural reform* policies overlap and are difficult to disentangle from one another. Development processes do not unfold in neat, clear-cut phases. This, undoubtedly, conspires against forecasting social costs on the basis of present information. These are the problems Oscar Altimir (1994) addresses in an extremely important article.

Altimir points out that the estimates for the whole of Latin America indicate that 41 percent of the population lived in poverty in 1980, with this figure rising to 43 percent in 1986 and reaching 46 percent in 1990. This first image Altimir presents of an apparent worsening of poverty is quite conventional and can be found, with little alteration, in many studies that describe and evaluate the so-called "lost decade" of the 1980s. Altimir questions the meaning of the first image, however, and concludes that the situation is far more murky than it appears at first glance. Why? Because this image of growing misery is built upon data that "incorporate the effects of adjustment, of institutional changes involving policy reform and underlying restructuring processes, as well as those failed adjustments and the acceleration of inflation" (Altimir 1994, 13). In short, behind the image of deepening poverty lie a variety of economic processes that make it difficult to discern consequences and social costs on the basis of aggregate data on changes in income distribution.

For some, of course, it would be sufficient to indicate that poverty has increased since the foreign debt crisis imposed the path of economic adjustment on Latin American countries. This conclusion can be useful as a political weapon in negotiations between the indebted countries and international financial centers. However, this assertion is conceptually insufficient, as it does not help "to disentangle those changes that are permanently reshaping Latin American societies from those related to people's transitory accommodation to hard times" (Altimir 1994, 24). Or, to put it differently, this claim fails to distinguish adequately the changes induced by neoliberal economic reforms from those associated with the vicissitudes of economic adjustment.

In responding to his own challenge, Altimir first proceeds to identify the different economic phases through which Latin American countries have passed during the 1980s, as well as the nature and depth of the policy reforms undertaken. He then compares distributive changes and the evolution of the principal macroeconomic variables within each phase. A first consequence of this methodological approach is that Latin America, as an object of analysis, vanishes: Not all countries implemented the same policy packages, and even when they did, they did not implement similar policies at the same time nor at the same pace. Moreover, the success of these attempts also varied considerably. Consequently, any assessment that takes Latin America as a whole is scarcely meaningful.

Comparison among countries also becomes problematic unless it takes into consideration the distinctions already mentioned regarding their macroeconomic evolution and patterns of policy implementation, since they have different welfare implications. Therefore, just to juxtapose poverty indexes for different countries in the same table may tell very little. For instance, to know where Brazil, Mexico, and Argentina stood in 1990 in terms of some distributive index may have some descriptive value, but that measurement can conceal a diversity of economic situations for which one needs additional information in order to draw significant conclusions.[3] This is especially true since the interest is in probing whether, and to what extent, changes in inequality during the decade of crisis and adjustment may have some permanence and if these changes are the results of the new neoliberal economic reforms and institutions.

Altimir's laborious and imaginative analysis will not be pursued here. Rather, note only that in order to distinguish the social impacts of adjustment from those due to broader processes of neoliberal reform, Altimir focuses on the distributive outcomes obtained in different countries *after* stabilization and adjustment policies and market-oriented reforms have been implemented fully and *after* a process of sustained growth has been achieved. The perspective of completed reforms provides the best vantage point from which to assess the social correlates of the new pattern of development. In the region, the country that best embodies these traits is Chile.[4]

Analyzing the Transformation Process

Which Chile should be examined? The Chile of President Augusto Pinochet and Finance Minister Hernán Büchi or the Chile of President Patricio Aylwin and his Finance Minister Alejandro Foxley? In both cases, the remarkable continuity of the less statist and more outward-oriented economy established in the 1980s means the principal economic institutions are the same under both authoritarian and democratic administrations. President Aylwin's administration, however, introduced a tax reform that produced resources that allowed some alleviation in inherited levels of poverty (Muñoz and Celedón 1993).

With this experience of continuity and discontinuity in mind, the question of "which Chile" is posed for an explicit methodological purpose: to warn against lapsing into the tendency to establish a necessary relationship between a given pattern of development and its social correlates. Altimir relates that those countries that have recovered from the crisis and its sequels, going on to complete structural adjustment and the implementation of market-oriented reforms, now exhibit a more unequal distribution of income and a higher incidence of poverty. This is an empirical proposition drawn from cases such as Chile, where distributive changes seem to be more permanent than those found in countries still laboring to leave recession and instability behind.

This permanency should be understood purely in statistical terms with no other implications, such as an "elective affinity" between neoliberal economic institutions and a fixed distributive pattern. There should be no rush toward making a parameter out of what is really a variable and, as such, is subject to the ebb and flow of different policy options. A close reading of the Chilean transition suggests that when a country consolidates its fiscal accounts and external equilibrium and begins to grow again, the degree of freedom of action available to governments increases; in this way, the potential space for renegotiating the terms of economic transformation is broadened. In this latter context, social and political forces may move beyond the dire strictures of "there is no alternative" to search for social policies that may enhance the political sustainability of market reforms by correcting the emerging pattern of unequal distribution.

In the face of an evolving process of adjustment and structural change, what is the best position from which to catch a glimpse of the future? As indicated above, some countries may be better observation posts than others. Yet looking at other countries, as at Chile, is likely to reveal an ongoing process of renegotiation developing within the new economic institutions, moving them toward *sui generis* social arrangements. The inchoate nature of this evolution makes assessment tentative and interpretation transitory. In order to express this argument more clearly, an historical analogy will be useful.

To identify the social correlates of what is known as the import-substitution pattern of development, which is a better year on which to focus, 1935 or 1960? From within the conceptual framework found in most of the contemporary literature on Latin America, the distinction between 1935 and 1960 may appear incomprehensible. Once the collapse of import-substitution industrialization (ISI) was declared, retrospective views of the development process that unfolded between 1930 and the debt crisis provide such a "stylized" sketch of ISI that the changes undergone by this model since the 1930s vanish. Instead of the rich historical texture of a development process evolving over time, adapting to a succession of domestic and international challenges, what is left is a flat landscape whose contours remain unchanged, sketched in coarse brush strokes of simplistic analytical content. From this perspective, it becomes difficult to distinguish the changing features of a development pattern between the moment of its installation (circa 1935) and the moment of its full deployment (circa 1960). Conversely, if a more sensitive historical approach were used, the differences between the two moments could be recognized.

This is an important distinction to make and is illustrated further by contrasting two views of the current transformation process. In a valuable essay published in Mexico by Sergio Zermeño (1989), the author poses the following question: "Is the current moment just a passing crisis, albeit a drastic one like the crisis of the 1930s? Or is it a darkness that, judging by some prognoses, will lead us to the new millennium in a situation of chaos and profound deterioration?" Two years later, the same author returns to this disturbing question in a new article (Zermeño 1991). His answer on both occasions is the same: Even granting that neoliberal policies may achieve positive indicators of economic performance, he warns that "upon corrobo-ration of the surprisingly devastating capacity of [neoliberal] measures, manifest in the destruction of social identities and their sequels of dehuman-ization and collective anomie, optimism [resulting from positive economic performance] turns into its opposite" (Zermeño 1991, 57).

In contrast to Zermeño's pessimism, Alvaro Díaz, writing from Chile but aspiring to speak about Latin America, observes, "the continent is in the midst of a transition in which the disarticulating effects of the crisis of the old model of international insertion is giving way to the emergence of new phenomena" (Díaz 1993). After providing some examples of this twofold movement in the fields of economic activities and of occupational structure, Díaz points out, "in societies that are experiencing simultaneous processes of structuration and destructuration, it is possible to employ, at the same time, concepts such as 'anomie' and 'social integration.'" Díaz then adds, "the social destructuration generated by unemployment or the loss of stable employment...seems to be associated with the loss of social identities....There also exist, however, processes of reconstitution of collective identities, of the recreation of social movements that will take years to manifest themselves" (Díaz 1993).

Assuming that both are fair descriptions, how can these two contrasting views be reconciled — Zermeño's view centered on the more somber aspects of the present reality and Díaz's broader perspective that simultaneously calls attention to both the negative and the positive phenomena embedded in the transformations generated by neoliberal reform? Why does Zermeño focus primarily on the effects of the destructuring process, while Díaz, without ignoring these effects, is also able to perceive more salutary consequences of the process of restructuring?

The clue may lie in a passage of Díaz's article, referring to "a double process that began in the seventies, earlier in some economies like Chile, and later in others, like the Brazilian economy" (Díaz 1993). This observation highlights the fact that what distinguishes these two viewpoints is the different time perspective from which they observe the transition toward the emergence of the new pattern of development. Zermeño writes from the perspective of a country still in the throes of the difficult and traumatic adjustment to market reforms.[5] Díaz, in contrast, writes from the perspective of a country in which the process of social and economic transformation was begun at an earlier date and has been carried out more thoroughly; from this latter vantage point, Díaz sees Latin American countries embarked on a process, no less arduous and conflictive, that may be leading not toward chaos but toward a new, stable social and economic equilibrium for their societies.[6]

These difficulties in interpretation, related to different temporal perspectives, are a useful warning to bear in mind if one hopes to sort out the divergent viewpoints regarding the consequences of the changes under way. However, it is necessary to resort to this methodological distinction with caution. Reducing everything to a question of perspective, whether temporal or national, mistakenly can create the impression that the process of change follows a linear sequence. As shall be demonstrated in the next section, the assessment of Latin America's current economic transformation must come to terms with the different paths and modalities through which the process of change unfolds.

On the Nature of Structural Change

A second problem in analyzing structural reforms in Latin America arises from the very nature of the changes being implemented. In order to provide descriptions of these changes, it is necessary, as David Stark (1992) suggests in one of the best approaches to the politics of transformation, to make a clean break with two conventional assumptions. The first is the view that conceives of processes of transformation as the consequence of the uniform application of a single recipe. It is true that there is a blueprint for market-oriented reforms, broadly reflected in the "Washington Consensus." This blueprint has had a pervasive influence, particularly through the conditions attached to the lending policies and practices of international financial institutions. However, in fact, there is no "common model" of policy reform being applied by all countries of the region. Although almost all governments in the region pursue goals of macroeconomic stability and international competitiveness, their strategies of reform have exhibited considerable differences, particularly in terms of their institutional content and the attendant style of state intervention, as well as in terms of the mix and sequencing of reforms.

To comprehend these differences of content, style, and sequencing of reforms, notions such as "transition to a market economy," which often function as catchwords of contemporary processes of change, are scarcely useful and should be discarded. Following Stark, it would be more fruitful if "in place of transitions (with emphasis on destination) we analyze transformations (with the emphasis on actual processes)" (Stark 1992, 22). Consequently, the best strategy would be to desegregate the more general problem of restructuring Latin America's economy by examining the different historical trajectories that countries may follow after launching reforms. Considering the transformations at hand from this comparative angle, the focus of the analysis would no longer be to assess whether a certain reform policy fits a prescribed model or not but to identify the different institutional configurations that emerge in the various countries as the politics of transformation unfold.

The second assumption to be abandoned is the notion of the existence of an unconstrained reform environment, as frequently implied by resorting to the concept of the "collapse of the model of state-centric and inward-oriented development." This assumption equates the reform process to the act of painting on a blank white canvas by following the instruction booklet accompanying a ready-made model. Although this is the demiurgical mirror in which reformist elites like to see themselves and their work reflected, it distorts the complex process of change now under way. To capture contemporary historical processes more accurately, the starting point should be to recognize that a *tabula rasa* never exists.

It is true that the devastating effects of the external crisis may create the impression of an empty stage ready for the introduction from above of a tailor-made capitalism. Yet a closer look at the actual process reveals that, as Stark (1992) argues, economic transformations follow the logic of *bricolage* rather than the logic of architectural design. In other words, the introduction of new elements usually occurs in combination with rearrangements of preexisting institutional relationships. Rather than mere replacement, the process of transformation resembles innovative adaptations that articulate seemingly discrepant elements, new and old.

Considered from this perspective, policy elites can be seen as motivated not in terms of the pursuit of a particular "end-state" but rather as acting to resolve dilemmas posed by the practical problems they confront. To summarize this argument in Stark's words, "instead of designating a future that shapes the present, we should examine how the future is being shaped by the pragmatic of the present" (Stark 1994). When examining contemporary changes in Latin America from the methodological perspective just outlined, two dimensions should be highlighted: The first refers to the differences in the strategies of policy reform, and the second concerns the relationships between existing economic institutions and the new ones being introduced. The following example of privatization policies should clarify these two dimensions and illustrate their historical meaning.

One of the market reforms that best symbolizes the new orientation of Latin America's political economy is the process of transferring property rights for productive assets from the state. In the context of the fiscal crises that dominated the region's economies, privatization has pursued various objectives: 1) to channel liquid assets to insolvent states no longer able (or finding it increasingly difficult) to issue public debt, 2) to eliminate the financial imbalances of public enterprises in order to reallocate resources to other areas, and 3) to transfer to the private sector the responsibility of modernizing infrastructure and public utilities.

Research has shown that countries differ in the policies adopted for effecting the transfer of ownership of the assets of public enterprises. For example, in some cases, all public assets have been sold, while in other cases, the state has retained partial ownership. In still other cases, popular capitalist schemes have been attempted, or pursuing the reverse course, large blocks of shares have been sold to a few investors. Limits may be imposed on the participation of foreign capital, or no restrictions may exist. Finally, the state may rationalize the enterprise (by reducing the workforce, for example) prior to sale, while in some instances, this task has been transferred to the new owners (Devlin and Cominetti 1994).

To understand these different strategies of privatization, it is necessary to focus on the diverse historical starting points in each country undergoing reform; at the time of the launching of reforms, each country faced different economic and political circumstances. Thus, for example, when President Carlos Menem took office in 1989, Argentina was in the midst of hyperinflation. Facing this dire predicament, the decision to privatize was swift, far-reaching, and included neither restrictions on the participation of foreign capital nor efforts to rationalize the state-owned enterprises targeted for transfer to private ownership. Argentina's alarmingly critical fiscal situation was a major determinant of economic expectations; authorities had to discount quite heavily future fiscal income, thus contributing to strong pressure in favor of privatization.

Nevertheless, the need for immediate revenue was not the only driving force behind the initial privatizations in Argentina (the sale of the state-owned airline and telephone companies actually raised little cash for the government). The other driving force was the need to bolster the government's credibility. Coming from a traditional populist party and having campaigned as a critic of economic adjustment, President Menem urgently needed to demonstrate pro-private enterprise credentials in order to consolidate his fledgling government vis-à-vis the local and international business communities.

Privatizations, together with other components of Menem's economic policy package, such as drastic trade liberalization, domestic deregulation, military participation in the Gulf War, and withdrawal from the G-77 group of developing countries, played a key role in his public relations efforts aimed at local business and the U.S. government. Neither General Augusto Pinochet in Chile nor President Carlos Salinas de Gortari in Mexico confronted a credibility problem of comparable magnitude. They were thus able to design their privatization strategies with greater leeway. Despite their strong neoliberal stance, both Pinochet and Salinas refrained from transferring to the private sector their main source of fiscal revenue — the state copper and oil monopolies, respectively.

Despite these differences, there is one feature that unifies and distinguishes the privatization wave currently sweeping Latin America: In most cases, the transfer of state assets to the private sector has not been accompanied by the implementation of appropriate rules to insure market competition. Concerned with maximizing fiscal income and securing future investment, governments generally have offered to many newly privatized firms the array of incentives that in the past had been reserved for the local business sector — captive markets and, on some occasions, fiscal privileges.[7]

There are numerous instances in Latin America of the privatization of natural monopolies (water supply, electricity distribution, and so on), but there are other cases in which privatization technically could have been implemented in such a fashion as to provide incentives for competition. Governments, however, generally have refrained from promoting competition, thereby fostering market concentration or the formation of monopolies with the new framework of neoliberal economic institutions. As a consequence, while regimes of industrial promotion have either been suspended or canceled outright and the domestic market opened to international competition, the new privatized firms stand as a case apart, a sort of hybrid that, incidentally, is quite significant given the share of resources in the local economy controlled by these firms.

Pablo Gerchunoff, the author of one of the best analyses of privatization in Argentina whose arguments are followed here, has stressed that, in the present circumstances, the objective of promoting competition conflicts with that of maximizing fiscal income for the state and encouraging future private investment (Gerchunoff 1993). The sale of public sector firms operating in a competitive environment under unstable economic conditions will entail 1) a strong reduction in the price of the assets to be transferred and 2) a high degree of risk that might discourage the new private owners from making significant investment commitments because the value of these investments can be recovered only in the long term. "Evidence of this rationale is found," G. John Ikenberry has noted, "when governments sell public enterprises under implicit or explicit guarantees that the firms' monopoly profits will be maintained. That is, states show more interest in dressing up a public enterprise to increase its asset value, even at the expense of not promoting the competitive breakup of the monopoly" (Ikenberry 1990, 91).

Privatization policies thus have generated a change in property relations but not in the relationship between the firm and the market; the newly privatized firms operate in a framework where rules of market competition are as alien as they were in the previous phase of import-substitution industrialization.[8] This is a true experience of *bricolage*, the "pragmatic of the present" — to use Stark's term — that guides governments (i.e., their demands for fiscal income and their desires to secure future investment in public utilities) compels them to combine the style of economic relationships of the past with the new reliance on the private sector. The historical conditions under which the reform process takes place are leading Latin American countries not so much toward a model of a market economy but toward a new type of economy with different combinations of market and nonmarket relationships.

To capture the main features of this new economy requires conceptual lenses less simplistic than those rooted in the conventional state-market dichotomy. As Alvaro Díaz points out, "Without doubt, markets have expanded enormously in Latin America, occupying far more space than they did in the past" (see Chapter 3 in this volume). However, Díaz also stresses that this trend does not exhaust all that is taking place as a consequence of the current economic transformation. The new literature on economic governance offers some useful clues by focusing on the variety of "institutional arrangements — including rule and rule-making agents — that regulate transactions inside and across the boundaries of an economic system" (Hollingsworth, Rogers, and Schmitter 1994, 5). For this analytical perspective, markets are just one among several mechanisms of economic governance, mechanisms that also include corporate hierarchies, the state, alliances, networks, and associations. Working within this framework should enable a better understanding of what is new in Latin American societies undergoing neoliberal restructuring, as well as what differentiates them from each other.[9]

A New Direction

The primary purpose of this chapter has been to make a methodological point by outlining some of the problems that emerge when describing and evaluating the changes produced by the process of economic reforms implemented by Latin American countries since the late 1980s. These reflections conclude by addressing an issue that progressively is coming to dominate the region's public agenda: the renegotiation of the terms of economic transformation.

Pressured by a sudden modification in their external environments and motivated by sheer political realism, Latin American governments have resorted to policies of adjustment and structural reform as a means of coping with a crisis of systemic proportions. Following Albert Hirschman's observations (1981) on an earlier period, public authorities in contemporary Latin America have reacted to pressing problems that left them with precious little room for maneuver. Not one Latin American president in recent years ran for office on a platform of free trade, privatization, and deregulation. Once in office, however, many committed themselves and their governments to these policies, guided by the strong arm of the International Monetary Fund (IMF), the World Bank, and their local financial markets. After a decade of economic turbulence, Latin American countries slowly are beginning to grow again, this time within a more stable domestic environment. A recent report of the Economic Commission for Latin America and the Caribbean (ECLAC) of the United Nations observed, "The year 1994 produced new evidence of the consolidation of a more dynamic economic performance in Latin America and the Caribbean. The growth rate of the gross domestic product in the region rose from an average of 3.2 percent a year in 1991-1993 to 3.7 percent in 1994, the second highest level in the last 14 years. Per capita income rose by 11.9 percent. Average inflation (excluding Brazil) fell to 16 percent, a record low in recent decades" (ECLAC 1994, 1).

Behind their satisfactory performance in recent years, however, all countries of the region have been experiencing a similar array of postreform problems. These problems point to the need for policy corrections (see Naim

1993). In most cases, for example, privatizations have led to the formation of monopolies or oligopolies without the counterweight of public regulations of antitrust legislation. In the case of trade opening, the sudden demand for modernization posed by the new economic incentives has not been met by state-sponsored policies of industrial reconversion and export promotion. Moreover, the fact that the economic reforms were carried out in an international environment characterized by an excess supply of financial capital led to subsequent exchange rate appreciation; this, in turn, explains why, in most countries except Chile, trade liberalization has resulted in a high rate of mortality for businesses, increasing unemployment, and persistent balance of payments deficits. In addition, efforts to sustain fiscal discipline have led to a contraction of public investment in both human capital and physical infrastructure. Consequently, the economies of the region have experienced an erosion of their competitiveness and capacity for technological innovation. By the same token, financial exigencies and budget constraints also have entailed cuts in social spending, antipoverty programs, and employment promotion policies.

In view of these emerging strains in the market-oriented reforms, it should not be surprising that efforts to redress the present asymmetrical relationship between the market and the state, in the direction of new roles for the latter, will dominate future Latin American scenarios.[10] Most likely, privatization, trade liberalization, and fiscal reform will remain the distinctive traits of the new economic organizations in most countries. However, these emergent economic arrangements will certainly be more institutionally complex and heterogeneous than those prescribed by the "Washington Consensus." Thus, as countries seek to address postreform problems, greater state involvement can be expected in areas such as regulatory frameworks, industrial reconversion, technological innovation, export promotion, infrastructure investment, and poverty-alleviation programs. The challenge of the new agenda will be to incorporate these policies without endangering macroeconomic stability and to enhance state capabilities without yielding to sectoral pressures, as was common in the past. It remains to be seen if these challenges can be met successfully, thus improving the economic sustainability and the social inclusiveness of the Latin American politics of transformation.

Notes

1. The work of Joseph Ramos (1984) deserves a special mention for his revision of previously well-established assumptions to show the great capacity of Latin American economies for incorporating the labor force between 1950 and 1980.

2. The perceptive observations of Albert Hirschman (1981, Chapter 6) may be usefully consulted on this issue.

3. Changes in poverty in the short run are strongly influenced by the intensity of growth (or recession) at the level of both formal employment and wages as well as underemployment. Therefore, to make synchronic comparisons between national economies undergoing different macroeconomic phases (such as recession, recovery, and sustainable growth) is untenable.

4. Colombia has also been growing along a full-capacity sustainable growth path, but policy reforms have been recent and limited. Mexico has introduced a wide range of reforms since 1987, and Argentina did the same around 1990, but both economies were still recovering at the time of the above-mentioned analysis. Their expansion since then has taken place with relative price distortions that still have to be consolidated eventually or corrected for growth to be sustained. In all three cases, it is too early to assess the longer-term effects of reforms. On this subject, see Mario Damil et al. (1993, 228).

5. Ten years ago, the somber tones of Zermeño's work were familiar in Chile. For example, Eugenio Tironi asked if "just as there was a sociology of modernization, wouldn't it now be fruitful to propose a sociology of decadence?" (Tironi 1986). In a more recent article, in collaboration with Ricardo A. Lagos, Tironi moves away from his previous opinion: "Until now, a great deal of socioeconomic research has concentrated on the analysis of the social disorganization that accompanies the transition; today, however, it seems necessary to pay more attention to the new social order that is born with the process of structural adjustment" (Tironi 1991).

6. Although in somewhat altered form, this difference in perspective between Zermeño and Díaz persists in their more recent work. See, for example, Chapter 3 by Díaz and Chapter 7 by Zermeño in this volume.

7. By captive markets, I mean markets that operate within a set of institutional rules that confer to the firms a monopoly position in the domestic economy.

8. This outcome can be read in a more political light, as Héctor Schamis has done in his analysis of the Chilean privatization process. According to Schamis, the compromises between the government and the main economic groups (around the privatization policies) were "a way of recomposing the ruling coalition through the distribution of, in most cases, monopolistic rents. This explains why, particularly in extraordinarily sensitive sectors, such as energy and telecommunications, the indus- tries were privatized as vertically integrated monopolies, including basic concessions on property rights of water for the former and exclusive access to the satellite for the

latter. This perpetuated the monopoly condition of the now-private companies and thus secured rents for the purchasing groups" (Schamis 1994).

9. In addition to Chapter 3 by Díaz in this volume, see also Eduardo Feldman (1995), which offers a more elaborated attempt to theorize this perspective.

10. See Chapter 4 by Ian Roxborough in this volume for thoughts along these lines.

References

Altimir, Oscar. 1981. "La pobreza en América Latina." *Revista de la CEPAL* 13 (April).

Altimir, Oscar. 1994. "Distribución del ingreso e incidencia de la pobreza a lo largo del ajuste." *Revista de la CEPAL* 52 (April), 4-32.

Cardoso, Fernando Henrique, and Enzo Faletto. 1969. *Dependencia y desarrollo en América Latina.* México, D.F.: Siglo Veintiuno.

Damil, Mario, José María Fanelli, Roberto Frenkel, and Guillermo Rozenwurcel. 1993. "Crecimiento económico en América Latina. Experiencia reciente y perspectivas." *Desarollo Económico* 130 (July-September).

Devlin, Robert, and Rossella Cominetti. 1994. "La crisis de la empresa pública y las privatizaciones." Working Paper for the "Proyecto Regional de Reformas de Política Pública." Santiago, Chile: ECLAC.

Díaz, Alvaro. 1993. "Tendencias de la reestructuración económica y social en Latinoamérica." Paper submitted to the Conference "Rethinking Development Theories." Institute of Latin American Studies, University of North Carolina. March.

ECLAC (Economic Commission for Latin America and the Caribbean). 1994. *Preliminary Overview of the Economy of Latin America and the Caribbean 1994.* Santiago, Chile: United Nations.

Feldman, Eduardo. 1995. "The Political Economy of the Transformation of Contemporary Argentine Capitalism, 1976-1994." Department of Political Science, University of North Carolina. Unpublished manuscript.

Frank, André Gunder. 1967. *Capitalism and Underdevelopment in Latin America.* New York: Monthly Review Press.

García, Norbert, and Víctor Tokman. 1985. *Acumulación, empleo y crisis.* Santiago de Chile: PREALC (UN Program on Employment in Latin America).

Gerchunoff, Pablo. 1993. "Privatization in Argentina." In *Privatization in Latin America,* eds. Manuel Sanchez and Rossan Corona. Washington, D.C.: Inter-American Development Bank.

Hollingsworth, James, J. Rogers, and Phillipe Schmitter, eds. 1994. *Governing Capitalist Economies.* New York: Oxford University Press.

Hirschman, Albert O. 1981. *Essays in Trespassing.* Cambridge: Cambridge University Press.

Ikenberry, G. John. 1990. "The International Spread of Privatization Policies: Inducements, Learning, and 'Policy Bandwagoning.'" In *The Political Economy of Public Sector Reforms and Privatization,* eds. Erza N. Suleiman and John Waterbury. Boulder, Colo.: Westview Press.

Muñoz, Oscar, and Carmen Celedón. 1993. "Chile en transición: Estrategia económica en la transición a la democracia." In *La politica económica en la transición a la democracia,* eds. Juan Antonio Morales and Gary MacMahon. Santiago de Chile; CIEPLAN.

Naim, Moisés. 1993. "Latin American Post-Adjustment Blues." *Foreign Policy* 92 (Fall), 133-150.

Ramos, Joseph. 1984. "Urbanizacíon y mercado de trabajo." *Revista de CEPAL* 24 (December), 63-81.

Schamis, Héctor. 1994. "Economic Reform and Political Process: The Case of Chile." Working Paper for the "Proyecto Regional de Reformas de Política Pública." Santiago, Chile: ECLAC.

Stark, David. 1992. "Path Dependence and Privatization Strategies in East Central Europe." *East European Politics and Societies* 6(1).

Stark, David. 1994. "Recombinant Property in East European Capitalism." Paper presented at a conference on Economic Liberalization and Democratic Consolidation sponsored by the Social Science Research Council, Rio de Janeiro, Brazil, June.

Tironi, Eugenio. 1986. "Para una sociología de la decadencia?" *Proposiciones* 6 (October-November).

Tironi, Eugenio. 1991. "Actores sociales y ajuste estructural." *Revista de la CEPAL* 44 (August).

Zermeño, Sergio. 1989. "El regreso del líder: Crisis, neoliberalismo y desorden." *Revista Mexicana de Sociología* LI, 4 (July-September).

Zermeño, Sergio. 1991. "Desidentidad y desorden: México en la economía global y en el libre comercio." *Revista Mexicana de Sociología* LIII, 3 (July-September).

Chapter 3

New Developments in Economic and Social Restructuring in Latin America

Alvaro Díaz

Introduction

Over the last 30 years, Latin America's transition from closed economies with nascent or advanced import-substitution policies to openness and relatively diversified exports has been a painful one. Economic adjustment has triggered a chain reaction, gathering speed in recent years, that is part and parcel of the rapid globalization of production, trade, and finance. As a consequence of these traumatic transformations, the state has ceased to be the only, or even primary, motor of change. Along with the rest of the world, Latin America is being buffeted by whirlwinds of change that in all likelihood will be greater than those of earlier periods. Karl Marx's description of the first industrial revolution may well apply: "All that is solid vanishes into air, and all that is sacred becomes profane."

As Latin America is seized by destabilizing changes, new socioeconomic structures flash into being, and groups who are not competitive have to either reinvent themselves completely or perish. Events during 1995 in Mexico, Brazil, and Argentina reveal that the transition is quite unstable and remains far from complete.[1] The region's less-developed nations may have to endure several more decades of the process, trapped in a "long wait" analogous to the post-independence period in the nineteenth century (Halperín Donghi 1969).

Moreover, there is no certainty regarding the type of social formation that eventually will be consolidated. It is, indeed, possible for export economies to combine growth with equity, democratic states, and broad social welfare coverage. On the other hand, it is also possible that the region will remain stalled in dualist economies and mired in systems that perpetuate social inequality and reproduce variations of authoritarianism, while reducing democracy to "delegative" electoral regimes.

For either of these tendencies to prevail is not preordained. Nor will it be exogenous "megatrends" such as globalization or the technological revolution that will define outcomes in each Latin American country, though these have surely transformed the region. The future will be determined by internal processes that either provide opportunities or close them off: Each nation's prospects will be decided by its capacity to build political, social, and economic institutions that facilitate stable and sustainable growth with greater equity.

From this perspective, the transition is marked by uncertainty and irregularity. Through the end of 1994, many observers argued that things were going well. Difficulties were minimized as simply the "costs" of a virtuous path, the benefits of which were on display in Mexico and Chile. Recent events have shown such confidence to be misplaced. The economic crisis that erupted in Mexico following the December 1994 currency devaluation and subsequent financial collapse hit some observers like a thunderbolt. Today a pessimistic climate prevails, and the down side of modernization is emphasized. The fluctuations of mood in the literature seem to make it appropriate to take a "countercyclical" stance and assume that uncertainty, heterogeneity, and inequality are inherent to this transition.

New Functions of the State

In Latin America, two processes shape the transition to a new economic model: regional integration and structural adjustment. In both cases, economic policy has an important role to play. Policymakers are obliged to negotiate the integration of their countries with other economies and to take measures to stabilize, open, deregulate, privatize, and streamline the social role of the state in order to free up markets and release the "animal spirits" of the entrepreneur. The impact of these changes profoundly alters the nature of production and socioeconomic relationships — with the paradoxical result that new interventions by the state in the economy are required.

For the purposes of this chapter, the term "structural adjustment" goes beyond the programs associated with World Bank conditionality to include the various economic policies tried over the years (1975-1990 in Chile, 1982-1994 in Mexico, and 1986-1993 in Argentina) and that brought structural change to the economies of Latin America. Receiving its initial impulse from the state, structural adjustment remade both the regulatory functions of the accumulation model and the economy's mode of insertion into the global economy.

Globalization and integration differ in that globalization is more abstract and refers to the convergence of events and forces that emerge and develop in new terrains of capitalism on a global scale. Integration refers to the policies, negotiations, agreements, and norms that in their early phases lower tariffs and eliminate nontariff barriers. Later on, integration policies pursue more advanced objectives that include customs unions, currency alignments such as the "monetary serpent" in Europe, and the coordination of finance policy.

With these definitions in mind, it is possible to put forth the following 10 hypotheses. These hypotheses provide a point of departure for considering the following issues: 1) the nature and direction of structural adjustment in Latin America, 2) the changes in Latin American economic institutions, 3) the trends in social structures around the region, and 4) the decline of some social actors in Latin America and the rise of others. This chapter, however, is a preliminary work that puts forth ideas intended for further research.

The first proposition is the following: Neoliberal ideology aside, economic adjustment (whether orthodox or heterodox) cannot be understood as the state's simple abandonment of its economic functions but rather must be seen as shifts in the way the state intervenes in the economy. In some areas, state intervention expands, such as in the case of macroeconomic policies to correct flaws in the "coordination" of markets. Elsewhere, state intervention recedes, as in the area of industrial policy, or is refocused, as in social programs.

Second, structural adjustment will be most consistent where government power is centralized and where the economic policy-making apparatus subordinates the rest of the public sector. While it is true that market forces in Latin America have become freer and more generalized, it is no less true that the *grupos económicos nacionales* (national economic groups) organized as conglomerates have grown in size and significance during the same period. While these economic groups face competitive markets globally, they enjoy oligopolistic control of local markets and dominate home production of exportable goods and services. Furthermore, the success of economic opening and export promotion relies on the strength and diversity of economic groups and the presence of transnational firms.

Third, whether neoliberal economic adjustment will be consistent, and thus successful, depends on how much power the state has over civil society and how autonomous its technocratic elites are vis-à-vis other elites, corporatist interests, and social movements.

Fourth, massive economic, social, and institutional changes have been tearing down some structures at the same time that new ones are being generated. This process will continue. Its dramatic consequences — the disempowerment of certain groups and the breakdown of certain relationships — have left some members of society marginalized or even excluded. The term "anomie" applies provisionally here, though only by way of description not explanation. Meanwhile, new groups have emerged that can be considered new fractions of the working class, or perhaps even new working classes, such as data entry operators, temporary workers, and *maquila* workers in export processing zones. These social categories constitute spaces in which management enjoys much greater power than in the rest of society. Recently, these new sectors have begun to construct collective identities and forms of action, silent though they may be.

So while large groups are being expelled from the social formation, new ones are being integrated into it. There seems to be an inverse relationship between dynamism in the economy and in the rest of civil society: Where capitalist change has been most rapid and advanced, social organization is least evident; where the economy is in crisis, social movements and diverse forms of political and social resistance (nonviolent or not) are most significant. This observation describes a particular constellation of current events and should not be taken as a law of history. (Brazil in the 1980s is a counterexample: There labor unions were the strongest and most militant in the most dynamic sectors of the economy.)

Fifth, another inverse relationship can be observed between the cyclical expansion and decline of social structures and the rise and fall of social movements. This relationship does seem to transcend the historical moment and, perhaps, is a generalizable law. The birth of new socioeconomic structures only very slowly gives rise to new forms of collective action. At the same time, the breakdown of old structures does not imply the prompt disappearance of organized groups and individuals and can even spur an increase in their capacity to resist or influence change. Nor has the middle class entered its heyday. The most pronounced trend is the expansion of bourgeois civil society, of the so-called business world, and the resurgence of the entrepreneur as the symbol of modernity.

Sixth, imbalances can no longer be attributed only to the debt crisis at the beginning of the 1980s. The structural reforms of the 1980s have not stabilized the economies of the region in a sustainable fashion. On the contrary, they generate new macroeconomic disequilibria because economies are more exposed to the instability of international financial markets whose "hot money" flows in and out of each country with amazing ease and speed with every fluctuation in international and regional markets. In response, governments implement new structural adjustment "packages" that accelerate structural reform, taking it to its logical outer limits. These packages are no longer the product of World Bank pressure; it is pragmatism that now obliges governments.

Seventh, neoliberal reform in Latin America is winding down because it is running out of objects for reform. In a few years, there will not be any state enterprises left to privatize; unilateral trade openings will have all culminated in negotiated regional integration processes, and the old regulations that restricted markets and capital movements will have been replaced by new regulatory frameworks for correcting market flaws. Chile, Argentina, and Mexico already are reaching the outer limits of neoliberal reform.

Eighth, the regional integration schemes, which have only been a factor since the end of the 1980s, act as substitutes for the industrial policies of yesteryear in that they favor certain sectors of the economy to the detriment of others. This trend violates the neoliberal tenet of tariff equalization similar to what formally exists in Chile. In other words, a "selective" trade policy like that of the industrial policies of the 1940-1970 period is emerging; these selective policies are not determined exclusively by technocrats but by political agreements between the government and pressure groups in civil society. The paradoxical result is the reactivation and rebirth of social actors. Regional integration also places new demands on the state by requiring a perspective that is increasingly strategic — in every sense of the word, including geopolitical.

Ninth, in a few years, Latin American countries will enter a post-neoliberal phase in which traditional prescriptions will no longer be useful. Latin America does not have the opportunities some Asian countries did back in the 1950s; they were able to achieve a powerful export dynamism while simultaneously protecting internal markets. Nonetheless, one should not rule out the potential for an innovative economic policy. Some of the smaller economies may not be able to expand their freedom of action because of their excessive dependence on the United States, but for mid-sized and larger countries that diversify their trade, there are compelling reasons to look beyond neoliberalism for a model that can provide greater stability. These countries should move toward new forms of economic policy, including technology policy, industrial policy, and new kinds of social policy. This effort could possibly be attempted on a regional scale, using the Southern Cone Common Market (MERCOSUR) as a vehicle, for example.

Tenth, and finally, the older welfare functions of the Latin American state proved to be unsustainable politically and economically because they only incorporated the urban middle classes, leaving out peasants and the urban poor. Furthermore, they relied on deficit spending, promoted inefficiency, allowed resources to be siphoned off by high income groups, and were used for clientelistic purposes by elected officials. They were doomed to enter into crisis in Latin America, just as they did in Europe and the United States. By the same token, however, neoliberalism has not succeeded in offering an efficient, effective alternative.

Granted, neoliberal reforms have allowed for more efficient and better quality services but only for higher and upper-middle income groups. In Chile, for example, one of the few successes of the streamlining of social policy was to lower infant mortality rates. However, the same reforms also increased social exclusion, and social spending continues to be used for electoral purposes. Access to basic services has become much more restricted, and the effort to focus resources on the extreme poor is very limited in scope.

In sum, the old welfare state has not been replaced by markets that respond to demand and achieve Pareto optimality. Markets in social services are indifferent to social inequalities, and they have numerous flaws and high transaction costs. Finally, the failure of the neoliberal model has consequences that reverberate not only in the social and economic spheres; the very legitimacy of the state is at stake, and a hard-earned space for crucial social compromise is being jeopardized. As in the United States, Latin America is searching for a new social welfare model to improve upon those of the 1960s or 1980s.

The Reconfiguration of Economic Institutions

The transformation of capitalism in Latin America has changed basic economic institutions not only within the public sector but also among private firms and organizations. Moreover, the rules governing the functioning of markets have been modified, and new forms of coordination among economic agents — via informal and formal contracts — have emerged.

These institutional changes were eclipsed until recently by the opening of trade, deregulation, privatization, and the dismantling of industrial and social policies. These dramatic changes lend themselves to a superficial and incomplete reading of what is actually occurring. The result is the widely held impression that the four processes marked a transition from highly protected, regulated, state-managed economies to new, open, unregulated economies with "subsidiary" states.

In other words, observers on both the left and the right saw Latin America as moving in the direction of "free market" economies, regardless of whether they viewed the movement as positive or negative. The understanding was that 1) markets (decentralized modes of coordination based on a price system) were expanding and 2) hierarchies (centralized modes of coordination based in authority and power) were being undermined.

Yet this view is reductionist. It reveals the shortcomings of an analysis born of the heated states versus markets debate in which markets and capitalism were taken to be synonymous — simplifying economic history to an extreme. Though markets may be the key economic institutions of capitalism, and a necessary condition for capitalism's existence, they are not sufficient, in and of themselves, to give the capitalist system its cohesion and durability. The essence of capitalism's success and longevity is a mix of markets and tightly interlocking hierarchical structures.

In the Latin American case, Alfred Chandler's thesis (1977) is highly applicable: To the "invisible hand" of the market, one must add the visible hand of institutions that, in countries such as Chile, control more than half the gross national product (the state and the large conglomerates). These institutions are not ruled by markets but rather by dictates emanating from hierarchical structures.

Moreover, the firm, the church, and the family are organizations that have a large impact on the economic life of a nation. Among other things, they guide individuals toward paths that may differ from those markets urge upon them. For this reason, many contemporary economic theorists recognize that just as there are millions of transactions via markets, so too are there millions of transactions that are not realized through markets.

Without a doubt, markets have expanded enormously in Latin America, occupying far more space than they did in the past. Latin American capitalism in its many manifestations has branched out toward international markets, developed land markets, fueled financial markets, and made labor markets more flexible. The intensive, extensive development of markets in Latin America deepened their role in every economy of the region.

Nevertheless, two parallel phenomena contradict the proposition that the region is advancing in the direction of free market supremacy. The first is the growth of powerful economic groups that has accompanied the expansion of markets. Why have the large economic groups grown so much? Infrequent transactions involving standardized goods are more efficient when markets are present. However, markets decrease the efficiency of frequent, specific transactions such as those between manager and worker or in subcontracts among firms. In cases such as those, firms and contracts that assume asymmetrical relations (where agents are positioned in a clear hierarchy) will be more efficient. On the other hand, the expansion and linking up of markets increase the potential for economies of scale and variety, favoring the big economic groups with greater room for maneuver.

The success of different kinds of capitalism does not lie in "free" markets but rather in the organizational and competitive prowess of firms and economic groups that can innovate and update their management practices, putting themselves on the cutting edge of new patterns of development. Highlighting the importance of the large conglomerates does not underestimate the role of competition. Access to larger markets, however, was facilitated by the emergence or renovation of large firms that were able to organize and maintain effective competitiveness strategies.

Thus, in several countries (Chile, Mexico, Argentina), a new generation of economic groups — new and renovated ones — is being consolidated. Compared to those of the 1960s, these entities are more professional, more diversified, and better managed financially. They also possess greater potential for internationalization, increased capacity for strategic planning, and more autonomy from the state. These firms may be "price takers" in the global economy, where their influence is marginal, but they are "price makers" domestically, and they dominate important sectors of the economies of Latin America.

The second phenomenon that challenges the notion that free markets are going to reign supreme in the region involves contested markets (Bowles and Gintis 1993). Market exchanges always contain the seeds of potential conflict, and no market can last indefinitely without implicit rules of the game being constructed. Needed are a mix of norms, and even explicit laws, that reinforce the rules of the game and public and private institutions to regulate these transactions. All these measures that seek to provide greater certainty or narrow the room for conflict carry both social and economic costs because rents that were destined to be allocated by markets are diverted. For this reason, it can be said that truly "free" markets do not exist except in specific historical conjunctures. For better or worse, all markets assume regulations that attempt to discipline agents, strengthen contracts, and minimize future risks.

The free market illusion already has begun to disappear in Latin America, even sooner than one might have thought, as it has become obvious that unregulated markets lead to ecological degradation and that the dismantling of the old public regulations has allowed private regulations to spring up that improperly appropriate rents — both at a hefty cost to consumers, workers, and other businesses. The concept of "regulation" thus reacquires legitimacy and becomes once again an accepted tool of economic policy.

In other words, not long after the expansion of markets in the region, many Latin American countries already are attempting to build a new regulatory structure. Chance will not determine how transparent the resulting institutions will be: Outcomes will be determined by clash of economic agents, conflicts among social and political actors, and most of all, the correlation of political forces.

In sum, the growth of markets did not precede but rather occurred simultaneously with two processes: first, the fortification of the power of the private sector (especially in the influence of hierarchies such as the large conglomerates) and, second, the reconfiguration of public power and the reorganization of the functions and forms of state intervention. Along the way, a highly centralized state apparatus was conserved, and before long new types of regulation were being developed.

Strong firms emerged most rapidly in those Latin American economies with the greatest possibility for a successful insertion into the global economy. Yet the possibility of sustaining this type of development requires, in turn, a new kind of relationship between the state and the private sector. This principle is demonstrated clearly in the tight links between the state and large economic groups in East Asia, but it is no less important in the United States, where close relations exist between corporations and the government (as in the military-industrial complex).

These realities should give one pause when considering the transformations that actually are occurring in Latin America, even if mainstream economists are blind to them. As Alfred Eichner (1985) has observed, "The megacorp remains the bastard child of economic theory."[2] The perspective embodied in this chapter, though unconventional, is consistent with a current that is gaining increasing theoretical importance in the field. It seeks to break out of the cognitive prisons positivism has imposed and requires new alliances with other disciplines such as sociology, political science, and history.[3]

Transformations in the Social Structure

The transformation of Latin American society in the 1970-1990 period was enormous. The most fundamental change was that of size: The region's population increased from 280 million to 440 million inhabitants. In the 1980s, employment in the tertiary sector increased from 47 percent to 55 percent of the economically active population; informal employment increased from 26 percent to 31 percent, and the percentage of salaried workers declined from 74 percent to 69 percent, while the level of public employment remained constant, and employment by small and medium-sized firms rose.

Citing general trends glosses over the diversity of particular cases. For example, in the 1980s in Chile, the region-wide indicators just mentioned moved in exactly the opposite direction. Whatever social homogeneity may have existed in Latin America at the time of the debt crisis (1981-1983), from 1985 on, social diversity multiplied exponentially. Yet despite the disparities, there were similar tendencies among Latin American countries, such as the breakdown of social institutions and the resulting dissipation of identities, as well as emergence of new sectors and the incipient construction of new identities.

The Expansion of Entrepreneurial Civil Society

It is often said that neoliberalism and its attendant crisis cause the disarticulation of civil societies, especially where neoliberal policies are implemented by an authoritarian state, such as the one in Chile from 1973 to 1990. Latin American experience indicates that while this observation holds true for the popular and middle classes, it does not for the business world — bourgeois civil society, if you will. At the same time that the structures of the popular classes and sectors were being rent asunder, a new type of entrepreneur was breaking free and taking off. This new upper class differed from that of the past with its corporatist schemes. More important, it was increasingly autonomous from the state.

Processes of privatization, deregulation, and economic opening to the outside create new spaces in which markets may expand into the public domain, into agriculture, and into global markets. In a process that began in the 1960s at a snail's pace and accelerated dramatically in the 1980s, the strength and legitimacy of the business class grew. The business explosion in Latin America hastened the emergence of new strata of entrepreneurs in expanding sectors, who were better educated than their predecessors, more proficient in information and marketing technologies, and more deeply and extensively linked to the export sector. The ranks of small and medium-sized business owners also swelled, particularly in the tertiary sector. These trends are fed by the "outsourcing" of services, a now nearly generalized practice.

The modernization and expansion of the entrepreneurial class have enhanced its social prestige. The business owner is no longer seen only as a power figure but also as a symbol of modernity: He/she and the profit motive, the market, competition, and possessive individualism have acquired great legitimacy in Latin American society.

The Transnationalization of Societies

In the 1980s, the globalization of civil society advanced further and more rapidly than at any other time in history. In the Americas, the spread of telecommunications was a leading catalyst. Seasonal and permanent migrations to the United States by millions of Latin Americans not only had a major impact on the receiving nation but also on all the countries of origin as well. The city with the second-largest concentration of Mexicans in the world became Los Angeles, and New York became home to the second-largest number of Ecuadorans.

Latin American migration is more complex than a simple export of labor. While migration is greatest from the northern portion of the region, southern countries such as Argentina, Brazil, and Chile also are affected. Nationals from this group are dispersed between the United States and Europe. Studies of the trend indicate that migrants always maintain ties with family in the home country, often sending money on a regular basis. The result is a new source of income and also a socialization effect in the sending society.[4] Last but not least, it is important to note that Latin American elites increasingly are sending their sons and daughters to schools in North America. The tendency to do so, well established in Mesoamerica, now also incorporates the Southern Cone.

Deepening Social Inequalities

Economic crisis and neoliberal economic adjustment have increased social inequality throughout Latin America, primarily by lowering median and minimum incomes. In a sample of 14 Latin American countries between 1981 and 1990, unemployment increased from 6.7 percent to 7.8 percent; the minimum wage dropped by 35 percent, and the median salary fell 17.5 percent. Colombia, Uruguay, and Chile represent exceptions to these disturbing trends: In the first two countries, income distribution actually improved somewhat, and in Chile, the concentration of income began to reverse at the end of the period in question.[5]

An approximate comparison of the concentration of income in specific countries is possible, although uniform statistics are not available for the entire region. In Mexico between 1984 and 1989, the income share of the wealthiest 10 percent climbed from 33 percent to 38 percent, while the share of income received by the poorest 40 percent eroded from 14 percent to 13 percent. In Brazil, the share of the wealthiest 20 percent went from 62 percent of income in 1979 to 66 percent in 1987. During the same period, the share of the poorest 40 percent of Brazilians fell from 18 percent to 15 percent.

The concentration of income also worsened in Chile in the 1978-1988 period: The share of the richest 10 percent jumped from 42 percent to 50 percent, and the poorest 40 percent saw their share decline from 11 percent to 9 percent. This trend diminished somewhat from 1988 to 1992. In the Chilean case, data are available only for individuals not households, which makes the concentration of income appear even more pronounced as a single poor household generally contains a relatively higher number of members.[6]

Within the context of the economic crisis that has devastated most of Latin America, increased economic inequality has meant higher levels of poverty, reversing three decades of progress in this area. It is no longer the case that the greatest misery exists in the hinterlands. Today the urban poor outnumber the rural poor, and the deterioration of living standards is more acute in cities than in the countryside.

Increased inequality of income distribution is a relative measure best evaluated using data, where available, on changes in the following: the distribution of power among groups, respect for civil rights, and access to education, health care, information, and education. Such an analysis goes beyond the scope of this chapter, especially since wide disparities exist among living standards for the different countries. Be that as it may, available research demonstrates clearly the erosion of living standards and the quality of life among the middle and popular classes in the region, with the deterioration being much more acute in some countries than others.

Precarious Employment and Informal Employment

In terms of employment and informality, the trends in Latin America are heterogeneous. On a regional level, unemployment has increased, although in Brazil and Mexico, which are both still in the midst of ongoing structural adjustment, unemployment has been clearly lower today than it was a decade ago.[7] In those two countries, along with Peru and Honduras, the work force that was expelled from the formal sector has been channeled into the informal sector. In contrast, in Colombia and Venezuela, unemployment rose, and the informal sector was stagnant. Argentina witnessed growth in the ranks of its unemployed and also its informal sector. Finally, in Chile, both contracted (ECLAC 1994).

Precarious employment is another situation altogether. A growing body of literature confirms that precarious employment in Latin America is rising. This trend is attributed to the deregulation of both formal and informal labor markets, and it manifests itself in diminished job security and the conversion of full-time positions into part-time or temporary work. Added to this is the growth in the number of workers in the informal sector, who are by definition outside or on the margin of employment standards and norms (PREALC 1994).

Precarious employment should not be viewed as the atypical case, an anomaly or an exception in the market. Nor is it the result of stagnation, nor does it prevail only in traditional sectors or small firms. A relatively recent phenomenon, precarious employment is the direct result of entrepreneurial decisions made in response to market signals. This specific type of capitalist development has taken root in many Latin American countries: for example, in the *maquila* industries of the Dominican Republic, Mexico, and Venezuela and in the natural resource (fruit, seafood, timber) processing industries of Chile. In other words, precarious employment is characteristic of "cutting edge" sectors of the economies in question.

Precarious employment has two origins. First, changes in labor legislation and the regulation of labor markets have given management greater flexibility in its use of labor. Second, new production and management techniques and a different dominant model for firm behavior have swept the region, creating a new paradigm (Díaz 1989, De la Garza 1990).

Structural Change and Social Actors

This chapter has sought to compare the impact of structural change on economic agents and social movements in Latin America. As the region makes its economic transition, the disarticulating effects of the crisis of the old model of international insertion are clearing the way for new modalities. This two-faceted process began in the 1970s — earlier in places such as Chile and later in countries such as Brazil. The nature of this process can be expressed in binary oppositions such as destructuration/restructuration, decline/expansion, break-up/reconfiguration, or destruction/creation. Structural adjustment, change in patterns of accumulation, structural reconfiguration, and economic reconversion are the terms best suited to describe what is happening in Latin America.

Processes of Destructuration

It is worthwhile to take a closer look at the disarticulation, break-up, and dissolution of productive systems and social relations seen in the decline of industries such as the Bolivian tin mines, the Chilean automobile industry and coal mining, the Peruvian fishing industry, and the Argentine capital goods industry. One could also include the abandonment of the cultivation of banana, cacao, sugar, and other traditional crops, some for export, some not. This process of disarticulation and dissolution is not a new phenomenon. In a country such as Chile, these processes have occurred repeatedly over the centuries.

Destructuration is a lengthy process that manifests itself initially in competitive backwardness and later as a precipitous decline marked by successive shocks. Its impact is sectoral as well as spatial. The industry characteristically suffers from capital flight, falling stock values, unemployment, and withdrawal from national and international markets.

Evident in numerous countries is an asymmetry between the industry's health and the level of organization of its workers. As in the United States and Europe, industrial decline often occurs where forms of social organization have consolidated over decades. For this reason, the process of destructuration always involves sharp social conflict that may or may not be expressed openly, depending on the national political context and the level of organization of the social forces affected.

The flight of capital and managerial talent from a sector in decline generally does not imply their immediate reallocation to other productive activities. They frequently are channeled into commercial or financial pursuits, swelling the tertiary sector. By the same token, the labor force that is expelled from one sector seldom is absorbed quickly by those sectors of the economy in expansion — least of all in economies where slow growth rates are the norm. Open unemployment soars, or alternatively, an informal sector burgeons. The process is a prolonged one as economic agents take years to adapt to new conditions.

Destructuration is not caused exclusively by market forces. In every Latin American country, the state plays an important role in structural adjustment, particularly when it promotes neoliberal strategies. The demise of an industry inevitably entails the successive defeat of those social forces — be they management, small producers, or workers — that emerged historically, acquiring social legitimacy, institutional space, and political or corporative representation.

Consequently, when a sector is in decline, the legitimacy of the state's actions in the economy are easily called into question. The state ends up intervening, either to detain or accelerate the process of destructuration. The state always provides a measure of compensation that, even if it is less than the norm in developed economies, remains significant.[8] Only in very small economies, such as those in the Caribbean, is the demise of an entire industry determined exclusively by market forces. To reiterate, industries in decline were at one time dynamic. Then they experienced an inability to compete and benefitted from direct or indirect state subsidies and protectionist barriers.

Neoliberalism and its measures to open and deregulate the economy presuppose an end to state protection. For state firms, privatization means their rationalization. For private firms, the process tends to be more complex. The state compensates the affected industries by deregulating the labor market, restricting union activities, and permitting the "flexible" use of the labor force. Despite this compensation, however, competition becomes more fierce, and many firms are driven out of the market.

In short, destructuration fuels the growth of the informal sector and the "spurious" tertiary sector (Pinto 1989). The process of structural disarticulation conceivably may result in the consolidation of a stable sector that is oriented primarily toward middle and lower income members of the population. It is possible, but at the same time less likely, for the economy in question to achieve reinsertion into global markets via this path.

Social Restructuring

New processes of social restructuring emerge parallel to the disarticulation described above. For certain individuals and groups, restructuring creates new possibilities for employment, for social integration, and for social mobility. New job categories are created, such as the *maquila* worker in Mexico, the female "temp" worker in Chile, or the employees in finance or informatics. The lives of the newly employed are changed as they work eight- to 12-hour shifts and earn regular wages, however low.[9]

There may be multiplier effects: altered life routines, new patterns of social relations, and extended families lifted out of absolute poverty. Old modes of social organization often become unsuitable for present needs. Some organizational forms change and adapt; others simply disappear.[10] New social identities are created in settings that are dominated by management and lack any corporatist pact (in the Mexican *maquila*) or any other pact associated with the state, as in the *estado de compromiso* characterizing Chilean democracy prior to 1970.

In this context, the construction of collective identities is slow, difficult, and silent. It may manifest itself initially as simply a search for collective space within the rules of the game defined by management. It would be an error to interpret the failure of popular groups to attempt radical change as a form of social "conformism," a term that proved to be less than useful back in the 1960s. The term does not capture the gradual accumulation of small conflicts and successive modifications in the collective consciousness that may require a long gestation period before they become apparent. It would also seem that the expression of this accumulated consciousness is hastened by the democratization processes, which exist to greater or lesser degrees in different countries of the region.

Anomie and Integration: Concurrent Trends

In those societies experiencing destructuration and restructuration simultaneously, it becomes possible to use both the terms "anomie" and "integration" to describe (not explain) what is occurring among some social groups.[11] Groups are being marginalized and expelled from political and economic systems at the same time that their upward mobility and social integration increase. Anomie is the other face of conformism. Both apply to equally significant sectors of the society.

Anomie can be understood as a social situation that uproots individuals and cuts them off from shared moral boundaries and that isolates and encloses them. Defined in this manner, anomie is more prevalent in the large urban areas of Mexico and Argentina than in the peripheral areas of those countries, such as Chiapas in Mexico or Santiago del Estero in Argentina. Anomie would not be an apt description of conditions in Brazil or Chile.

The disarticulation of social structures caused by unemployment or the shift to less stable forms of employment generates deep traumas in the conditions and social relations of the popular classes in both rural and urban areas. Processes of social dissolution are associated with the loss of collective identities and a process of social atomization. Individuals lose the old ways of relating to each other and are forced to construct new social relations in a more hostile and precarious environment.

Yet at the same time, new collective identities are indeed being reconstituted, and social movements are being reconstructed, tardy though the process may be. The structural changes of the 1980s are manifest in a whole new class of managers and workers. These new social actors constitute a very different social and cultural configuration than that of 20 years ago. Moreover, in many countries of the region, contrary to what one might assume, both classes have expanded.

Unlike the new worker class, however, the new management class is organized, conscious, and endowed with an identity as the nation's modernizers. Even so, there is an awareness among the new entrepreneurs that the golden age of their absolute power is waning, and they sense the old ghosts surrounding their enterprises. The working classes, for their part, only appeared to be destined to vanish. Instead, they are undergoing a process of reconfiguration that is far slower and quite distinct from the ideal types imagined by the left. Having failed to generate grand social movements, this new class of workers nevertheless is traversing new and unknown paths that it will have to chart for itself.

Notes

1. The word "transition" refers here not just to the political transition but also to the historical changes and transformations occurring in economic, social, and institutional structures. "Structures," for purposes here, refer to the economic institutions of capitalism: the state, markets, firms, and economic groups and agents.

2. The importance of these new economic groups has not been fully recognized in conventional economic theory. As Alfred Eichner observes, "Despite the doubts which both Schumpeter and Galbraith have tried to implant in the minds of their colleagues, economists — whatever their other differences — are still inclined to view the megacorp and its accompanying oliogopolistic market structure as a departure from the ideal of multitudinous enterprises competing in atomistic markets. The megacorp remains the bastard child of economic theory...." (Eichner 1985, 23).

3. Over the previous two decades, a more adequate theoretical analysis has emerged focusing on the simultaneity of coordination through markets and through public and private hierarchies. The leading proponents of this current thought are the economic historian Alfred Chandler(1961, 1977); Oliver Williamson(1975, 1985), who has laid the groundwork for the neoinstitutional theory of transaction costs; and the post-Keynesian economist Alfred Eichner (1985), who placed the new microeconomics at the center of new macroeconomic approaches. There is no uniform theory, however. For example, the neoclassical analysis of these phenomena considers that coordination through hierarchies occurs due to "market failures" that raise transaction costs. This follows a long tradition that analyzes really existing markets as "deviations" from an ideal model. An alternative approach argues that in all capitalist economies, both forms of coordination develop simultaneously. Paraphrasing Alfred Chandler, it could be said that the "invisible hand" accompanies the "visible hand." What can be considered a "market failure" could also be seen as an "organizational success" and vice-versa (Lazonick 1991). See Bowles and Gintis 1993 for a more radical perspective on these same ideas.

4. See the excellent essay by Alejandro Portes (1996) on the emergence of "transnational communities."

5. The data in the next several paragraphs may be found in ECLAC 1994 and CEPAL 1991. For important analysis, see Oscar Altimir 1994.

6. Also, the Mexican data result from surveys only of urban areas over a 15-year period, while the Chilean data came from national surveys over only a decade.

7. The December 1994 financial collapse in Mexico resulted in sharp increases in unemployment and may reverse the previous trend toward lower rates of unemployment.

8. For example, intense pressure from farmers led the Pinochet government to establish a price floor for traditional agricultural products after the crisis in 1982-1983.

9. When workers acquire relatively stable employment, not only their incomes rise but also their access to credit. For example, in Chile, there are now three million credit cards in circulation — in a country with a labor force of five million.

10. Youth groups in Chile and Brazil are a divergent example. In Brazil, the campaign to impeach President Fernando Collor de Mello was led by the student movement, which took on new and original forms while using the protests of the 1960s as its model. A Brazilian journalist observed, "the streets beat the shopping malls" for a while. In Chile, by contrast, the shopping malls are beating the streets, at least for now.

11. Desalarization, unemployment, and informality do not necessarily imply that anomie will always be reproduced. The social movements that emerged in Latin America in the 1950s show that in popular neighborhoods, alternative forms of identity reconstruction are possible and sometimes are able to build social movements that are potent and even antisystemic.

References

Altimir, Oscar. 1994. "Distribución del ingreso e incidencia de la pobreza a lo largo del ajuste." *Revista de la CEPAL* 52 (April), 4-32.

Bowles, Samuel, and Herbert Gintis. 1993. "The Revenge of Homo Economicus: Contested Exchange and the Revival of Political Economy." *Journal of Economic Perspectives* 7 (1).

CEPAL (Comisión Económica para América Latina). 1990. *Magnitud de la pobreza en América Latina en los ochenta.* Santiago: CEPAL.

CEPAL (Comisión Económica para América Latina). 1991. *Cadenas agroexportadoras en Chile: Transformación productiva e integración social.* Santiago: CEPAL.

Chandler, Alfred. 1961. *Strategy and Structure.* Cambridge, Mass.: MIT Press.

Chandler, Alfred. 1977. *The Visible Hand: The Managerial Revolution in American Business.* Cambridge, Mass.: Harvard University/Belknap Press.

De la Garza, E. 1990. "Reconversión industrial y cambio en el padron de relaciones laborales en México." In *La modernización de México,* ed. A. Anguiana. México: Universidad Nacional Autónoma de México.

Díaz, Alvaro. 1989. "Regimen de empresa y modernización autoritaria en Chile." *Revista Proposiciones* 20.

ECLAC (Economic Commission for Latin America and the Caribbean). 1994. *Social Panorama in Latin America.* Santiago: ECLAC.

Eichner, Alfred. 1985. *Toward a New Economics: Essays in Post-Keynesian and Institutionalist Theory.* New York: MacMillan.

Halperín Donghi, Tulio. 1969. *Historia contemporánea de América Latina.* Madrid: Alianza Editorial.

Lazonick, W. 1991. *Business Organization and the Myth of the Market Economy.* New York: Cambridge University Press.

Pinto, Aníbal. 1989. "Notas sobre industrialización y progreso técnico en la perspectiva Prebish-ECLAC." Santiago: ECLAC.

Portes, Alejandro. 1996. "Transnational Communities: Their Emergence and Significance in the Contemporary World System." In *Latin America and the World-Economy,* eds. Roberto Patricio Korzeniewicz and William C. Smith. Westport, Conn.: Greenwood Press.

PREALC (UN Program on Employment in Latin America). 1994. "Empleo precario en América Latina." Santiago: PREALC.

Williamson, Oliver. 1975. *Markets and Hierarchies: Analysis and Implications.* Glencoe, Ill.: Free Press.

Williamson, Oliver. 1985. *The Economic Institutions of Capitalism.* New York: Free Press.

Part II.

Social Change, Social Actors, and Citizenship

Chapter 4

Citizenship and Social Movements under Neoliberalism

Ian Roxborough

Introduction

The neoliberal economic project has complex and contradictory implications for social movements and, more generally, for civil society.[1] Since neoliberalism increases the role of the market and decreases, or at least redefines, the role of the state, there should be far-reaching effects on civil society and on the relations between civil society and the state. Some analysts see the primary impact of neoliberalism as one of disarticulating civil society in a variety of ways. Others argue that current trends should be seen as a *re-*articulation of civil society and its relation to the state.

This chapter speculates about the complex and paradoxical impact of neoliberalism in Latin America in the next few years on the state, on civil society, and on state-civil society relations.

To begin, a caveat: Neoliberalism has not been and will not be applied in a total or uniform manner in Latin America; within neoliberalism, there is and will continue to be considerable scope for a wide range of state-civil society institutions and processes. Moreover, even in cases of considerable application of neoliberal economic reforms, there also will be trends toward the strengthening of certain forms of political organization in "civil society" and toward an increasingly tight integration of parts of "civil society" and the state. The chapter argues that there will be pressures for the state to expand its role in society and that this could perhaps lead to increased links between civil society and the state.

Social Movements, Both New and Old

The 1970s and 1980s were a period of flowering of "new" social movements throughout much of Latin America. In addition to established labor movements and political parties, an effervescence of grassroots mobilization led to a dramatic expansion of all sorts of organizations. Some of these were responses to rapid urbanization, seeking land or access to urban services. The "urban question" came to the fore in these years (Castells 1983). The political nature of these urban social movements varied from country to country. In some countries, radical and revolutionary parties were able to establish a dominant presence; in others, urban social movements rapidly entered into a form of clientelism with the state (Handelman 1975). Other "new" social movements arose in response to human rights and citizenship issues. Protests against the military governments of Chile and Argentina, for example, were led by organizations of women, the most famous being the *Madres de la Plaza de Mayo*. There were broad civic pro-democracy movements in Brazil (the *direitas já* campaign), in Chile, and elsewhere. This period saw the growth of movements on behalf of indigenous peoples, blacks, the environment, women, and gays.

Some of the new social movements had their origins in religious change and took on a deeply religious coloration. The 1970s and 1980s saw the rise of Catholic radicalism and the theology of liberation. In Brazil and Mexico, radical sections of the Catholic Church were involved heavily with the more militant sections of the labor movement, both urban and rural. Radical Catholics were important in the guerrilla movements of the 1970s in Central America, most notably in Nicaragua.[2] Another important dimension of religious mobilization in these years was the dramatic expansion of evangelical Protestantism throughout Latin America. Although often nominally apolitical, Protestant fundamentalism is an important social movement with considerable political ramifications. (Evangelical Protestants are greatly over-represented in the Brazilian Congress, for example, and in areas affected by massive violence and civil war, Protestant fundamentalism offered a rejection of "politics" that may have been supportive of right-wing authoritarianism. This seems to have been the case in some parts of rural Brazil and in Guatemala.)

Within the ranks of organized labor, generally believed to have been coopted as a conservative junior partner of corporatist regimes, there emerged new, grassroots currents. This "new unionism" appeared in Peru, in Argentina (in the *Cordobazos* of 1969 and 1971), in the struggles for democratization of the electricity workers' unions in Mexico, and, most famously, in the rank-and-file union insurgency in Brazil that led eventually to the formation of the Central Union of Workers (Central Única dos Trabalhadores — CUT) and the Workers Party (Partido dos Trabalhadores — PT). As the "new unionism" expanded, widespread efforts were made to link unions with residentially based movements. In some countries (Mexico, Colombia, and Peru), various forms of coordinating organizations were established. Women played a major role in many of these new social movements.

Nor were all social movements rural. The 1960s, 1970s, and 1980s saw widespread peasant movements, movements of indigenous peoples, rural unionization, and the operation of a number of guerrilla organizations in rural areas.

There were also changes in the political parties, with the emergence of new parties (and sometimes a revitalization of established parties) struggling against authoritarian regimes — the National Action Party (Partido de Acción Nacional — PAN) and the Democratic Revolutionary Party (Partido de la

Revolución Democrática — PRD) in Mexico and the Party of the Brazilian Democratic Movement (Partido do Movimento Democrático Brasileiro — PMDB) and PT in Brazil, for example. Throughout Latin America, civil society seemed to be on the move, challenging the old corporatist and elitist political systems, heralding a vastly expanded democratic and participatory polity.[3]

The newness of these movements should not be exaggerated. While some were, indeed, of recent origin and were quite different from older movements in that they adopted a more participatory political style, others had roots going back to the period of the import-substitution industrialization (ISI) project. In large part, the state sponsored and regulated many social movements during the ISI project. This was particularly true for the labor movement and for movements that have been labeled "populist." Corporatist mechanisms of tripartite negotiation and conflict resolution were employed frequently to mediate state-civil society relationships.

Other social movements, however, did grow up in opposition to the state and developed discourses and repertoires of action that were explicitly anti-statist. This is one sense in which they were "new." In some countries, though by no means universally, this was the case with some aspects of urban ameliorative movements that took on a self-help coloration. In the struggle against military dictatorships and authoritarian governments, parts of the labor movement also adopted anti-statist positions. Identity-based movements also might seek a sphere of autonomy from the state and develop some form of anti-statist discourse. These "new social movements" and the "new unionism" have been seen as the organized representation of civil society against the state and as the harbingers of new political arrangements.

Some theorists of "new social movements" seem to have deposited great hopes in these social movements as the generators of a new and fuller kind of democracy. Increased popular participation, greater egalitarianism in decisionmaking, the devolution of power to the grassroots, and greater accountability were all expected to enhance the quality of democracy in Latin America (Escobar and Alvarez 1992). While there is certainly some truth to this position, it was, understandably perhaps, greatly exaggerated.

In any case, these hopes for greatly expanded participatory democracy via new social movements were rudely shaken in the aftermath of the 1982 debt shock, the subsequent economic collapse, and the eventual widespread adoption of the neoliberal model.

Both participants in these new social movements and academic observers who chronicled their meteoric rise saw in neoliberalism their death-knell. On the one hand, the *substance* of the neoliberal project is seen as opposed to the interests of much of civil society. The reduction of state expenditures on social questions and the adjustment costs attendant on both the debt shock and the shift to neoliberalism are seen as placing civil society in general, and these new social movements in particular, on the defensive and as increasing the tensions between civil society and the state. On the other hand, the new *style* of politics inaugurated by state managers committed to neoliberalism had no place for widespread citizen mobilization. The new style of politics under neoliberalism has tended to be either technocratic (Chile and Mexico) or a sort of personalistic, authoritarian, and plebiscitary populism (Brazil, Peru, and Argentina) (Roxborough 1992a). In neither case is there much encouragement for widespread involvement by citizens.

Such a perception is somewhat paradoxical, however, since neoliberalism is, of course, a form of liberalism. That is, it seeks to return to society and to individuals functions that have been "inappropriately" taken over by the state. One would have thought that this result would be applauded by the theorists of new social movements. Some of the writing on new social movements seemed to imply that corporatism and clientelism were antithetical to democracy, which in turn was identified with participation. In this view, democracy would be strengthened if new social movements could break away from state tutelage. This line of argument was perhaps most pronounced in Mexico and Brazil in criticisms of the *charro* and *pelego* pro-government labor leaderships. This strand of thought had a number of interesting coincidences with neoliberal arguments coming from conservative quarters. By reducing (or redefining) the role of the state, neoliberalism would return power to society as a whole. There should be more space for the autonomous action of a wide range of social actors, including labor and a variety of social movements. Unfortunately, this benign vision of a rebirth of civil society was belied by the harsh facts of continual crisis, weakly institutionalized polities, and fragmented and incomplete citizenship.[4]

Not only has there been much less movement toward grassroots, participatory democracy than might have been hoped for, there has also been, it seems, a general demobilization of new social movements as a result of the implementation of the neoliberal project. In this project, there is little room for diffuse movements of civil society. Politics in neoliberalism is about macroeconomic control of the economy, deregulation of the economy, and a withdrawal of the state from civil society in general. As a result, most analysts of neoliberalism tend to focus on the state and on the more organized social actors (business and labor) and devote little attention to the more diffuse types of social movements. In a way, this relative neglect mirrors the pessimism of some theorists of new social movements, who see little scope for such movements under neoliberalism except in a purely defensive and contestatory manner. The view of these theorists is that neoliberalism leads to disorganization of social movements.

The economic crisis and neoliberal transformation have pushed some social movements onto the defensive (this is true of several labor movements, particularly in Peru and Argentina), while increasing the prominence of others (soup kitchens in Peru, old-age pensioners in Argentina), and has, in addition, focused the attention of society and analysts alike on the key state decisions about economic reform. In this way, the economic crisis and neoliberal transformation have displaced partially the locus of political concern from civil society to economic decisionmaking. On the other hand, the current transformations in the role of the state are calling forth new social movements (beneficiaries of social security systems, for example) as a response to state initiatives.

Schematically, neoliberalism is producing 1) some renewed develop-ment of social movements as they respond to attacks on previous privileges and 2) a process of disarticulation and rearticulation of more established social movements. Moreover, the process of disarticulation itself is complicated and worthy of closer examination.

The disarticulation produced by neoliberalism is threefold: 1) a gener-alized sense of crisis and despair, leading to an erosion of the cultural and organizational bases for stable democracy; 2) a reduction in the role of organized labor; and 3) a general perplexity among political parties and their electorates as the old lines of cleavage disappear and have yet to be replaced.

How serious the first form of disarticulation, the generalized sense of crisis and despair, is remains still to be seen. It should not be minimized, and Guillermo O'Donnell's description of the steady descent into "delegative democracies, weak horizontal accountability, schizophrenic states, brown areas, and low-intensity citizenship" is powerful and convincing (O'Donnell 1994b, 176). On the other hand, to argue that there is a sort of Durkheimian crisis of moral authority is hard to establish empirically. When large numbers of citizens are integrated only weakly into the political system, it is not at all clear that their views matter very much in terms of concrete political outcomes. In any case, it is also plausible that there can be a fairly rapid turnaround in public attitudes if an upward spiral of growth and democratic accountability can be initiated.

The second form of disarticulation is more apparent than real: Unions are on the defensive, and there are moves to restructure radically both plant-level industrial relations and the role of unions in national-level collective bargaining, but this should not be taken as meaning that unions will cease to be important political players. In any case, with the exception of Chile and Argentina, which have implemented radical neoliberal labor legislation, it is by no means clear as yet how widespread these changes will be. In Mexico, for example, there have been discussions of labor law reform for a number of years now without any concrete result as yet.

The third form of disarticulation, political parties in search of new definitions, while serious, may be a purely transitional phenomenon. As the neoliberal project settles down, it would be reasonable to predict that political parties also will settle down along new lines of cleavage. This will take time, but there is no reason to assume that the present state of flux and uncertainty in the political party system will be permanent.

At the same time that the economic crisis and neoliberal restructuring have transformed the region, a general process of democratization (or redemocratization) has also had a major impact on the nature of social movements in Latin America.

With redemocratization, a number of things have happened. First, some of the conjuncture-specific social movements (*Direitas Já, Madres de la Plaza de Mayo*) have ceased to play central roles. This sort of movement emerged during authoritarian episodes, sometimes in response to the actions of the authoritarian government directly and sometimes because of the lack of alternative spaces for political mobilization as a result of the closure of Congress or the banning of political party activity. However, some of these movements have continued to flourish. Here the rapid expansion of radical Catholic organizations is notable. However, where this was the case, most of these movements had a longer and more complex history. They were not all, in any simple sense, new. The rise of Catholic radicalism, for example, must be traced back at least to the early 1960s, while the rapid growth of fundamentalist Protestantism, which also must be included as a new social movement, seems to have had little direct connection with authoritarianism.[5] Second, the revival of the arena of political parties and parliamentary debate has brought back a number of arenas for political debate and mobilization and has, as a direct result, led to a reduced role for those new social movements that grew up in alternative settings, such as radical church groups. Finally, some new social movements have become more institutionalized and have adopted strategies oriented toward strategic bargaining rather than simple contestation (the CUT). Routinization has set in and with it the development of more bureaucratic and less participatory organizational forms. These phenomena stem directly from the return to democracy.

The picture, however, is by no means uniformly bleak. Different kinds of social movements have suffered different fates in the new conjuncture. While some have been weakened radically or have disappeared, other social movements continue to flourish. Those that continue generally have undergone a process of institutionalization. None of this suggests a uniform process of "disaggregation" of civil society. Civil society always has been somewhat incoherent, and its movements always have been heterogeneous, poorly articulated with political parties, and often diffuse. Is the present situation any worse?

The State

The reduction in state intervention in the social sphere reduces the total amount of resources available in the polity. It does not merely *transfer* resources or power from the state to other actors. Some of these resources simply are lost to society as a whole along the way. The roll-back in social welfare programs reduces the ability both of the state and of organizations, such as labor unions, to alleviate the widespread failures of markets to provide an acceptable level of social justice in terms of access to health care, education, and social security. The state's renunciation of certain instruments of economic policy — various forms of price control, subsidies and transfer prices, and protectionism — not only weaken the state; they also weaken those organizations in civil society that represented their members' interests by constant lobbying within the policy-making arena. During the post-Second World War period, and often before, employers' associations were represented regularly in the councils of state. The mechanisms of corporatist concertation, whatever their faults, were ways that organized labor and small business could lobby for the representation of their interests in the formulation of economic policy.[6] In contrast to the general acceptance of state intervention in the post-World War II period, both the new left and neoliberals now are opposed to corporatism and wish to set civil society free from state tutelage. While this, in principle, enables organizations in civil society to set their own goals, it also reduces some of their power.

In these ways, both the state and civil society lose power capacities. If Latin American states hew closely to the ideological prescriptions for a minimalist state as advocated by doctrinaire neoliberalism, in the current context of fiscal penury, disempowerment of the state could lead to the disempowerment of civil society as well or at least to the disempowerment of certain elements of civil society. Of course, the roll-back of the state is unlikely to be "class neutral": Big business is likely to gain, and small business and labor are likely to lose. In a market-oriented society, those groups that can dominate markets will do well, while others will lose.

However, while some Latin American states may stick with the neoliberal prescription for a minimalist state, there will be considerable temptations for state managers throughout Latin America to try to expand their power resources. These moves will be aided and abetted by significant sectors of civil society. It is reasonable to predict a net *increase* in state capacities in Latin America in coming years rather than a continuation of a minimalist approach.

In part, this will be because some states will deviate from a pure neoliberal model. It will happen because the expansion of state capacities will stem from the fact that neoliberalism itself requires a redefinition of the powers of the state. As Carlos Acuña and William Smith say, "Affirmations that state power in Latin America is 'weakening' say very little...greater orthodoxy may imply not less but *more* effective coordination and oversight of the private sector...and concentration of expanded administrative power in the hands of state managers and technocratic elites" (Acuña and Smith 1994, 21). This will involve a redefinition of the tasks the state will attempt to undertake. The aim will be not simply to minimize the role of the state but rather to redefine what is appropriate for the state.[7] Whether neoliberal state managers succeed in reshaping the state so that it is both leaner and more effective from their point of view will depend in part on the degree to which they can ignore pressures (both domestic and international) for ideological consistency at the expense of pragmatism.

Acuña and Smith argue that neoliberal states are likely to assume new regulatory roles so that markets function smoothly. There are also other reasons why state managers might attempt to increase their power capacity (in the most abstract sense) once again. Politics is, after all, a matter of accommodating interests. The notion of a Bonapartist neoliberal state standing above all the contending interests of civil society is a description of an exceptional period. This is not normal politics: It is the description of a society in crisis. Sooner or later, the need to form electoral alliances or to gain support for particular policies will lead state managers toward a resumption of bargaining. To do this, they will be forced to expand their power capacity in order to have something they can offer groups in civil society. At present, they can offer big business the immediate rewards of privatization and deregulation, but it is most unlikely that state managers will be able to ignore small business, middle classes, and labor indefinitely.

There are potentially great gains to be made, both from the point of view of state efficacy and from the point of view of the general welfare of society, as a result of streamlining and restructuring the state. Unencumbered by inefficient state-owned industries and by a mass of inappropriate and inefficient transfer payments and subsidies, untrammelled by blanket protectionism and complex regulatory systems, unburdened of a bloated and inefficient (not to say, corrupt) state bureaucracy, the state, after its neoliberal purging, is now in a position to expand its functions once more.

If the state were to expand its functions rationally, there would be a tremendous gain in autonomy and coherence of the state apparatus. This either could tend in the direction of elitist and exclusionary technocracy or could increase pressures for fuller democratic control over state policy formation. Which will occur depends on a great many factors; the concern at this point is simply to note that reform of the state could perhaps be beneficial for society as a whole.

For this to occur, many of the neoliberal reforms would need to remain in place. Markets are often more efficient than state allocation. There are compelling reasons in many areas of the economy for moving away from centralized political decisionmaking and toward increasingly decentered markets. However, markets are often imperfect, and there are many ways in which states can and should attempt to remedy market failure. Within the overall framework of neoliberalism, there is room for considerable state intervention. Obvious areas include the following:

- Industrial policy;
- Market intervention in the non-tradables sector, particularly health and education; and
- Wage and price policy.

These are areas in which Latin American states can expand their capacities within a neoliberal framework. Whether they will do so will depend on the perceived political risks involved and the constraints on successful state intervention in these areas. Two key constraints are the fiscal and administrative capability of Latin American states. Both of these are extremely difficult matters; tax reform is politically risky, and improvements in administrative capacity are unlikely to be subject to a quick fix. A sustained effort to reduce corruption and clientelism needs to be mounted, and a core of permanent civil servants needs to be built up. These problems are not new; they were identified by the early modernization theorists in the 1950s and 1960s. They still remain unresolved. They are dealt with in more detail below.

Industrial Policy

It should be possible, even in a region fixated on neoliberal ideology, to develop the sort of state-civil society relationships that will foster rapid economic growth. Latin American governments ought to be able to build on their tradition of the state playing a leading role in sponsoring industrialization and industrial exports. The accumulating evidence from the Asian newly industrializing countries (NICs), plus the example of Colombia, suggest that the key to rapid economic growth lies in developing the *right* kind of links with private business (Evans 1995 and Thorp 1991). It is not a question of maximizing or minimizing the role of the state in the economy or of maximizing or minimizing the influence of economic elites on the government. As Peter Evans (1995) has argued, developmentalism requires getting the balance right between private business and the state. This means either strong employers' associations or oligopolistic industry, together with well-functioning corporatist institutions, to ensure smooth two-way flows of information between government and industry. It also requires a competent state technocracy capable of maintaining continuity in a *dirigiste* approach. Both parties need to be strong, and both need to be able to communicate with each other in a permanent and regular manner.[8]

Market Intervention

Historically, both social democracy in Europe and ISI-oriented states in Latin America have operated in economic regimes that have enabled governments to insulate the national economy somewhat from international economic forces. This has been done partly by intervening in the foreign exchange markets. The buffer between the national and the international economy enabled these governments to pursue Keynesian or structural-developmental policies. Governments were able to distort market prices in a number of ways, through subsidies and stimuli, and were able to create some semblance of a welfare state. Its form in Latin America was different from its form in Europe, with a greater reliance on tariffs and regulations in Latin America and a greater coordination of exchange rate policy with other key economic variables in Europe. Particularly in Latin America, this created a large non-tradables sector in the economy. In general, in the non-tradables sector, the government could interfere in the setting of prices without immediate and massive problems. Transfer payments could be made without incurring huge problems, and this was an important mechanism for redistribution of income.

Since the 1970s, this situation has been changing gradually, and for Latin America in the 1990s, it has changed considerably. The degree of internationalization of markets has increased markedly. In principle, nearly all goods are now tradable, and capital flows are much greater, less subject to government control, and more volatile than at any point in the past. There is, however, still an important sector of the economy that has not been thoroughly internationalized: personal services such as health and education. This means that there is room for raising wages for teachers and health workers and also for increasing subsidies to consumers of health and education. Given the importance of both health and education in long-term development, this could be an important area of government intervention.[9]

Wage and Price Policy

Wage and price control policies will continue to be a possible and useful weapon in any government's economic arsenal. Many neoliberal governments will adopt exclusively orthodox (i.e., purely market) policies to deal with inflation. Some, however, most notably Mexico, will continue to use wage and price controls *in addition* to monetary and fiscal measures. Taken as part of a larger package, there is often a strong case to be made for the utility of incomes policy as an anti-inflationary device. Wage and price controls are not a panacea, and there are considerable difficulties, both technical and political-organizational, in making them work. At the risk of some repetition of previous work (Smith 1989 and Roxborough 1992b), some of the conditions will be briefly summarized here.

It is helpful to conceptualize price and income policies as a slightly expanded Prisoners' Dilemma. There are three actors: organized labor, organized business, and the government. It is assumed that there is a stable solution that will lead to positive results for all actors and that the problem is for each actor to pursue a strategy that will lead to this solution.[10] If repeated iterations of the Prisoners' Dilemma are assumed, then a learning process and the adoption of tit-for-tat or similar procedures would lead to a stable solution (Axlerod 1984). However, in real politics, the time frame is limited, and there will be very few iterations. It is important, therefore, for each actor to move rapidly toward the optimal solution without "mistakes" that would set back this process. There appear to be two principal prerequisites here. First, each actor must be able to operate in as coherent and unitary a manner as possible. This means extensive organizational coverage, strong peak associations with the ability to sanction dissident and free-riding elements within their ranks, and a leadership that is not blinkered by dysfunctional ideological preconceptions. The second prerequisite is a degree of mutual trust among the three actors. With each successful iteration of the game, this mutual trust may be assumed to grow and to take on institutional embodiment. The problem is in the initial stages of the game. If there is little mutual trust, one or more actors may attempt to free ride or to sucker the other(s), and this will produce a suboptimal solution that, in turn, may begin a downward spiral well-nigh impossible to arrest.

Trust among business and labor will depend on the previous history of industrial relations. They may well have a clear adversarial posture, but as long as each sees the other as sticking by agreements, trust is not incompatible with conflict. In Brazil, for example, despite the violent confrontations between labor and business in the late 1970s and early 1980s, both actors felt able to rely on the other to keep their word.

The actor that has the greatest difficulty in generating trust is the government. For other actors to trust the state, there has to be a clear history of both consistency and coherence in policy.[11] This is not easy to achieve when control of the economy is difficult, as in periods of high inflation and hyperinflation, or in periods of political transition, when the basic rules of the game are up for grabs. In these circumstances, state managers often are tempted to impose a solution on the other actors. The sudden introduction of heterodox shocks in the Austral Plan in Argentina and the Plan Cruzado in Brazil illustrates this attempt by state managers to cut the Gordian knot and attempt to establish new rules of the game. However, these experiences also suggest that unilateral imposition by the state is unlikely to succeed unless (among other things) there is also a serious effort to get the various parties around a bargaining table in order to begin to build up working relationships. While there were several reasons for the failure of both of these heterodox plans, the fact that they were developed as unilateral state strategies rather than as a result of some form of concertation meant that any minor shift in policy was likely to lead to sudden collapse.

State Capacities

State capacity is largely an organizational question. While Latin American states chronically are under-resourced, the road to increased efficiency and capacity in the state runs through institutional reform. There are several areas where action is needed: creation of a permanent civil service (particularly, the managerial cadres); increased fiscal capacity through tax reform; improved mechanisms for links between the state and key economic actors; improved internal functioning of the state apparatus, including reduction of over-manning, clientelism, and corruption; and improved balance between the executive and the legislative/judicial powers.

Concretely, this program of reform means reviving or reinvigorating some corporatist institutions and establishing a ministry of technology. It will involve the creation of civil service career patterns for state technocrats. Some of the formal structures are to a considerable degree already in place; what is required is to produce the sense of a stable career open to talent that will make these structures function effectively.

Guillermo O'Donnell is eloquent on the ways in which the service of the state has become less and less attractive. As he says, "In addition to diminishing salaries, there are indications of a severe degradation not only in the functioning of the public sector but in the very ideal of public service....If to be a state official was at one time a sign of high status, nowadays it is nearly the opposite" (O'Donnell 1994b, 168).

A major difficulty is the limited fiscal resources available for administrative reform. In one way, this fiscal stringency can be an advantage, since it may force the reduction of supernumerary clientelistic personnel whose marginal efficiency may actually be negative. In practice, however, it is often the most qualified personnel who leave first, since they can get jobs elsewhere, thus compounding the problem. Unless salaries in the public sector are raised once more (and raised substantially), even a slimmed-down state apparatus will have enormous difficulties in attracting the right kind of personnel.

Tax reform, of course, will be high on the agenda. This should have substantial backing from the "post-Washington Consensus" policymakers in the United States. There is considerable mileage, as the Carlos Menem government has demonstrated, in improving tax collection, even without changing the system of taxation itself. There is also a major reward for any government courageous enough to implement a radical change in the overall tax burden.

An anti-corruption drive is also likely to garner considerable international support and will yield considerable payoffs both in terms of improved administrative capabilities and in terms of more effective use of scarce state resources. However, cleaning up corruption is notoriously difficult, since corruption not only creates vested interests and institutionalized practices but also, as O'Donnell (1994b) has argued, enables state managers to make political deals with the various particularistic interests that have colonized parts of the state apparatus.

This is a massive agenda that will produce benefits for the state primarily in the long run. As a result, although the long-term benefits may be appealing, there is little incentive for any particular government, concerned with short-term political survival, to embark on these reforms. The immediate risks and costs are perceived to be high, and the benefits are seen to accrue only in the long run.

There is one circumstance in which Latin American governments might embark on these long-term reforms. If there existed a strong movement in civil society aimed at making the state responsive to its citizens, it is possible that this could be institutionalized in a number of civic movements and in the programs of some political parties in a way that might give state managers some incentive to embark on these reforms. However, this is to anticipate the argument of this chapter.

In sum, at least some state managers may be tempted to revive the state in ways that increase its general power capacity. What effect might this have on civil society? First, the issue of social movements is addressed and then citizenship concerns.

Citizenship

In terms of the coherence of civil society, the present situation may perhaps be worse than the past. However, there are reasons to believe that it may, at least potentially, be better. Much will depend on the future evolution of social movements and their relation to the state.

Before discussing this issue, some distinctions need to be made. An electoral democracy is a way of choosing a government;[12] this should not be conflated with the regular and continuing participation of the citizenry in the day-to-day functioning of that democracy. The quality of that democracy is dependent on a variety of factors: on the extent of participation (as suggested by theorists of new social movements), on the type of civic culture and the existence of norms of tolerance and civility, on the effective operation of the rule of law across the entire territory and for all social strata, and on the institutionalization of both popular and elite participation in decisionmaking so that there is something approximating a legitimate and rational process of policy formation.

A high-quality democracy with full citizenship is a society in which many people hold strong beliefs about the rights and duties of citizens, both vis-à-vis one another and with regard to the state. It is one in which there is rule of law and equality before the law, one in which arbitrary and antisocial acts by the state or by citizens are actively contested, one in which there is a general concern for justice (understood in a broad sense), and one in which there is rational and tolerant discussion of public issues. Expanded participation by social movements is only *one* aspect that needs to be considered when judging the quality of a democracy and not necessarily the most important. Indeed, under certain circumstances, expanded participation may have unintended consequences that are deleterious for the consolidation of democracy and for the improvement of its quality. It may well be that a high-quality democracy has a fairly low level of political mobilization. Politics in a high-quality democracy may, sometimes, be quite institutionalized and a little dull.

In many, if not all, of the countries of modern Latin America, substantial numbers of people are, in some sense, not full citizens. They are marginalized from or not fully incorporated into the body politic. These people do not enjoy adequate access to the rule of law or have insufficient educational, organizational, or other resources to ensure that they get a fair deal.[13] Guillermo O'Donnell (1994a) has emphasized the importance of rule of law for the constitution of a stable democracy. He has stressed the fragmentation of power and authority, the privatization and colonization of parts of the state, and the correlative atomization of civil society. In this scenario, there is little reason to be optimistic about the development of a well-functioning citizen democracy. The paradox is that while the quality of democracy in practice leaves a great deal to be desired, at the same time demands for an enhancement of citizenship, rather than automatically becoming the central issue of politics, may well be relegated to a marginal position.

How then, under neoliberalism, do citizenship issues become articulated politically? Will they be taken up by political parties, or will social movements develop around particular citizenship issues?[14] Clearly, there is scope for political parties to adopt citizenship issues as part of a broader package. The scope for social movements is much more limited, though by no means nonexistent. The principal issue is whether demands for fuller citizenship can lead to a conceptualization of citizenship issues that stimulates mobilization around concrete, attainable goals. To put it slightly differently, will social movements primarily be oriented to concerns that can be articulated in public discourse as general citizenship concerns, or will they primarily pursue particularistic aims, whether material or symbolic?[15]

Insofar as concrete demands can be linked to a general argument for better quality citizenship, there will be a point of convergence between social movements and the interests of state managers. As argued earlier in this chapter, there are good reasons for state managers to want to enhance the efficiency and capacity of the state. The ways in which this might occur are congruent with a generalized demand stemming from the public that the state be answerable to its citizens. There are multiple points of possible coincidence of interest between state managers and (some) citizens. What some of these might be has been discussed from the point of view of state managers. They include reform of the state, industrial policy, incomes policy, and substantial state intervention in health and education.

While there is not necessarily a direct parallel, these reforms have their counterparts if seen from the side of civil society. Large numbers of citizens have an interest in an efficient and competent state, partly in terms of government services and also in terms of the administration of justice. They also will be concerned about sustainable and equitable economic growth. There is, moreover, possible convergence of interest in the area of social policy. If these sorts of issues are presented as a package of citizenship issues, as matters of rights and justice, rather than as a set of incremental reforms, the likelihood of effective political mobilization will be enhanced.

In terms of concrete policies, obvious areas include health and education. Another important area concerns crime and policing. There may be still other issues that can link immediate concerns and a broader notion of citizenship, but the present discussion will be limited to these.

With regard to health and education, there is a possible convergence of interests between state managers and the public. For many Latin American states at the present time, the fiscal crisis of the state is the key determinant of social policy, leading to reductions in spending in these areas. However, should reforms in fiscal and administrative areas, together with stabilization of the economy and growth, lead to less urgency to cut government spending, then increased expenditure on health and education could, conceivably, fit in with a broader neoliberal project. While doctrinaire neoliberalism calls for a reduction of state intervention across the board, more pragmatic versions well may focus on improving the efficiency of markets, particularly those concerned with tradable goods and services. To the extent that health and education lie within the non-tradables sector of the economy, governments can intervene in massive ways that will bring them both considerable political support and long-run improvements in growth prospects.

It is important to repeat that adoption of a major program of reform in health and education will be most likely to improve the quality of democracy if these reforms are articulated politically as citizenship issues and not as incremental and largely economic reforms.

Similar arguments apply to crime. Law and order issues involve two separate dimensions that are often hard to link together in terms of political practice. On the one hand, all citizens want a reasonable level of protection from crime. While this is often articulated as either a middle-class moral panic or as petit-bourgeois vigilantism (assassinations of small crooks and "marginals," often with the active involvement of the police), there are other ways in which law and order issues might be articulated. Responses to a perceived failure of the state to guarantee law and order need not always be of a "do-it-yourself" kind. Are anything other than episodic movements demanding better policing likely to develop? Apparently, largely middle-class demonstrations for greater physical security have occurred in Brazil. Whether these remain simply episodic outbursts or whether they become institutionalized in the form of a social movement, as opposed to being taken up by political parties, remains to be seen.

The second aspect of law and order issues concerns proper treatment of citizens by the police and courts. Reform of the police already has become an important political issue in both Mexico and Brazil. In general, all citizens have an interest in having more police on the streets where they are needed and in developing forms of community control over the police. Reform of the criminal justice system is less likely to become a political issue, much less something around which a social movement is able to crystallize, though there is certainly a great need here. It is, however, an issue around which there can be considerable osmosis between social movements and political parties.

Points of convergence will not always involve all citizens. Rather, following Ernesto Laclau (1985), concrete class and sector (and identity) issues could and should be framed with a discourse of citizenship. There should be contestation of the content of citizenship and, in this way, a higher-quality democracy might develop together with a greater responsiveness of the state to the material interests of many citizens.

Conclusions

There are many grounds for pessimism about the future of Latin America as far as state-civil society relations are concerned. Many analysts argue, using the logic of rational actors and Prisoners' Dilemmas, that the most likely outcome of attempts to implement neoliberal economic reforms will be some sort of suboptimal "dual democracy" (Acuña and Smith 1994) or "delegative democracy" (O'Donnell 1994b). It is hard to disagree with this as a statement of probabilities. The same analysts therefore urge an effort to move Latin American societies along a more desirable, but minimalist, path (see also Cavarozzi 1994). In line with the general thinking of these authors, the impetus for such a shift toward sustained improvement, both in terms of sustained growth with equity and in terms of improved quality of democracy, need not depend on some *deus ex machina* or on luck or an act of political will. Rather, internal pressures from the state itself, in its drive to increase its power capacities, could perhaps generate a mutually reinforcing spiral that will force social movements to respond.

This discussion suggests that it is both desirable and likely that Latin American states seek to expand their power capacities in the foreseeable future. It is also both desirable and likely that social movements will become more institutionalized. The combination of these trends will be an increased organizational density in state-civil society relations. This could increase the possibilities for various forms of stable consensus politics at the expense of both "populist" mobilization and exclusionary elitist projects.[16]

This is a paradoxical conclusion, since neoliberalism is generally seen as a new form of elitist exclusion and as an attempt to roll back many popular gains. It is frequently held that popular responses to neoliberalism are likely to be of a more disorganized kind and that the organized left and its constituencies are likely to find themselves on the defensive. This is unlikely to happen, however, because the present situation of limited state capacity is unlikely to endure. States will expand their power capacities, forcing civil society to respond. The outcome is likely to mean a more structured form of politics, with greater regularity and a denser intermeshing of state and civil society. This is entirely compatible with authoritarian politics, but it could also strengthen and improve the quality of democracy. This will happen to the extent that a whole series of rather specific issues become articulated as part of a larger demand for enhanced citizenship.

If the present trends toward the consolidation of the neoliberal project continue, there are a number of likely possibilities in terms of the enhancement or otherwise of the quality of democracy in the region. In one scenario, large sectors of civil society find themselves locked in permanent conflict with a state that continues to push through a neoliberal model even though the social costs are high. The state continues to adopt a minimalist posture with regard to direction of the economy. Under such a scenario, the more organized sections of the society, particularly labor, will adopt defensive postures, and the less organized sections will resort to apparently random and spontaneous manifestations of discontent.[17] This is a scenario in which one outcome is Behemoth — an overmighty state and a disorganized and defensive civil society, incapable of adopting any transformist project.

In another scenario, a government comes into office that makes a sustained effort to implement policies of a more equitable sort, but without opening up the polity to broad citizenship participation. Here would be included a government such as that of Carlos Salinas of Mexico, whose National Solidarity Program (Programa Nacional de Solidaridad — PRONASOL) gave credence to the administration's claim to be engaged in a form of "social liberalism." Despite the centrality of the clientelistic and electoral aims of PRONASOL, it had an important impact in reducing poverty in particular areas. However, it also had the (intended) effect of strengthening the hold of the Institutional Revolutionary Party (Partido Revolucionario Institucional — PRI) on an authoritarian political system. The PRI seems to have won the 1994 presidential election in part because of the relatively good performance of the economy during the year prior to the election, in part because of PRONASOL and other "social liberal" measures, and in part because of risk aversion in the electorate.[18] Mexico may now be classified as a weakly institutionalized and somewhat authoritarian democracy. Yet even though it may now be a democracy, Mexico remains a country where the quality of that democracy is extremely limited.

A third scenario is one in which expansion of the state triggers a response on the part of civil society. Both for its own purposes, and partly as an unintended effect, the state fosters the increasing institutionalization of many actors in civil society. If social movements and political parties rise to the challenge and fight for enhanced citizenship, then there is some possibility of a self-reinforcing upward spiral. This may be a real possibility in contemporary Latin America. It may not be the most likely outcome; it is a possible option.

Notes

1. Before proceeding further, it is perhaps salutary to draw attention to a certain reification implicit in the use of the binary notion of the state versus "civil society." The use of these terms suggests that state and civil society can, at least in principle, be clearly conceptually (if not empirically) demarcated. It is doubtful whether this is possible theoretically, except perhaps at a very abstract level; at an empirical level, it is impossible.

The term "civil society" is used for want of anything better. It is well-nigh impossible to break free of this entrenched vocabulary. However, despite my continued use of these terms, I do not mean to imply a clear dichotomy, much less a conflict, between "civil society" and "the state." These are analytic constructs that are not coterminous with concrete social actors, institutions, or processes. As Michael Mann says, "Where does the state end and civil society begin?" (Mann 1993, 61). In modern states, there is a complex institutional and processual interpenetration of the analytic categories of "state" and "civil society" such that it is difficult, if not impossible, to distinguish one from the other in concrete ways. When groups in "civil society" organize and act politically, they, by definition, become part of the political sphere. As they organize, their activities are regulated by law and administrative fiat; the state enters into the constitution of these organizations of civil society. The more they expand their activities, and the more institutionalized they become, the more the boundary between these "civil society" organizations and the state becomes porous. Moreover, even if it is still possible to delineate a boundary between the two, their relations are not simply or exclusively adversarial. These political organizations emanating from civil society want outputs from the state. This necessarily involves them in strategies of both conflict and cooperation with various parts of the state. The notion of "civil society" versus the state is a sociocultural construct and should not be a sociological one.

2. While to some extent the fact that these authoritarian regimes precluded most "normal" forms of political organization meant that grassroots mobilization was directed perforce into the church (there was nowhere else to meet), it would be a mistake to underestimate the authentically religious dimension of this mobilization.

3. See, for example, Evers 1985 and Escobar and Alvarez 1992.

4. This situation has led analysts to a careful exploration of the impact of the withdrawal of the state. Here the weakness of liberalism as a form of sociological analysis becomes apparent. Liberalism as a philosophy cannot satisfactorily answer the question about which groups or classes benefit from the reduction in the role of the state. Liberalism works with a concept of atomistic individuals or, at best, a plurality of mutually balancing groups and interests. Typically, the argument is that pluralist competition generates outcomes that resemble some sort of Pareto-optimum equilibrium. Society, however, is composed not only of atomistic individuals (if there are any at all) but also of groups and organizations, of vastly unequal power and influence, many of which are created in relation to the state. As a result, optimality in social welfare requires state intervention.

5. There are arguments that both political and domestic violence and a general sense of anomie are the fundamental causes of the expansion of fundamentalist Protestantism in the region (Martin 1990). The superficial apoliticism of fundamentalist Protestantism, with its injunction to "give unto Caesar that which is Caesar's" and the ascetic but inner-worldly orientations of the faithful (Weber 1968, 542), should not blind us to its very important impact on politics. For example, a disproportionate percentage of Brazilian members of Congress are fundamentalist Protestants.

6. Carlos Acuña (1994) argues this for Argentina.

7. The extent to which restructuring of the state was a response to a fiscal emergency as well as a response to a sea change in ideology should not be understated. In large part, states shed functions as a response to fiscal crisis. They got rid of state enterprises in order to balance their books.

8. While in these matters, labor is less important than business, similar arguments can be made about the utility of having a strong and well-organized labor movement that is committed to ongoing negotiation with the state.

9. It may also be the case that certain foodstuffs can be considered as non-tradables (in which case, there is scope for government price-setting or subsidies), but with increasing international trade in all kinds of foodstuffs, this is less and less likely as a policy option.

10. A further complication is added by noting that actors are not, in fact, unitary and that there are a variety of internal struggles within each actor that increase the difficulty not only of arriving at the optimal strategy but even of arriving at any coherent strategy at all.

11. Coherence refers to the internal relationships between the various component parts of a policy package; consistency, to regularity over time.

12. I am taking a narrow definition of democracy. In this context, democracy happens when there is universal suffrage and when free and fair elections are regular and institutionalized — when the electorate has the formal possibility to choose among its leaders.

13. Thinking of these concerns as "human rights" issues makes a lot of sense in political terms, since it is politically illegitimate to deny anyone their human rights. Whether this is a very helpful social-scientific way of thinking about the issues is perhaps more problematic. It is more useful to conceptualize these matters as aspects of citizenship. This has the political corollary of casting demands as a matter of contention vis-à-vis the state.

14. I do not see social movements and political parties as in any sense antithetical to one another. They are simply different ways of institutionalizing interests in a complex political system.

15. Ernesto Laclau (1985) has written extensively on the ways in which class and citizenship discourses might be articulated together.

16. By stable consensus politics, I mean such things as Christian Democracy, Social Democracy, and pragmatic forms of conservatism. What they all have in common is an agreement on "the rules of the game" of a mixed economy and a commitment to democracy. This is not true of radical authoritarianism, populism, and certain movements within the Left.

17. In mind here are the sorts of rioting against austerity measures analyzed by John Walton (1989).

18. While there is general consensus that such abuses as may have occurred in the 1994 presidential elections in Mexico could not have substantially altered the final outcome, it is also reasonable to note that the quality of Mexican democracy leaves a great deal to be desired. In other words, while the 1994 election produced a democratic result, there are still serious doubts about how firmly institutionalized democracy is in Mexico and how widespread notions of full citizenship are in that country.

References

Acuña, Carlos H. 1994. "Politics and Economics in the Argentina of the Nineties." In *Democracy, Markets, and Structural Reform in Latin America: Argentina, Bolivia, Brazil, Chile, and Mexico,* eds. William C. Smith, Carlos H. Acuña, and Eduardo A. Gamarra. Coral Gables, Fla.: University of Miami North-South Center.

Acuña, Carlos H., and William C. Smith. 1994. "The Political Economy of Structural Adjustment: The Logic of Support and Opposition to Neoliberal Reform." In *Latin American Political Economy in the Age of Neoliberal Reform,* eds. William C. Smith, Carlos Acuña, and Eduardo Gamarra. Coral Gables, Fla.: University of Miami North-South Center.

Axelrod, Robert. 1984. *The Evolution of Cooperation.* New York: Basic Books.

Castells, Manuel. 1983. *The City and the Grassroots.* Berkeley: University of California Press.

Cavarozzi, Marcelo. 1994. "Politics: A Key for the Long Term in South America." In *Latin American Political Economy in the Age of Neoliberal Reform: Theoretical and Comparative Perspectives for the 1990s,* eds. William C. Smith, Carlos H. Acuña, and Eduardo A. Gamarra. Coral Gables, Fla.: University of Miami North-South Center.

Escobar, Arturo, and Sonia Alvarez. 1992. "Introduction: Theory and Protest in Latin America Today." In *The Making of Social Movements in Latin America,* eds. Arturo Escobar and Sonia Alvarez. Boulder, Colo.: Westview Press.

Evans, Peter. 1995. *Embedded Autonomy: States and Industrial Transformation.* Princeton, N.J.: Princeton University Press.

Evers, Tilman. 1985. "Identity: the Hidden Side of New Social Movements in Latin America." In *New Social Movements and the State in Latin America,* ed. David Slater. Amsterdam: CEDLA (Centre for Latin American Research and Documentation).

Handleman, Howard. 1975. "The Political Mobilization of Urban Squatter Settlements." *Latin American Research Review* 10, 2.

Laclau, Ernesto. 1985. "New Social Movements and the Plurality of the Social." In *New Social Movements and the State in Latin America,* ed. David Slater. Amsterdam: CEDLA.

Mann, Michael. 1993. *The Sources of Social Power, Volume II: The Rise of Classes and Nation-States, 1760-1914.* New York: Cambridge University Press.

Martin, David. 1990. *Tongues of Fire.* London: Basil Blackwell.

O'Donnell, Guillermo. 1994a. "The State, Democratization, and Some Conceptual Problems." In *Latin American Political Economy in the Age of Neoliberal Reform: Theoretical and Comparative Perspectives for the 1990s,* eds. William C. Smith, Carlos H. Acuña, and Eduardo A. Gamarra. Coral Gables, Fla.: University of Miami North-South Center.

O'Donnell, Guillermo. 1994b. "Delegative Democracy." *Journal of Democracy* 5 (1): 55-69.

Roxborough, Ian. 1992a. "Neoliberalism in Latin America: Limits and Alternatives." *Third World Quarterly* 13 (2).

Roxborough, Ian. 1992b. "Inflation and Social Pacts in Brazil and Mexico." *Journal of Latin American Studies* 24.

Smith, William C. 1989. "Heterodox Shocks and the Political Economy of Democratic Transition in Argentina and Brazil." In *Lost Promises: Debt, Austerity and Development in Latin America*, ed. William Canak. Boulder, Colo.: Westview Press.

Thorp, Rosemary. 1991. *Economic Management and Economic Development in Peru and Colombia*. Pittsburgh: University of Pittsburgh Press.

Walton, John. 1989. "Debt, Protest and the State in Latin America." In *Power and Popular Protest: Latin American Social Movements*, ed. Susan Eckstein. Berkeley: University of California Press.

Weber, Max. 1968. *Economy and Society, Vol. 1*. New York: Bedminister Press.

Chapter 5

Emergent Citizenship or Exclusion? Social Movements and Non-Governmental Organizations in the 1990s

Elizabeth Jelin

Introduction

During the 1970s and early 1980s, a concern for the study of *new* social movements emerged in Latin America, as it had in Europe. What was specific to Latin America, however, was that the emergence of new forms of collective action coincided in several countries with the establishment of military dictatorships that closed down the institutional channels for the expression of social demands, denied political parties their role as interest articulators in society, imposed political repression targeted at labor unions and other popular organizations, and transformed state agencies into entities unresponsive to the demands of the population. For analysts and researchers, the issue then became whether these forms of collective action were a genuinely "new" phenomenon or rather a more temporary response to the closing of institutionalized channels of participation.

The enormous intellectual enthusiasm generated by the new forms of collective expression in the 1970s and early 1980s is now in the past: It is clear that they did not produce long-term political or social alternatives, in either form or content. The return of democracy implied a reinvigoration of political parties and a renewed commitment to institution building, a trend that emphasized the construction of institutions within the political system, guided by the logic of "governability." This effort often clashes with the less-institutionalized collective means of expressing old and new social demands and even with the more participatory pressures in the process of democratization. At the same time, neoliberalism and the corresponding expansion of a market-oriented economy imply the strengthening of individualism and a trend toward defining social relations in market terms, according to a logic of individual interests, weakening the basis of collective actions and movements. Adjustment policies and economic restructuring imply, in fact, the postponement of social demands and the exclusion of social justice and equity from the priorities of the political agenda.

In this context, one could expect an eclipse of collective action, a halt in the process of emergence and the symbolic strengthening of the identities of "new" collective actors. However, it would be somewhat hasty to assert, without qualifications, that this has indeed been the case. It becomes necessary to look more carefully into what is going on, trying to reveal and uncover social processes whose main actors do not occupy the center of the sociopolitical stage — one that is indeed dominated by institutional politics and by the adjustment and restructuring of the economy.

This chapter examines social movements from a perspective that privileges the relation between political democracy, economic equity, and social democracy — issues that are all central to this book. At the outset, this chapter rejects unilateral perspectives and linear interpretations of social movements and instead focuses on the tensions and contradictions (both internal and external) that are present in their development and action. Social movements can, at times, be forces that push the (formal) limits of political democratization; they may be mediating agencies between disadvantaged and unprotected social groups and the state apparatus; they may also be part of the institutional framework of the state or reproduce clientelistic patterns of political relations. In addition, social movements are not impervious to the institutionalization process that permeates them, and thus, tensions often are generated between more bureaucratic and more movement-oriented approaches to the articulation of demands. In sum, social movements and collective actors are not always neat, rational, and unitary; rather, they contain and express a multiplicity of meanings, varying according to context and historical conjuncture.

This chapter takes up several distinct issues, all of them related to the capacity of various social sectors to express themselves in the public-political arena. The first three points are general in nature. They deal with the conditions that facilitate or constrain the presence and action of collective actors and social movements: the limits placed by "democratization-with-adjustment," the twofold trend toward globalization and localization, and the social dynamics generated by the tension between equality and the right to difference. Following this analysis, the chapter takes up two issues related to social movements in the context of transition: the institutionalized and noninstitutionalized forms of expression of collective identities and social demands (that is, movements and their relationship with political parties and non-governmental organizations) and the specific role of solidarity movements in the process of the construction of democracy.

Democracy and Exclusion: Polarization, Fragmentation, Marginalization

The issue is a classic: Can there be political democracy without guaranteeing a basic minimum level of economic well-being? Are basic economic rights part of the contents of basic human rights? What is the "right to development"? Can people enjoy their civil and political rights if they do not have access to the basic conditions (eliminating hunger and pain, but also access to the relevant information) that ensure the possibility of exercising such rights?

These themes are the subject of permanent debate. The argument that postulates economic rights as a precondition for the existence of human rights is expressed by many in response to neoliberal individualism. Indeed, one of the main documents prepared for the 1993 International Conference on Human Rights, held in Vienna, affirms:

> Poverty is associated with the negation of fundamental rights, insofar as the poor are marginalized and do not have the capacity to fight for themselves. Whereas in the West, workers were able to secure their basic rights through their struggles and organization, at the current historical juncture of recession and injustice, those who live at the margins of the system are powerless and do not have the capacity to make themselves heard....In sum, economic growth is imperative for the consolidation of new democracies. However, growth alone is not enough. More attention should be paid to the distribution of resources and of the benefits of economic growth and to the need of profound changes in the socioeconomic structure and in the political system. Without a sustained effort on the part of the state and of all sectors of the population to eliminate the worst manifestations of human misery, the demise of authoritarianism and the existence of democratic institutions will not, by themselves, guarantee the economic and social rights of the poor. (Pinheiro, Poppovic, and Kahn 1993, 25)

This theme is not concerned solely with the relationship between political democracy and economic dimensions such as equity or growth. Rather, it is a key aspect of the conditions for the emergence of individual and collective self-reflective subjects (of rights).

The theoretical and ideological debate about the nature of rights and the definition of human rights, especially whether it includes socioeconomic rights, tends to obscure a few central questions: What is the limit? Is there a "threshold of humanity"? What are the minimum qualifications that human beings, defined as a biological species, must meet to qualify as "human" social subjects? Obviously, mere physical survival is such a condition. Hunger, physical pain, torture, bodily injury, and extreme victimization all serve to transform the human subject into a body, annihilating its cultural dimension.

At another level, the human condition involves a sense of belonging to a political community, referred to by Hannah Arendt:

> The fundamental deprivation of human rights is manifested first and above all in the deprivation of a place in the world [a political space] which makes opinions significant and actions effective....We became aware of the right to have rights...and a right to belong to some kind of organized community, only when millions of people emerged who had lost and could not regain those rights because of the new global situation....Man, as it turns out, can lose all so-called Rights of Man without losing his essential quality as man, his human dignity. Only the loss of a polity expels him from humanity. (Arendt 1949, quoted by Young-Bruehl 1982, 257)

The sense of belonging and the possibility of interaction lie at the core of humanity. In other words, human society exists when there simultaneously exist "the other" and a public sphere of interaction.

In this light, faced with extreme poverty, how can one be sure that he/she is still within the realm of humanity? Isn't extreme poverty a sign of dehumanization? Exclusion and indigence lie at the opposite edge of democracy, implying the denial of fundamental rights. It is the contrary of social actors and scenarios. Those who are excluded are outside society or are simply defined as nonexistent.

The data on poverty and exclusion in Latin America are well known. It appears that "democratization with adjustment" is leaving out masses of people and that this does not seem to be a passing, frictional phenomenon but rather part and parcel of a process of structural marginalization.

This poses a puzzle: Defined as outsiders by the powerful, subordinate peoples (even slaves) always have been part of the political and social community. Historically, they have gained access to the public sociopolitical space through their struggles. Yet social struggles involve collective actors and resources. However, these variables seem to be absent in cases of extreme poverty and exclusion. No social movement of the oppressed can grow without having first gained a minimum of access and a minimum of humanity, in the sense of belonging to a community and of a self-reflexive capacity involved in identity building. A first response of the excluded, then, is apathy and passivity, followed by isolation and the loneliness of misery, the lack of social ties among destitute people.

However, history and anthropology have both documented everyday forms of protest and boycott among subordinate groups. When power relations are extremely hierarchical and asymmetric, subordinate people develop hidden forms of action, alternative social spaces where they can express their dissidence with the discourse of domination. In such spaces, in the backyards and alleys, in the invisible shapes and shadows, in what James Scott (1992) calls "hidden transcripts," a sense of dignity and autonomy vis-à-vis domination and power is constructed and sheltered. These spaces are the proto-forms of politics, the "infrapolitics of the powerless," through which dignity and a sense of community are constructed. In a sense, such practices already show some degree of autonomy and reflexive capacity. Insofar as these are hidden practices, it becomes difficult to recognize them and distinguish them from apathy and subservience, until they become more explicit or when a process of transformation into collective movements is underway, that is, when the process of formation of social actors and movements already is taking place.

During the last two decades, the human rights movement and the feminist movement have both evolved in this way and are outcomes of what were initially resistive practices. The initial stages of the labor movement, the anti-slave movements, and the indigenous and peasant movements were also similar. In all these cases, boycotts and hidden resistances converged with

ideologically driven "liberating" proposals, evolving into collective movements with a clear presence in the public space. Many other "proto-
movements" remained in the backyards and graveyards of history.

During the dictatorships of the 1960s and 1970s, many activities of
political opposition had the character of resistance practices. Insofar as
political opposition was multi-class, economic survival was not an issue, at
least for a good part of the opposition movement. Practices of resistance to
dictatorship easily transformed themselves into political acts. Or rather,
resistance was, from the very beginning, a political act. Under authoritarianism,
the logic of domination was clear, and the lines of the "us" and the "them"
could be drawn easily. There was not the pretense of inclusion of "the other."
Yet the transparent nature of political opposition obscured the other face of
domination: poverty and the economic violations of human rights.

The transition to democracy brings with it confusion and bewilderment.
A new space opens up for democratic discourse, for elections and participation. While democratic discourse becomes hegemonic, the reality of economic relations is in contradiction with it. Indeed, there is a double discourse:
a discourse of participation and a non-discourse of economic exclusion.

Under such conditions, the historically constructed "threshold of
humanity" is threatened. Marginalized and excluded people may refuse then
to accept the rules of the democratic game or accept them only partially. Their
response then may become social violence. The economically excluded do
not become individual or collective subjects in the newly emerging public and
political sphere: They may resist and protest, living under different rules, the
rules of violence. Their (limited) energies and resources are not geared toward
integration; at times, they may choose to "act out" instead of participate. (This
often manifests itself in forms of communitarian resistance.)

There are other forms of violence found in groups that are not
economically excluded. On the one hand, there are those who do not accept
democratic rules for personal or group interests (drug traffic, corruption); on
the other, violence is generated by the totalitarian rejection of the right of
"others" to participate in the public sphere, with attempts to annihilate the
other — state terrorism or racist violence, which do not disappear magically
with political transition to democratically elected governments.

Processes of impoverishment and exclusion, and their consequences in
hampering the formation of social movements ready to articulate conflicts in
terms of societal tensions and of social relations, create the conditions for the
emergence of racism. Downwardly mobile social sectors live the threat of
those below (immigrants, blacks); elites define social problems in racial terms
(it is "foreigners" who create problems), as a form of disguise of domination
and class exclusion (Wieviorka 1992).

Often, violence is understood as a last resort, when words and dialogue
become impossible. It also can be conceived as a form of discourse, as an
extreme way of talking, as a language of expression of conflicts and social
relations, in an attempt to participate in the definition of the political scenario.

In such cases (the Zapatista uprising in Chiapas, Mexico, is perhaps the most recent and clearest case), it is the voice of a collective actor with a strong sense of identity, resorting to a political discourse that will have to be heard by the powerful. In this way, the actor gains a place in the theater of the sociopolitical game. A real breakthrough in managing social and political conflict will take place if and when the discourse of violence is transformed into a discourse of dialogue and negotiation. The powerful must learn to listen to other languages before messages are translated into the discourse of violent action.

Accepting the line of reasoning just presented has significant implications for the challenges faced by emerging democracies: Political democratization does not produce automatically a strengthened civil society, a culture of citizenship, and a sense of social responsibility. In fact, the vitality of civil society requires that people not be allowed to fall below the thresholds that mark the possibility of participation in the political community. This lack of participation in the community can be brought on by exclusion or through choice (alternative, unlawful, channels). At the same time and in a circular way, the vitality of civil society becomes the guarantee for the functioning of political democracy.

In summation, the range of responses to exclusion and economic marginalization that accompanies democratization is quite wide: violence, apathy, resistance, formation of new collective identities, and other struggles. However, at present, given the way in which the world economic and political scenario is shaped, it is hard to expect that new creative social forces will emerge easily from these social sectors. Rather, extreme poverty and exclusion become priority issues in economic and political processes when they are expressed by the powerful: be it out of moral indignation (in his inaugural speech, Fernando Henrique Cardoso exclaimed that he was "horrified" by extreme poverty in Brazil), out of calculus of economic rationality (in terms of the return to investments in specific sectors, such as education and health),[1] out of fear of outbreaks or threats (as exemplified by the Chiapas uprising in Mexico and the riots that erupted in various Argentine cities during 1994). Apparently this theme is becoming a priority on the national, regional, and international agenda.

Globalization and Regionalization

At the threshold of the twenty-first century, powerful trends toward globalization and transnationalization coexist with others pointing toward the revitalization of locality. On the one hand, it is an era of supranational institutions and of increasingly globalized communications, economic interests, environmental hazards, and arms races. On the other, it is an era of renewed sensitivity to local roots and identities, revealed violently sometimes in rivalries among ethnic and cultural groups, as more people choose to identify themselves with cultural and other narrowly defined symbols.

The tension between the two is unmistakable, yet globalization and intensified concern with the local are closely related. This calls for a reconceptualization and reformulation of central issues related to collective action. First, it is necessary to rethink the relationship among different spheres and competing blueprints for action — that is to say, what is taking place at the international, national, community, microsocial, and interpersonal levels of social identity and interaction. Second, it is also imperative to revisit and reanalyze the tensions between universalism and relativism and between collective identities and human rights.

The changes taking place in recent decades have disrupted traditional units of analysis. No transformation is more noteworthy than that involving the notion of the nation-state. The nation-state was construed during the last two centuries as the "natural" focus of loyalty, the locus of citizenship and solidarity, of political power, and of sovereignty. Today, this centrality is strongly questioned: National boundaries at times seem irrelevant in the face of the globalization of production, trade, finance, and culture. The result is that national governments have lost much of the control they once exercised over events within their boundaries. Sovereignty is curtailed further by changes in regional and supranational alliances and blocs. Meanwhile, and partly as a result of the state's weakening, states are being challenged at a subnational level by the rebirth of solidarity groups grounded in a variety of sources of collective identities — regional, linguistic, religious, ethnic — as well as by innumerable social movements that generate solidarities of their own. They contend with the state for citizens' loyalty and, at times, for territorial authority.[2]

The erosion of traditionally fixed boundaries and the proliferation of new units of analysis and identity imply a diversification of the sites and arenas in which public action takes place. To analyze this phenomenon, Boaventura de Sousa Santos (1991a) resorts to a cartographic model, one which recognizes that in contemporary societies different sets of normative standards operate simultaneously, varying in terms of which groups they regulate, their duration and degree of institutionalization, and the way in which they are practiced and enforced. The model is designed to analyze the plurality of juridical arrangements, but it also can be applied usefully to social norms more generally. As in cartography, what counts is the definition of the scale:

> The modern state is based on the assumption that law operates according to a single scale, the scale of the state....Research on juridical pluralism calls attention to the existence of local rights,...forms of infra-state law, informal, unofficial, ingrained through habitual practice...[and] an international juridical space where different types of agents, whose behavior is regulated by new international rules, operate....This system of law is generally quite informal....What sets these forms of law apart from each other is the size of the scale in which they regulate social action. (de Sousa Santos 1991a, 222-223)

This means that there are multiple spheres and arenas for social processes and public action, with complex interaction patterns:

> [B]oth at the intrastate level and at the suprastate level, there have been emerging forms of law that are explicitly liquid, ephemeral, ever negotiable, and renegotiable, in sum, disposable....[We have seen] the emergence of a contextual legality, finely tuned to the momentary interests of the parties involved and to the power relations among them. (de Sousa Santos 1991b, 113)

Extending the application of this model to societal norms in general, the interaction among the different scales implies that any concrete historical circumstance entails a mixture of codes, complex patterns of symbolization and syncretisms, with meanings that are seldom transparent. Although intercultural exchanges and processes of social change linked to international or global phenomena have always existed (as exemplified by the expansion of commercial capitalism, colonization and formation of empires, and forced migration of slave and semi-slave laborers), communication improvements and the proliferation of information during the last few decades have altered significantly the dynamics of interaction among regions, times, actors, and levels of interaction. More than ever before, expressions of collective demands at the local level (be they labor demands voiced by a union, neighborhood demands for state services, protests against pollution or environmental hazards, or whatever) embody the multiplicity of meanings that result from the articulation and overlap of different levels. Conversely, grand international conferences and events that garner worldwide attention reveal their human message only when the global themes are interwoven with specific local conditions. The personalized, intimate story of the suffering and pain of an experience of rape in Bosnia, transmitted via television to a universal audience (as occurred during the International Human Rights Conference in Vienna), puts this multiplicity of meanings and levels at center-stage, demonstrating the potential to impact attitudes and behaviors not only in Bosnia but throughout the world.

Globalization, as it pertains both to the nature of the social demands and to the speed of communications, involves important transformations in the configuration of social movements. Indeed, the days when European militants and organizers arrived in the Americas to foster the emergence of a "workers' consciousness," entering factories by posing as workers in order to proselytize the labor force in face-to-face exchanges, are long gone. The growth of international organizations, of international summits and conferences, and of non-governmental organizations (NGOs) has combined to produce an entirely different picture. Direct collective participation is only one of the elements — and, in most cases, not even an indispensable one — in the emergence of social movements and new collective actors. Today has witnessed the creation of international issue networks composed of international, national, and local NGOs, intergovernmental organizations, government agencies, philantrophic foundations, churches, militants, and intellectuals of diverse academic and ideological backgrounds. These networks do not depend necessarily on widespread grassroots participation or on how rooted the issues they champion are in a society or among certain segments of it. As Kathryn Sikkink (1996) observes in relation to the area of human rights, these networks are made up of various groups, informally and non-hierarchically linked, that generally lack a high degree of coordination among themselves. Rather, to be able to talk about a network, the component groups have to share values and objectives, as well as participate in a dense flow of information and services.

The flow of information among human rights organizations reveals an extremely dense web of interconnections. In most cases, this flow of information takes place informally through the exchange of reports, telephone calls, and attendance at common conferences and meetings. In other cases, the connections are formalized, as when NGOs with official consultative status with intergovernmental organizations present reports to those organizations. Second, the members of the network share allegiance or loyalty to similar values and principles, which in the human rights case are embodied in international human rights law. A third type of interconnection among these organizations is the flow of funds and services. (Sikkink 1996, 61-62)

Undoubtedly, something similar is taking place in the international women's movement and, in a more incipient manner, in groups linked to indigenous, environmental, and "sustainable development" issues. What remains to be seen is the nature of the links and the articulation mechanisms connecting these social networks with their constituencies and with society-wide movements and processes.

Equality and Difference

A different global issue, which at times is seen in connection with what was discussed above, is the tension between the universality of rights and the respect for cultural pluralism and diversity. The *Universal Declaration of Human Rights*, proclaimed by the United Nations in 1948, sets the basic framework for universalism, which has since become the banner of movements seeking the expansion of the social base of citizenship (i.e., granting voting rights to women or illiterates), the inclusion of minorities, of discriminated or dispossessed social groups as members of the citizenry, and the claim of "equality before the law." The most visible and best-known international examples of these social struggles for inclusion are the campaigns against the "final solution" of Nazism, the civil rights movement during the 1960s in the United States, the struggles against apartheid in South Africa, the demands of feminism to end all types of discrimination toward women, and the claims to full citizenship and legal pluralism of ethnic minorities. Other examples abound around the globe.

Modern history, with its colonialism and racism of the past two centuries, was the ideological backdrop for the *Universal Declaration*. For some intellectual groups (of well-meaning anthropologists, humanists, and progressive people), the urgency was to enter the era of cultural pluralism, to demonstrate scientifically the falsehood of white racial superiority, and to discover the complexity of "primitive" cultures. Recognition of pluralism was to become an antidote to the recurrence of massive crimes (genocide and cultural annihilation), committed on the basis of ideologies and interests that implicitly or explicitly denied victims the condition of "human being with rights." The ideology of universal human rights was therefore designed to serve as a protection of both potential and actual victims. To raise the flag of universalism in defense of the rights of those who were different in a struggle against those who wanted to impose uniformity and the idea of universal progress in the world was, in a sense, paradoxical.

How was it possible to reconcile cultural relativism with the defense of universal human rights? How could the alleged objectivity of science be combined with an ethically committed defense of principles? Very soon, the *Universal Declaration* began to be criticized on the basis that its underlying notion of human rights was Western and individualistic and that the will to extend it worldwide was an act of an imperialistic, discriminating, and ethnocentric power. This anti-Western argument, in turn, would be used politically to justify aberrant violations, under the shield of cultural relativism and the insistence on national sovereignty and self-determination, all of which could lead to a rejection of humanitarian interventions, international monitoring, and controls. At the International Conference on Human Rights (Vienna, 1993), several countries relied on the argument of cultural pluralism in their attempts to curtail the scope of "universal human rights" and the international efforts to control violations.

Today, after years of debate and dialogue, the issue of cultural diversity can be approached in a different way. If the original idea of universal human rights responded to an individualistic view of rights, it now pivots on communities. To speak of cultural rights is to speak of groups and communities: the right of societies and cultures (self-defined as such) to live their own life-styles, speak their own languages, use their own clothes, pursue their own objectives, and receive fair treatment from the laws of the nation-state in which they happen to be living (almost invariably, as "minorities").

The emergence of demands for indigenous peoples' rights based on ethnicity is one significant field where these issues are being discussed (Stavenhagen 1990 and 1996). To think about the agenda of ethnic rights implies a profound revision of the original notion of human rights, so far conceptualized in an abstract way, with a bias toward universality and individual subjects. The statement that indigenous peoples and minorities have rights implies that the very notion of "human rights" can only acquire meaning in specific cultural circumstances, which thus become requisites for, and part of, human rights. In this framework, to speak about human rights of indigenous peoples or of traditionally oppressed or marginalized groups of the population (to which women obviously belong) implies the recognition of a history of discrimination and oppression and an active commitment to reverse this situation.

Advancing this point entails the recognition of the inevitable tension between individual and collective rights. A good portion of ongoing global conflicts can be analyzed from this perspective. There are circumstances in which individual rights cannot be achieved fully unless collective rights are recognized and respected. In other cases, individual and collective rights are in direct contradiction to each other. In fact, the enforcement of universal human rights does not guarantee the enforcement of collective rights of peoples, and vice-versa: The right of a people to live in accordance with their own life-style can be rooted in the negation of basic human rights to certain social categories within that culture. How can this conceptual bottleneck be overcome? How can the parameters and criteria for evaluation of violations best be determined? Faced with the dilemma of having to establish priorities between individual and collective rights, Rodolfo Stavenhagen proposes a "provisional and normative" conclusion:

> Group or collective rights must be considered human rights to the extent that their recognition and exercise also promotes the individual rights of its members [for instance, the right to use their native language]....A corollary of this conclusion: collective rights that violate or diminish the individual rights of the members of a society should not be considered as human rights [as, for example, the case of the sexual mutilation of female children in some African societies]. (Stavenhagen 1996, 152)

There is an increasing danger that efforts to establish the rights of people will foster the emergence of fundamentalist ideologies and the formation of exclusionary and racist communal identities. These, in turn, can take the form of a defensive posture looking for scapegoats or an expansionist approach rooted in conquest and self-aggrandizement (Wieviorka 1992). These fundamentalisms can be interpreted in terms of the opposition between social movements and communitarian action, pointing to the weakening of social movements and the strengthening of communitarian action in the contemporary world (as experienced in Europe and elsewhere), a tendency clearly associated with the growing threat of racism. This opposition, however, is not an absolute one. Rather, the way out of this dilemma may be found in "advocating for the transformation of tensions and difficulties that very frequently or disproportionately are experienced according to non-social, communitarian, and more concretely racial ways, into societal conflict situations" (Wieviorka 1992, 266). The idea is not to destroy community identities in the name of modernity but rather to "support, with sympathy, the efforts of those actors that resist dissociation and seek to devise integrative formulas in which the reference to a collective identity in no way impedes progress and participation in modern life" (Wieviorka 1992, 266-267).

Within this context, Latin America is experiencing in the 1990s a noticeable growth and expansion of indigenous movements pressing for the recognition of their "right of identity," and of their right to participate more fully in the global society (Strobele-Gregor 1994), linked among themselves in a dense international network. There is also a tendency to seek acceptance of racial identities, particularly among the black population of Brazil (Hasenbalg 1996) and among the many "Latino" communities of the United States. These demands for the recognition of different identities are taking place in a context of national societies and states that (at least formally) embraces the principles of citizen equality, which is also a key demand of these movements. This dialectic between citizens' equality and cultural pluralism generates new tensions and sociopolitical dilemmas.

Finally, differences may be viewed as a function of social relations, which means that they cannot be analyzed properly at the level of the individual but rather demand analysis in terms of social institutions and existing laws (Minow 1990). The social demands of the "different" (that is to say, inferior) consist, first, of a demand for equality. There are various ways of approaching the issue of difference and equality. A first approach conceives difference as inherent in some persons, becoming significant when identified with inferiority: Persons who are different cannot enjoy rights and are seen as "dependents" and "non-citizens." A second approach strives to secure "equality before the law" but defines equality in terms of a single set of (masculine?, Western?) traits, which implies overlooking, and even denying, many traits that indicate differences.[3] Yet since differences do exist, this approach eventually leads to a search for the "real" differences, i.e., those that deserve a "truly differentiated" treatment. In a third approach, difference is a function of social relations and therefore cannot be situated in categories of individual persons but in social institutions and in the legal norms that rule them (Minow 1990).

Social demands on the part of the "different" (inferior) actor — for instance, women — express themselves first in a call for equality. This has manifested itself during the last few decades in the demand for increased access to places and positions that hitherto had been barred to them (ranging from membership in exclusive clubs to occupations traditionally deemed as appropriate only for males), denunciation of discriminatory practices (for example, the placement of obstacles to the attainment of high positions in politics and the work place), and inequality (in which "equal work" by no means entails "equal pay").

Much remains to be done to attain equality for women before the law. However, a literal interpretation of equality can be misleading or insufficient in many situations. For instance, in cases of workers' pregnancies, is equality — in the sense of denying the difference between men and women — called for? Or should the law recognize the need for "special" treatment? To pose the issue in a different area, what does equality of educational rights mean for a disabled child or for one whose mother tongue is not the language used in public schools?

Emphasis on the norm of equality reinforces a conception grounded in universal natural law: It reasserts that all human beings are naturally equal. This is politically effective insofar as it allows opposition to certain forms of discrimination, asserts individualities, and limits the exercise of power. However, there is another side to social reality: Not all individuals are equal, and hiding or denying differences eventually serves to perpetuate the implicit notion that there are two essentially different kinds of people: those who are "normal" and those who are "different" (which almost always implies "inferior"). Maintaining the illusion of equality and stating this issue in universal terms entail risks: They may lead to an excessive formalization of rights, isolating them from the social structures in which they exist and acquire meaning. The passage from the universal to the social, historical, and contingent then becomes difficult.

One of the major contributions of feminism has been its profound critique and unmasking of the assumptions implicit in the dominant paradigm that takes (Western) men as the universal reference point and makes women (and others) different or invisible.[4] By so doing, feminism treads on contradictory grounds: On the one hand, it has claimed equality of rights and equal treatment vis-à-vis men; on the other hand, it has demanded the right to a differentiated treatment and to the social recognition of women's uniqueness. This implies an unavoidable tension between the principle of equality and the right to difference. Recognizing this tension has important payoffs and poses the challenge to find a way to conceptualize difference without making it hierarchical (Minow 1990). Both from a theoretical point of view and from strategic considerations, the way out will not be found in the irreconcilable juxtaposition of the discourse of equality and the discourse of difference but rather in conceptualizing equality of rights within contexts of social relations in which differences, including those of power and marginalization, reveal themselves (Valdés 1990).

Spokespersons and Mediators: Social Movements, NGOs, Political Parties, Democratic States

The social actors in the world scene have changed profoundly during the last two decades. Up until the 1970s, the primacy of the political system was undisputed: Political parties, elections, and revolutionary wars were the strategies for change. The state was at the center: The question was the best strategy to use to gain state power. Even traditional corporatist actors (entrepreneurs and the labor movement, the military, and the clergy) were analyzed in terms of their capacity to intervene in the political space of the state. Other actors were weak, and social demands were put directly to the state; what was left outside the formal political arenas (spaces for sociability and local cultural reinforcement) was thought of as less "important."

Internationally, states were also the central actors and agents. There were numerous international conventions and pacts that were promoted and ratified by democratic governments. Society had little room in these accords; there was limited societal space. Underneath this reality, however, something different was boiling up — something hidden and muddled. In 1975, at the time of the International Conference on Women, the world witnessed with astonishment the ferment of women in Mexico. The action was not in the intergovernmental conference but outside, in the multiplicity of events and proposals with which the international movement of women challenged the official conference. Since then, this pattern of parallel activities has become a widespread practice, and the power of non-governmental social organizations started to grow. At the United Nations Conference on Environment and Development (UNCED) in Rio de Janeiro in 1992, at the Human Rights Conference in Vienna in 1993, as well as at Cairo, Copenhagen, and Beijing, the struggle of non-governmental organizations is not for the right to have a forum but for the incorporation of the demands and voices of the parallel forums in the official proceedings and resolutions. This international visibility and recognition of NGOs are indicators of broader organizational and institutional changes.

Since the 1970s, even at the national levels, new forms of interest articulation and expression have emerged in the public sphere: They direct their claims to the state yet do not act through political parties. This was understandable under dictatorial regimes, where political parties had very limited room for action. Social movements could then emerge as opposition forces to dictatorship, as democratizing agents, although this was not always the case. Very often, they actually were collective actions with quite specific and limited objectives and demands.[5] During the transition to democracy, some urban movements become institutionalized social actors, especially at the level of local governments. There are now many arenas that provide opportunities for the expression of citizens' demands, for citizens' control and monitoring of municipal administration, and for joint participation of social organizations and local government in city management (Raczynski and Serrano 1992).

Other social movements followed a different path during the 1980s. Several demands of the women's and human rights movements were incorporated into the sociopolitical agenda of the transition. Thus, the socially critical stands of the feminist movement have penetrated state bureaucracies, labor unions, business organizations, the state, and the church. The debate on issues such as sexual discrimination, the logic of equality, and judicial reform — including political and social recognition of a number of violations of women's rights such as domestic violence (although not yet marital rape) — undeniably has taken root in Latin American societies. Even the debate about reproductive rights (with the exception of abortion) is voiced openly in the region.

Also, insofar as the human rights discourse is adopted by large sectors of society and is no longer limited to a small group of militants and activists, the very definition of success or failure of a social movement is under question. Indeed, both the women's and the human rights movements actually weakened and deteriorated during the transition.[6] There were conflicts around strategies, among those who wished to penetrate the power structures of the state and those inclined not to negotiate, even at the cost of remaining outside the loci of power. At the same time, the issues raised by these movements expanded significantly and became much more generalized in the population, which is clearly an indication of success. The result is new themes absorbed and appropriated by society in large, weak, and conflict-ridden organizations.

In more general terms, when the "new" social movements began to gain visibility on national and local scenes, the question that generated interest and attention was the future of the links between these new demands and the political system. Will they be able to maintain their autonomy? Would they ultimately be coopted by political parties? Will their demands be appropriated by existing political and social institutions? Clearly, the links between social movements and political institutions — state agencies, political parties, and the like — are extremely unstable. The scenarios are quite heterogeneous. Some significant trends, anchored on transnational processes, can nonetheless be detected.

As was already mentioned, during the last two decades, international solidarity networks (from north to south), poised to intervene in situations of economic exclusion and political oppression in the South (and increasingly in Eastern Europe), emerged and strengthened. Although some of these networks are highly asymmetrical (the donors of the North define the targets and select the recipients and channels of aid in the South), others are beginning to evidence greater reciprocity and symmetry not only in terms of the flow of resources but also in terms of ideas and priorities. This is seen most clearly in the areas of human rights and women; the environmental movement is younger but is moving in the same direction.

In Latin America, the collective protests and localized movements that prevailed two decades ago began to change, evolving into more formal organizations — the so-called third sector. This sector is different from the state and from the market; it is composed of private non-profit organizations, is self-managed, has some degree of solidarity action, and is geared to intervene in favor of discriminated and dispossessed social sectors (Scherer-Warren 1993, Fernándes 1994). Structurally, these organizations are intermediaries and are related to each other through networks. At the local and national levels, these organizations are becoming the mediators between the excluded and the state, between international movements and organizations and local demands, and between international cooperation and the final recipients of aid. These networks, at both the national and the international levels, have a substantial organizational structure with their own rules. They increasingly are recognized as legitimate organizations by governmental agencies. In some countries, NGOs are even selected by international programs as channels for the transfer of resources, preferring them over governmental agencies in recipient countries. In that vein, local and national NGOs and their international links, through the formation of a class of professional staff and volunteer workers, are turning into major actors in the social scene of the processes of democratization.[7]

The density of organizations and the presence of international aid organizations vary among countries: They are more visible and have more impact in the smaller countries, such as Bolivia, Nicaragua, and currently El Salvador. In larger and more developed countries, international cooperation has less economic and political weight, and the local NGOs constitute only one of the many organizational forms of civil society. Their dynamism and strength depend, then, on the way the state, political parties, and other organizations relate to each other and how they define the space for NGOs. In the 1990s, given the prevalence of neoliberal economic policies that curtail the scope of welfare and social policies, the actual role of NGOs is expanding: They are becoming intermediaries between the dispossessed and the state. They also act to "compensate" or fill the vacuum left by the curtailment of state services. While assuming the role of representing the voiceless, they become authorized voices; at times they are self-appointed, speaking out on behalf of various victims of human rights violations under authoritarian regimes, of economic exclusion in dictatorships and democracies, of discrimination against minorities, of alienation or expropriation of natural resources, of pollution, and so on, representing them vis-à-vis the power structure. At times, these processes are part of the democratizing movements; at other times, they reproduce patriarchal, populist, or authoritarian forms of relations between subordinate and powerful sectors of society.

Thus, as is the case with most social organizations, the nature of social movements and of NGOs is quite heterogeneous. They not only vary in their aims and ideological commitments; they also vary in the degree of grassroots participation, in their degree of centralization, in their democratic or authoritarian practices. Cases of "authoritarian technocracy" for the poor ("We know what is good for you and will make sure that you comply.") are innumerable.

Within the hegemonic neoliberal discourse (including that of the international financial community), in which the state is "subsidiary" and should be as small as possible, this third sector is put forth as a model, as the basic road to strengthen civil society. There are several dangers in identifying this third sector with civil society (a conceptual danger, but with significant political and ethical implications), a position that prevails even among international agencies and financial institutions. The fact is that NGOs and "private-yet-public" organizations do not have a built-in mechanism of accountability. They do not have a constituency or membership composed of "sovereign citizens." They are financially accountable to those who provide funds, to their own ideology and consciousness, hopefully (but only hopefully) based on "good" values, solidarity, compassion, and commitment.

Given this relative absence of institutional and societal accountability, there is always the danger of arbitrary action, of manipulation, and of lack of transparency in their objectives and practices. Although this is generally not the case, and NGOs are playing a major role in the processes of democratization, a word of caution is necessary given this built-in structural difficulty. Nobody obliges NGOs to guide their actions according to democratic and participatory principles nor to promote citizenship and rights. There is no mechanism of accountability vis-à-vis the recipients, who have no say in the elaboration of projects and programs. Who elaborates the third sector's agenda? Individuals operating on good will and a communitarian conscience? All this implies that the state cannot and should not renounce its function and obligation to promote citizenship rights and participation. It also implies that social movements and collective participatory action cannot and should not be institutionalized totally, be it through state-oriented channels or through "concerned" NGOs. Despite these risks — which are more potential than real — this sector plays an important role in democratization processes, as shall be discussed next.

Actors and Scenarios of Transition: Victims and Social Movements in the Democratic Transformation

Thus far, this chapter has analyzed the middle-term tendencies and processes of continuity and change, extending over the course of the last two decades. An important, and different, theme focuses on the specific processes taking place within the contexts of the transition to democracy, especially when the key challenges are the very transformation of the state (from authoritarianism and state terrorism toward social responsibility and accountability of those in positions of power). In this process, social movements are called upon to play a very specific and crucial role.

In periods of transition, the legitimacy of the state cannot be taken for granted. Strong authoritarian enclaves persist and have to be challenged by democratic social forces. What are these forces? How can civil society accomplish the democratization of everyday practices in state institutions? How can authoritarian and arbitrary practices in the exercise of power change and evolve into practices guided by legality? And how can the rules, norms, and patterns of behavior of the state itself be democratized? One hypothesis, which should be tested comparatively, is that social movements anchored on solidarity mechanisms — that is, anchored in a shared sense of responsibility toward others — play a central role in challenging authoritarian norms and in opening up new institutional spaces that promote the expansion and strengthening of citizenship (Jelin 1996).

When the state itself has been a major violator of rights — whether through direct action or through complicity or silence — the victims (even those who are officially acknowledged as such, which does not happen often) have no one to take their cases to in the search for justice. In those cases, solidarity movements play a central role: They give legitimacy to the victim's claims, and they transform the meaning and understanding of state action in terms of the violation of fundamental rights. To the extent that this effort is successful (and the mobilization of international support has, in this regard, been extremely important), it can generate conditions favorable for the transformation of the state apparatus itself. The most successful scenario resulting from this interaction between victims, solidarity movements, and the state would entail the emergence of a new state actor pledged to uphold and respect the rule of law. This would imply the transformation of the judiciary and the introduction of new institutional procedures and mechanisms for citizens' control of state action and for the accountability of state agents.

The clearest example of this mode of operation is the human rights movement (Jelin 1994, Sikkink 1996). Nevertheless, this is not necessarily the only model of action, nor is it operational solely in a context (strictly defined) of democratic transition. On the contrary, democratic construction is a continuous task. Furthermore, given the current context of exclusion and social polarization, the expansion of space for citizens' participation is becoming an increasingly urgent challenge. As is well known, the transition to democracy does not end automatically with state violations of the rights of citizens. Various new forms of human rights violations are to be added — civil rights (Caldeira 1996, Jelin et al. 1995) and rights associated with the environment — to the list of unsatisfied needs linked to growing poverty and unemployment.[8]

In this limited field of action within democratic regimes, the mediation of non-governmental organizations and solidarity movements, the independent media, and international pressures (be it of international agencies, of bilateral state-to-state relations, or of international solidarity networks) are all part of a wide spectrum of social manifestations capable of influencing the state. At the same time, however, there is a strong tendency on the part of the population to be apathetic and to develop an individualistic and consumption-oriented outlook on life. Such perspectives, needless to say, run contrary to the values espoused by solidarity movements and thus tend to undermine their success.

In short, the expansion and strengthening of citizenship are a task and a challenge in the process of democratic consolidation. From a societal perspective, democratic consolidation implies the normal functioning of the rule of law as it is expressed in the elimination of arbitrary and abusive forms of state power, in the normal functioning of institutional mechanisms for the resolution of social conflicts, in the effective control of citizens over their own living conditions, and in a measure of predictability in everyday life. These conditions are not the automatic result of institutional change. In fact, in the current context of fiscal austerity and heavy influence of private interests on the state apparatus, the expansion of citizenship cannot be promoted effectively by the state itself. Democratic citizenship can, nonetheless, be furthered as a result of collective activities initiated and sponsored by movements and organizations of civil society. Thus, initiatives and movements emerging from social actors can play a significant role in shaping the democratization agenda.

Social Movements at the Turn of the Century

From a medium-term perspective, the social demands expressed in collective movements in Latin America have changed their profile. The labor movement and peasant movements had, at their peak, projects for "total" societal transformation (Calderón and Jelin 1986). Since the 1970s, with the end of the developmental model of import substitution and the expansion of authoritarian political regimes, the space and scope of social movements have been changing. The heterogeneity and multiplicity of actors and meanings turned more visible; grievances became more specific; the "identity" face of social movements (Evers 1984) began to surface, and patterns of everyday life became the focus of attention. What attracted the attention of analysts was that these specific and very concrete everyday-life concerns and demands often turned into major challenges to the basic principles of social and political organization (Calderón 1986, Escobar and Alvarez 1992). These were highly heterogeneous and diversified movements, which combined the logic of collective identity at the symbolic level with specific instrumental interests and demands.

Recent transformations and current processes — marked by the transition to democracy and to an open-market economy — point to new changes, to still more diversified patterns, to multiple meanings, and to fragmentation. One often hears the argument that links apathy and the weakening of the social bond to individualistic market economies. However, this is not a linear and total process. There is room for other expressions and other meanings, for collective actors who are searching for their identities and struggling for their legitimate space in the sociopolitical scenario: indigenous groups, youth, women, and racial and ethnic minorities. There are also themes and issues that attract and convene: human rights, the environment, poverty, and exclusion.

In this new context, social actors and movements have a double role. They represent collective systems of reciprocal recognition, expressing old and new collective identities with important cultural and symbolic components. They are also non-party political intermediaries, who bring the needs and demands of unarticulated voices to the public sphere, linking them to state institutions. The expressive role in the construction of collective identities and social recognition and the instrumental role that challenges the existing institutional arrangements are both essential for the vitality of democracy. Rather than interpreting the inability shown by political parties and formal institutions to coopt them as a weakness of democracy, social movements and non-party or state organizations should be seen as a way to insure a dynamic democracy — one that has within itself the means for the continuous expansion of its own frontiers.

Notes

1. In this same category, one can include the calls to further "investment in women," justified in terms of the benefits to be obtained, especially the decline in the levels of infant mortality. Currently, such arguments are better received than the claims justified in terms of the need to correct social injustices or expand women's rights.

2. The growth of the global economy, however, does not necessarily entail the disappearance of the state. In Craig Calhoun's words, "States remain the organizations of power through which democratic movements have the greatest capacity to affect economic organization...states remain the highest level of institutional structure at which programmes of democratization themselves can constantly be advanced. States also remain the most crucial objects and vehicles of efforts to achieve 'self-determination' or autonomy as a political community" (Calhoun 1993, 390).

3. Michael Warner's (1992) argument with regard to the public sphere is relevant here. The author claims that insofar as the (bourgeois) public sphere is presented as abstract and impersonal, the bodily marks and signals of the subject are also lost. On the contrary, the "others," the excluded from the hegemonic sphere — blacks, women — become identified by their bodily signals and foster a "politics of identity."

4. The feminist critique of the predominant "androcentrist" view of equality has been quite clear and explicit (Facio 1991, Bunch 1991). There is also the need for a reconceptualization: "The re-conceptualization of equality not only implies the redefinition of the concept of citizenship, but the very concept of 'human being,' because when one speaks about 'equality' of the sexes, one is generally thinking about 'raising' women's condition to that of man, paradigm of humanity" (Facio 1991, 11). The importance of the "right to have rights" view and of the role of the democratic debate on legitimacy and non-legitimacy is, precisely, that they open up the space for that reconceptualization.

5. Analyzing Brazilian urban movements, Ruth Correa Leite Cardoso (1983) shows that they invariably approached the state in terms of specific demands. Insofar as their demands were met by the authoritarian state, they rapidly lost their belligerence, and their potential oppositional stands waned. Her analysis was important to demythify the alleged contestatory nature of urban social movements. Also see Assies 1994.

6. For a discussion of the human rights movement in Argentina, see Jelin 1994.

7. This statement needs to be qualified. NGOs' fragility is linked to the lack of financial autonomy. It is international aid organizations (governmental, NGOs of the North that channel governmental funds, or international private financial links) who ultimately decide what their priorities will be. The current emphasis on "organizational sustainability" should be seen with concern as a prelude to a restriction of funds leading to a change in orientation toward projects where efficiency and economic returns will become the measuring rod of investments (Scherer-Warren 1993).

8. In Argentina, for example, the "heroic" behavior of a few individual judges investigating flagrant cases of pollution and other environmental transgressions has played a significant role in legitimizing victims' claims within a framework that, at least at first glance, seems more anchored on liberal individualism than on the defense of collective rights. Such actions may have important repercussions on the environmental movement, legitimizing its demands and its modes of operation. The 1994 Argentine constitution, similar to those of Brazil and Colombia, recognizes the existence of various environmental rights. This constitutional recognition, however, does not become internalized automatically as part of the consciousness of the larger population (Fuks 1994).

References

Arendt, Hannah. 1949. "The Rights of Man: What Are They?" *Modern Review* 3 (1).

Assies, Willem. 1994. "Urban Social Movements in Brazil: A Debate and its Dynamics." *Latin American Perspectives* 21 (2). Issue 81 (Spring).

Bunch, Charlotte. 1991. "Hacia una revisión de los derechos humanos." In *La mujer ausente: Derechos humanos en el mundo,* eds. Xiema Bunster and Regina Rodríguez. Santiago, Chile: Isis Internacional (Ediciones de las Mujeres No. 15).

Caldeira, Teresa. 1996. "Crime and Individual Rights: Re-framing the Question of Violence in Latin America." In *Constructing Democracy: Human Rights, Citizenship, and Society in Latin America,* eds. Elizabeth Jelin and Eric Hershberg. Boulder, Colo.: Westview Press.

Calderón, Fernando, ed. 1986. *Los Movimientos sociales ante la crisis.* Buenos Aires: FLACSO.

Calderón, Fernando, and Elizabeth Jelin. 1986. *Clases y movimientos sociales en América Latina: Perspectivas y realidad.* Buenos Aires: Estudios CEDES.

Calhoun, Craig. 1993. "Nationalism and Civil Society: Democracy, Diversity, and Self-Determination." *International Sociology* 8, 4 (December).

Cardoso, Ruth Correa Leite. 1983. "Movimentos Sociais Urbanos: Balanço Crítico." In *Sociedade e Política no Brasil Pos-64,* eds. Bernardo Sorj and Maria H. Tavares de Almeida. São Paulo: Brasiliense.

Escobar, Arturo, and Sonia E. Alvarez, eds. 1992. *The Making of Social Movements in Latin America: Identity, Strategy, and Democracy.* Boulder, Colo.: Westview Press.

Evers, Tilman. 1984. "Identidade: A Face Oculta dos Novos Movimentos Sociais." *Novos Estudos,* CEBRAP, 2 (4).

Facio, Alda. 1991. "El principio de igualdad frente a la ley." *El Otro Derecho* 8.

Fernándes, Rubem Cesar. 1994. *Privado Porém Público: O Terceiro Setor na América Latina.* Rio de Janeiro: Relume-Dumara.

Fuks, Mario. 1994. "Theoretical and Practical Considerations on Environment-Related Litigation." *International Sociology* 9, 4 (December).

Hasenbalg, Carlos. 1996. "Racial Inequalities in Brazil and Latin America: Timid Responses to Disguised Racism." In *Constructing Democracy: Human Rights, Citizenship, and Society in Latin America,* eds. Elizabeth Jelin and Eric Hershberg. Boulder, Colo.: Westview Press.

Jelin, Elizabeth. 1994. "The Politics of Memory: The Human Rights Movement and the Construction of Democracy in Argentina." *Latin American Perspectives* (special issue on social movements and political change in Latin America: 1), 21 (2). Issue 81 (Spring).

Jelin, Elizabeth. 1996. "Citizenship Revisited: Solidarity, Responsibility and Rights." In *Constructing Democracy: Human Rights, Citizenship, and Society in Latin America*, eds. Elizabeth Jelin and Eric Hershberg. Boulder, Colo.: Westview Press.

Jelin, Elizabeth, et al. 1995. *Justicia cotidiana, justicia institucional*. Buenos Aires, manuscript.

Minow, Martha. 1990. *Making All the Difference: Inclusion, Exclusion, and American Law*. New York: Cornell University Press.

Pinheiro, Paulo Sergio, Malak Poppovic, and Tulio Kahn. 1993. *Poverty, Marginalization, Violence, and the Realization of Human Rights*. São Paulo, mimeograph.

Raczynski, Dagmar, and Claudia Serrano, eds. 1992. *Políticas sociales, mujeres y gobierno local*. Santiago, Chile: CIEPLAN.

de Sousa Santos, Boaventura. 1991a. "Una cartografía simbólica de las representaciones sociales: Prolegómenos a una concepción posmoderna del derecho." In *Estado, derecho y luchas sociales*, ed. Boaventura de Sousa Santos. Bogotá: ILSA.

de Sousa Santos, Boaventura. 1991b. "The Postmodern Transition: Law and Politics." In *The Fate of Law*, ed. Austin Sarat and Thomas R. Kearns. Ann Arbor, Mich.: University of Michigan Press.

Scott, James C. 1992. *Domination and the Arts of Resistance: Hidden Transcripts*. New Haven, Conn.: Yale University Press.

Scherer-Warren, Ilse. 1993. "ONGs na América Latina: Trajetoria e Perfil." Mimeograph.

Sikkink, Kathryn. 1996. "The Emergence, Evolution, and Effectiveness of the Latin American Human Rights Network." In *Constructing Democracy: Human Rights, Citizenship, and Society in Latin America*, eds. Elizabeth Jelin and Eric Hershberg. Boulder, Colo.: Westview Press.

Stavenhagen, Rodolfo. 1990. *The Ethnic Question: Conflicts, Development, and Human Rights*. Tokyo: United Nations University Press.

Stavenhagen, Rodolfo. 1996. "Indigenous Rights: Some Conceptual Problems." In *Constructing Democracy: Human Rights, Citizenship, and Society in Latin America*, eds. Elizabeth Jelin and Eric Hershberg. Boulder, Colo.: Westview Press.

Strobele-Gregor, Juliana. 1994. "From Indio to Mestizo to...Indio: New Indianist Movements in Bolivia." *Latin American Perspectives* 21 (2). Issue 81 (Spring).

Valdés, Teresa. 1990. "Mujer y derechos humanos: 'Menos tu vientre.'" Santiago, Chile: FLACSO, Documento de Trabajo, Serie Estudios Sociales No. 8.

Warner, Michael. 1992. "The Mass Public and the Mass Subject." In *Habermas and the Public Sphere*, ed. Craig Calhoun. Cambridge, Mass.: The MIT Press.

Wieviorka, Michel. 1992. *El espacio del racismo*. Barcelona: Paidos.

Young-Bruehl, Elizabeth. 1982. *Hannah Arendt: For Love of the World*. New Haven, Conn.: Yale University Press.

Part III.

Comparative Case Studies

Chapter 6

Economic Restructuring and New Forms of Market Participation in Rural Latin America

Liliana R. Goldín

Introduction

This chapter is an analysis of recent developments observed by students of Latin American rural issues as structural adjustment policies have impacted on culture and economy. A Guatemalan case study is presented in the context of larger world developments, corroborating many existing studies and highlighting the risks of uneven and exclusionary development. The Guatemalan case shows how the debate over the future of the peasant sector can be enhanced by microanalyses of the effects of adjustment policies on rural areas.

Adjustment policies in Latin America have been precipitated by many events including the increase in oil prices in the 1970s and the rise of interest rates in the early 1980s, followed by significant decreases in demands for imports (Edwards and Teitel 1986). Before addressing the impact of adjustment policies on rural areas, it is necessary to describe the kind of rural sector that adjustment policies affect. Little interaction exists between scholars conducting "national" analyses of individual Latin American countries and those interested in the rural sector. The rural/urban dichotomy is painfully obvious, and the biases of researchers are evident in their debates. The identification of the rural with backward, feudal, pre- or non-capitalist is alive and well in academia, particularly among non-specialists. For example, consider a comparison of the white collar worker in Montevideo with the Central American peasant, supposedly placed at very different places within the class spectrum. The need to incorporate class analysis into interpretations and predictions of social and political action is evident, but the way in which researchers work with static and outdated categories can undermine interpretations. The white collar worker from Montevideo is a dependent wage worker, dispossessed of all means of production and only free to sell his/her labor in a limited labor market for low wages. In contrast, the Central American peasant may be landless and poor or landed and wealthy. Often, he/she will be a petty commodity producer, with some access to limited land ownership, who may hire temporary workers. He/she may produce for national or international markets, and his/her income is directly dependent on the whims and fluctuations of national policies and the world market. The Central American peasant may work for a rich landowner or may be an artisan who owns his/her weaving looms or ceramic oven. Many seasonal wage workers may own some land in their home townships where they own a site and some animals. Central American and other Latin American peasants still are endowed with the capacity for making decisions about how to survive or take advantage of the larger economy. The suggestion that peasants such as those who recently rebelled in Chiapas are outside the project of structural adjustment policies is misleading. Students of peasant movements throughout history know that through diverse forms of resistance or active engagement, peasants have made themselves part of governments' or elites' projects. The exploited sectors have been excluded from all projects, particularly since the Spanish invasion, but these sectors have figured out ways of becoming heard (see, for example, Hobsbawn 1965 and Scott 1990). Some sectors of the peasantry may indeed be disappearing, as the process of semiproletarianization develops. However, the disappearance of the peasant is far from a reality, with new small and middle sectors, as the one described below, still developing (see Deere and de Janvry 1979).

The general guiding ideology of neoliberal policies has been toward downsizing the state. Measures have included restrictions on social expenditures, such as health, education, and other social services; the privatization of public enterprises; and the denationalization of resources. Since the 1980s, the number of Latin Americans living below the poverty line has increased dramatically. At the same time, an increase in the standard of living of the top 25 percent of the population has been observed. Most of the decreases are found in the rural areas of Latin America (Petras and Vieux 1992).

Of all the domains discussed below, Guatemala probably represents the most extreme on all dimensions. As it is widely known, Guatemala has one of the most inequitable land distribution ratios in Latin America as well as the highest levels of urban and rural poverty. Profound problems of malnutrition, health, environmental degradation, and rural unrest are combined with high levels of political repression. In a country such as this, peasants have not totally lost agency, and even with limited resources, a few have been able to take advantage of some of the market opportunities that the new policies present. Indeed, in the case discussed here, some rural inhabitants have taken advantage of their skill base and the increased prices for nontraditionals in foreign markets, including other Latin American markets. The experience of one small community in the western highlands of Guatemala emphasizes at the microlevel the issue of uneven or exclusionary regional development. This is a case of increased differentiation within towns and also increased regional differentiation, with consequent fewer opportunities for most rural inhabitants. Guatemalan peasants lost land to large estates throughout the colonial years, just as other countries in the region. In the nineteenth century, laws were passed so that communal lands, identified as *tierras baldías* or unused lands, could be expropriated, and "vagrancy" laws were enacted to institute a system of forced labor in public works and in private commercial landholdings. Land loss and fewer opportunities led to increased seasonal labor in the coastal plantations and a prolonged system of debt peonage under extreme conditions, which are well documented in the literature (Handy 1984, Burgos Debrais 1985, Cambranes 1985).

In Western Guatemala, I have been studying aspects of economic development in several townships. San Pedro Almolonga, with a population of about 12,000, is located five miles from Quetzaltenango, Guatemala's second-largest city. The town as a whole is doing relatively well when compared with neighboring townships. The population of the township has quadrupled in the past 100 years, and the current high birth rate portends a continued rapid rate of growth in the future. Families are faced with the prospects of having to support themselves and maintain an already substandard existence in the face of fewer resources. For example, inheritance traditions within the township dictate that land be equally divided among the living children. This means that each generation has less land to work with, as the land is divided into smaller and smaller plots.

The next section provides an overview of ways in which structural adjustment policies have affected rural sectors, contrasting this case study with other Latin American cases. The effects of such policies on land and food production, migration, nutrition and health, forms of labor, culture, political developments, and the environment are discussed. By focusing on one small subregion within Western Guatemala, I hope to clarify the ways in which global and local conditions converge and shape the life of rural inhabitants.

Land and Food Production

There are ongoing debates about the future of the peasantry. While some analysts contend that small farms are doing quite well, others predict the disappearance of small farms and therefore the peasantry, as a result of increased marginalization and landlessness. Some see the peasantry moving toward total displacement, eventually becoming completely dependent upon food imports (De Janvry 1981). Limited domestic production is often due to limited domestic demand and an increase in food imports (Wise 1987). The forecast of stagnation or declining food production is true for some countries but not for all Latin American countries. Mexico, for example, shows signs of increase in food production. South America is doing better than Central America, the Dominican Republic, and Peru (Wise 1987).

In those areas where changes in the international economy are generating an increase in the import of grains, peasants are pushed out of the market and out of production or, at the least, out of traditional production. In those cases, peasants have pursued alternatives. In Guatemala, there are many examples of communities and regions oriented toward the export of new cash crops and crafts. Peasants have resorted to strategies that require small amounts of land and that are labor-intensive, often taking advantage of knowledge and skills inherited through traditional means. For example, Guatemalan and Mexican peasants have adapted the weaving techniques learned and passed through generations to the tastes and styles of new international markets (Rosenbaum and Goldín 1993). The people from Western Guatemala chose to intensify the production of vegetables, of which they had some knowledge since colonial times. Increasing commercialization is another form of capitalization chosen by peasants who have little or no access to land. In Guatemala, the most successful sector is one that combines the production of nontraditional crops with commercialization. However, not all farmers have access to international markets and are often unable to sell their surpluses (Helwege 1990).

In spite of discussions on the disappearance of the peasantry, an increase in the number of large and medium-sized farms that use capital extensively and labor sparingly have been observed. However, a dynamic small farm sector in several parts of Latin America has also been found. William Thiesenhusen and Jolyne Melmed-Sanjak (1990), for example, found an inverse relationship between farm size and agricultural receipts per unit of land in Brazil. This results from more intensive land use in small farms. Small farms are reaching the point of land exhaustion and overuse, but despite this, they appear to be among the most active farms. The conflict between large farms and smaller farms makes agrarian sectors compete against themselves. Left to their own devices, peasants are unable to compete with commercial landholders (i.e., fruit companies, sugar mills), and they are pushed away from the land and into the commercial market.

Land reform always has been in the minds of peasants and policymakers but is rarely fully instituted. Scholars suggest that reforms do not change the basic unequal social relations nor do they resolve any existing contradictions (De Janvry and Ground 1978). In general, reviews of the literature (Thiesenhusen 1982) document the limited effect of land reform efforts (Chile, Ecuador, Costa Rica), in particular, in those cases where peasants have little or no access to decisionmaking and to the power structures. There have been attempts at land reform in El Salvador, Guatemala, and other parts of Central America. Efforts also have been implemented on the Atlantic coasts of Colombia and Ecuador. While reports indicate that the peasants' agency has generated some policy changes, their effects have been limited. Land reform has been seen by peasants as another form of state control and intervention. By providing credit and setting terms on land ownership, states increase their control as peasants see their own control over production disappear. On the other hand, liberalization policies, by "freeing" the peasantry from obligations toward the state, have led peasants to resort to the dubious freedom of separating themselves from their life-long land-related production and moving into alternative sources of income, such as commerce, which in turn have resulted in the creation of new relations of production (Canak 1982).

Need for New Exports

In the 1980s, the agricultural sector found itself reduced in size, and many of its traditional exports declined. There was a clear need to generate new exports. There are concerns about the policy of adhering to nontraditional exports, however, because the North American market is quite small. Nontraditional products are directed toward the U.S. market, and some also are sent to Europe and other countries in Latin America. Examples of these exports are horticultural products and light manufactures, such as textiles and clothing. They represent, for example, 40 percent of all exports in Costa Rica (Timossi Dolinsky 1990). In Peru, the level of contribution from nontraditional exports to fiscal revenue went from 7.6 percent in 1978 to 12.3 percent in 1980, which represents 8.0 percent of the gross domestic product (GDP) (Shydlowsky 1986). It is clear that the short-term benefits and growth potential of nontraditionals are good. However, many question the long-term impact related to socioeconomic differentiation and environmental degradation. These new production strategies are associated with new styles of production that heavily influence peasant class relations. One of the main issues that derives from the analysis of the production and export of nontraditionals throughout Latin America is that the benefits do not flow to the whole society. There is a dangerous combination of great monopolies and multinational corporations with little chance for redistribution at home. Often, these styles of development have no regional policies, and they benefit only a local area. That is the case of the areas of food production in Chile, Mexico, Costa Rica, and Guatemala, where the benefits are small and only reach local elites and foreign capital (Paus 1988). In Costa Rica, the leading firms producing nontraditionals (pineapples and flowers) are all foreign. In Chile, the production of fruit is also in the hands of foreign companies from Japan, the United States, Norway, and Scotland, among others. There, the production of fruit, forestry, and salmon has increased the demand for labor since 1984, and it also has changed the demographic composition of the work force by incorporating women, urban inhabitants, and youths.

In Guatemala, the production of nontraditionals has progressed in several ways. Some export operations are growing crops on rented or purchased land, hiring help, and then exporting the crops directly to the United States or Europe. Exporters who contract directly with the growers, setting high standards of quality, also have been observed (Barham et al. 1992). In the case that I observed, independent producers and local middlemen themselves are marketing local products in bordering countries of Central America and Mexico. The price of traditional products, including traditional vegetables and grains sold for national consumption, has dropped, and imports of cheap grain from the United States have lowered dramatically the profitability of grain production. The emphasis on nontraditionals was caused by the need for export diversification, mentioned above, combined with a push by development agencies to expand exports as development strategy (AVANCSO 1992). Almolongueños, however, are not interested in offers from the U.S. Agency for International Development (USAID) to help them establish trade relations with foreign buyers. The conditions set by importers in the United States are too stringent and constraining for the people of Almolonga. Almolongueños prefer their independence, and they prefer to emphasize quantity over quality.

Limits of Nontraditionals

According to academics and political analysts alike, nontraditional agricultural products pose threats to the development of peasant communities in Guatemala. Nontraditional products are "accelerating the concentration of land in fewer hands in the countryside, benefitting a small group of *campesinos* who own land, while increasing the number of those who are landless" (Calí 1992). A large part of the vegetables produced in Western Guatemala are exported to Nicaragua, Mexico, and El Salvador, as well as the United States and Europe. Depending on international prices, the price of some vegetables has increased considerably and so have the prices of land. Wealthier peasants purchase these lands, generating concentration of land and capital. This is the case not only of Almolonga but of several townships in the valley of Chimaltenango.

Why aren't more peasants pursuing nontraditionals by cultivating vegetables, instead of selling or renting out their lands? The answer seems to be their "lack of knowledge," as vegetable production requires a high skill investment and is knowledge-intensive. Land must be irrigated constantly, and large amounts of fertilizers and pesticides must be used. Long ago, Almolongueños developed a creative irrigation system with the aid of wooden shovels and canals that are dug out around the plots. This system requires full community cooperation in the upkeep of the canals. The initial capital, which is lower than needed for other crops, since a small amount of land will produce several crops a year, is still considerable for the poor peasant, who also needs to purchase an abundant supply of chemicals. This is the explanation provided by some people of San Cristóbal Totonicapán, who supply the people of Almolonga with land, some labor, and even new homes. Thus, the poor farmers from townships like San Cristóbal, Zunil, and Concepción Chiquirichapa, among others, lose their land and all possibilities for improvement. They are left with the option of wage labor on the coast or migration to Guatemala City or to the United States, questionable options that reinforce unequal social relations and comment on a very limited form of economic development. Many of the developments described for Guatemala apply to other countries in Latin America that opted for the production of nontraditionals. A sector of the population is benefitting from the possibilities of vegetable production at the expense of the large peasant sector of the region, at high human and environmental costs.

In sum, many peasants have experienced marginalization and landlessness. Pushed out of production, some have found an alternative in the commercialization of nontraditional crops and artisan products. While many point to the disappearance of the peasantry, the process is far from complete, with new and active small and medium-sized farms. Land reform efforts have stopped short of any radical change and have been limited. The production of nontraditionals, requiring less land and more labor, is not proving to be the solution for rural people, as differentiation and land concentration increase.

Migration as an Option

A depressed situation in the countryside — no land, no credit, and no work — leads to migration. The outpouring of peasants into cities, documented for most countries in Latin America, has been influenced by a combination of complex factors, of which economic and political variables have been found to be crucial. Fear of repression and the lack of economic opportunities, when combined with family and friendship networks, can lead to an increase in migration (Morrison 1993). The most affected areas are those that depend on single or minimum sources of income. For example, migration differences have been observed between the population of coastal and highland Ecuador; where coastal women work as domestics or opt to migrate, highland women find options without resorting to migration (Phillips 1987). Migration was acute in Chile during the Augusto Pinochet years, as a result of the lack of agricultural options in the country (Hojman 1989). The migration trends in Brazil and Mexico are truly impressive. There again, lack of agricultural policies, infrastructure, and other rural options have depressed the countryside. In Guatemala, the striking migration to Guatemala City is creating great instability. Increased poverty, unemployment and subemployment, pollution, homelessness, and delinquency are the direct results of an impoverished rural population looking for alternatives. The dream of the Guatemalan peasant, however, is to migrate to the United States. The most developed areas of Western Guatemala are sources of migrants to the United States, and some townships are now observing improvements because of remittances from immigrants within the United States.

In sum, migration is changing the landscape of Latin America and the world, as rural sectors move to the cities of their own countries and abroad as dubious alternatives for economic success.

Problems of Nutrition and Health

Many of the studies assessing the impact of structural adjustment policies on the poorer sectors address problems of nutrition and health and the need to protect those sectors being affected the most. Some consider Chile and Peru as partial exceptions (Pfefferman and Griffin 1989). Chile has a long history of welfare intervention, and in Peru, the poor are not affected much by privatization policies because few of them are in public service. Some of the poor actually have benefitted from lower wheat and sugar prices, compared to the higher price of maize (Glewwe and de Tray 1989). David Hojman (1989) points to the interesting correlation between the decline of social and economic conditions in Chile and the fall in infant and child mortality rates, due, in part, to the reduction in birth rates but also as a result of migration to the cities where there is better access to hospitals. Bolivia's emergency social fund (Graham 1992) is an example of the measures developed as a reaction to neoliberal policies. Many consider such policies a "band-aid" approach. Even in areas that show some improvement due to returns from nontraditionals, there are no indications of changes in nutrition levels (Immink and Alarcón 1993, Barham et al. 1992). The township of

Almolonga, Guatemala, is seeing an increase in birth defects and neurological disorders. These are probably related to the excessive and inappropriate use of pesticides in their land, a phenomenon that is not exclusive to this region.

The new economic policies translate into a decrease in the health status of rural peoples as poverty and intensification of production create new dangerous conditions.

New Forms of Labor and Relations of Production

In the process of adapting to the new conditions related to access to land, population shifts, and new forms of production, peasants and capitalists have developed new forms of labor exploitation, depending upon the products sought. An example from Chile is the growth of contract farming in the production of fruit, specifically grapes (Korovkin 1992). Instead of wage workers, there is growth in contract farming, a system that gives flexibility to the land owners (Collins 1993). Contract farming results in differentiation; it converts rich peasants into peasant capitalists, and it affects all aspects of local organizations. Tanya Korovkin (1992) notes that the fruit boom in the 1970s and 1980s in Chile increased the gap between rich and poor peasants. Jane Collins (1993) observed the same in Brazil in the San Francisco Valley, where the firms involved in the production of fruit and vegetables are experimenting with alternative labor arrangements that they find both more suitable and economic. Often making use of unpaid family labor, forms of contract farming and sharecropping are considered flexible and tend to discourage political mobilization of the workers. Fruits and vegetables require great care and more intense investment of labor. For that purpose, growers use women and undocumented workers instead of a stable wage labor force (see also several examples in Deere and León 1987, in particular Lago). Contracting represents a de-skilling of labor as opposed to the peasant farmer. Contract farmers may need fewer skills and do not have as much control over production as petty commodity producers. Many of the contract farmers observed in Brazil, for example, are both direct producers or employers and operate small capitalist farms. Sharecropping is being used in small to medium-sized farms, taking advantage of the work of the whole family. Richard Tardanico (1993) observes the same effect on women and children in Costa Rica, where job downgrading, underemployment, and unemployment are also taking place. This is especially true in agriculture, where there is a large amount of informal employment. Market inequality has increased in many countries of Latin America in terms of gender, age, and social class as a result of liberalization policies. Unequal terms are more profound in the countryside, however, deepening the already existing unequal relations of production.

The case of Almolonga does not seem to support the notion of a supposed internal capacity of peasants to resist differentiation (Llovet 1987) and instead confirms cases from other Latin American countries where increased differentiation has been noted. In Almolonga some households do accumulate capital and invest their surpluses to expand their means of production (i.e., trucks and lands elsewhere). In this fashion, these small entrepreneurs develop into petty capitalists, who hire wage laborers to contribute to their businesses. However, these wage laborers do not constitute a permanent proletariat since these workers almost always are temporary and occasional, which prevents the possibility of extraction of a large surplus. Differentiation is then only limited to the extent that it does not generate separate rural bourgeois and proletarian classes. Surplus in Almolonga is extracted through the use of land and labor from other communities, which explains the overall "improved" performance of Almolonga in contrast to other townships in the region. The high prices for land in Almolonga are no doubt due to its scarcity. Compared to most neighboring villages, Almolonga has the lowest rate of land per capita, 30 persons per manzana (1980 census, 1 manzana = 1.7 acres), compared to a range of seven to 10 inhabitants per manzana in most neighboring villages and 20 persons per manzana in the more urban township of Salcajá. In examining internal distribution of land in each of the neighboring townships, there are some interesting features. While in Almolonga lots of less than one manzana represent 86 percent of the total number of lots, they comprise 51 percent of the land. The ratio in all other neighboring townships is much more skewed, so that a few people in the townships own most of the land (few plots).[1] The more equitable distribution of land observed in Almolonga gives a sense that the between-towns differentiation was more acute than the differentiation within the town. It also suggests that internal differentiation should be measured in external resources (land rental and ownership outside Almolonga and access to capital through trade) rather than land ownership in Almolonga. The marked differentiation between townships creates distrust and resentment from other towns and in turn reinforces within-town solidarity. Today, there are several townships in the surroundings of Almolonga that obtain a significant part of their subsistence from renting or selling land to Almolongueños. Almolongueños complain that people in other townships do not like them because of their practice of renting and purchasing land elsewhere, but they see other villages as sources of land and labor. Almolongueños proudly emphasize that they do not work in the plantations on the coast or for other people but that other people work for them.

In the pursuit of alternative production strategies, Almolongueños have not developed into two distinct classes of proprietors and workers within the village. Some people work as peons for a few days a month, but overall they cannot be considered as exclusively wage workers. If anything, there is exploitation of other villages through the use of their land and occasional wage labor. As between- and within-town differentiation takes place, incipient indications of class formation center around production forms and town specialization.

In the town, producers and traders of nontraditional crops (*comerciantes* or *gente de negocios*) tend to see themselves as more intelligent and equipped to succeed than others, and they are in fact wealthier, on average, than traditional (corn) agriculturalists. Traders state that they are good for the town in that, by taking vegetables for sale to El Salvador and other markets, they generate demand and are thus able to keep the price of vegetables high. The aura of progress and interest in innovation resulting in an advantaged position in the town creates a new faction around traders and middlemen and the potential for developing into a full differentiated class. This group has explored new alternatives (nontraditionals) provided by the market, has been open to change and innovation in social and economic terms, and has experienced large ideological transformations (religious change, individualistic attitudes, competitiveness, profit orientation).[2]

New forms of exploitation of labor give room for arrangements such as contract farming, sharecropping, and diverse forms of temporary work and use of family as unpaid labor. In all, these forms promote rural differentiation, increased friction between sectors, and increased uneven regional development.

Environmental Impact

Some of the environmental problems noted result from the emphasis that nation-states place on national development rather than local and regional development. The Amazonian case (Kyle and Cunha 1992, Binswanger 1991) shows how Amazonian policies are generating local poverty and concomitant destruction of the environment. In fact, tax policies and tax incentives guide the rules of land allocation and credit systems that accelerate the deforestation of the Amazon. For example, Brazilian landowners receive tax credits for acts of deforestation by establishing livestock ranches. In areas of limited land for agriculture, rural people are finding themselves pouring vast amounts of chemicals into the ground so as to sustain, if not increase, their production. Guatemala is a good example of this, especially in areas dedicated to export production. The international quality requirements are very high, and the need for steady production is such that peasants are now risking future low yields due to land exhaustion.

Cultural Changes Related to Structural Adjustment Policies

In addition to the developments previously discussed, ongoing cultural changes are truly impressive. The processes of capitalization, semiproletarianization, and general reorganization of the economy of rural peoples has taken place in the context of ideological changes that support and provide an interpretive framework for the economic changes and, at the same time, result from them. One of the areas where cultural changes are more noticeable is religion. For example, many Latin Americans are seeking out the new pentecostal and other evangelical churches for support (Stoll 1990). The new churches are constructed on ideologies that support the changes in production relations and new household strategies. They provide a framework for change, further stratification, and a sense of "brotherhood" that the Catholic Church is unable to offer (Goldín and Metz 1991). In Almolonga, 50 percent of the population has converted, most of them in the last 30 years. There are now 15 evangelical churches in the town. The largest one, located in front of the market and beside the Catholic Church, was built in 1993 and has a capacity for 4,000 people. It is clear that Almolonga has a larger evangelical population than most neighboring townships, where estimates suggest that conversion rates range from 10 to 30 percent. There is an observable correlation between changes in production strategies, and in particular the practice of trade in nontraditionals, and the rate of conversions. Consequently, as people turn to commerce and find themselves traveling to new places and are exposed to new ideologies, they become more open to accepting new ideas (Goldín 1992).

The actors involved in new economic strategies experience cultural transformations. However, these do not always imply a drastic change from one form to another or from some precapitalist form to a capitalist one. Instead, the new cultural forms often present new interpretations of traditional beliefs in the context of the new conditions. The presence of cultural variability in the midst of capitalization trends should not be surprising. New meanings are attached to older practices, and different interpretations are attributed to the new. Studies of oral tradition show how people reinterpret the world around them in the context of new practices and transformed ideologies (Warren 1989, Goldín and Rosenbaum 1993, Wachtel 1994).

In the area of gender relations, major changes are taking place as more women become partly employed or underemployed, generating new gender (and power) relations in the household (see Nash 1993). Men have benefitted more than women in most cases. Men often are involved in the new forms of production. Attempts to reform or redistribute land systematically have benefitted men over women. Often, women are not given titles to land and are not beneficiaries of land distribution. In the midst of changes in production, women and men are reconceptualized, and conflictive gender relations are creating the path for new socioeconomic positions for men and women.

Therefore, in search of economic alternatives, simultaneously, peasants have experienced profound cultural changes that have provided new interpretations and support systems for their new practices.

Political Implications of Structural Adjustment Policies

What are the consequences of economic and cultural changes in the political arena? The success at the polls of neoliberal governments are both the cause and effect of the new economic policies. How much of that support comes from the rural areas? In Guatemala, with a large rural population, the election of President Jorge Serrano Elías (1990-1993) is an example of the strengthening of right-wing evangelical sectors of the country and among the Mayas. The areas of larger economic development, as discussed in this chapter, are used by conservative sectors as examples of what "good Indians" can do. They are often referred to as hard-working and progressive sectors who are willing to innovate, change, and take advantage of developing economic opportunities. The contrast between the successful few and the larger numbers who are losing their lands and using multiple strategies to survive is striking. The latter are the sectors that are sometimes forced to comply or that take political action. Several researchers have observed recent peasant activity and rebellions as a reaction to the extreme poverty in the countryside (Edelman 1991, Brockett 1987). Currently, in Chiapas, Mexico, rebel peasants react against unfair conditions among the native peoples. Land occupations and protests are reported throughout Latin America (examples come from El Salvador, Mexico, Guatemala, Paraguay, Colombia, and many other countries). Changes in the legislation of *ejidos*, leading to privatization of collective ownership and the end of land distribution in Mexico, are a good example of some of these policies. The Mexican state, in an attempt to continue balancing exports and staple products through the use of incentives, has benefitted large commercial enterprises and allowed cattle ranching to continue expanding (Gates 1988). The impact of modernization policies on peasant agriculture in Mexico has been severe, turning more peasants into proletarians or semiproletarians and intensifying peasant marginality. In Costa Rica, the growth of a "politically heterogeneous peasant movement" and a clash between state and peasant organizations are thought to be the result of economic structural adjustment (Edelman 1991). In Honduras, for example, the proportion of landless and land-poor rural families continues to increase at the same time that the production of food continues to decline (Brockett 1987). This has led directly to the mobilization of peasants, which, in turn, has led to some reform policy measures. The measures, however, stopped short of land reform (Pino 1993).

Conclusions

The experience of Almolonga seems to confirm much of the research from other parts of Latin America. As peasants resort to alternative occupational strategies, there is increased differentiation within and between villages and regions, further increasing uneven development, underemployment, and conflict between formerly interdependent communities.

It is interesting to observe that much of the deregulation and steps toward the reduction in the size of the state have led to some of the same results that derived from previous policies of state intervention oriented toward the incorporation of the peasant sector into the capitalist economy. Both types of policies have benefitted a small elite, sometimes providing credit and advice by means of state intervention or by depriving sectors of access to credit or other options to continue with local production. A limited elite, although not necessarily the same one, benefits from either set of policies. Under both sets of policies, the ultimate goal is the incorporation of rural peoples into the capitalist market, a goal relatively easy to achieve even when the end result is marginalization due to the pervasiveness of the system in the world economy. The results are larger differentiation and a bigger gap between the rich and the poor, an increase in unemployment which has, in turn, increased migration to the cities and to the United States, land concentration in the hands of commercial export enterprises, and larger amounts of landlessness and semiproletarianization.

In the search for solutions, the emphasis in the literature has been placed on encouraging local development by developing infrastructure and industries and by the promotion of more credit. Many conclude that the situation for rural people has worsened in the last 50 years or that trends that began in the nineteenth century are continuing. A resolution of the existing contradictions well established in the nineteenth century between peasants and capital partially may be achieved by combined or mixed systems that include some state participation with free market policies. The large control by multinationals associated with the production of nontraditionals can only be diminished partially by some form of state controls. Current observation shows a marked double structure of development around export areas and underdevelopment around those areas associated with local and traditional types of production. Furthermore, there is a decline in food production, increase in food imports, and low purchasing power in the hands of the rural populations. Results may have been different by increasing infrastructural developments or establishing a more developed agricultural policy that would lead to some change in the agricultural structure rather than instituting wage suppression policies (Adelman and Taylor 1990).

Profound cultural changes, expressed in part by religious and political shifts, are at once expression of economic policies and also impulse for further changes. As the Chiapas peasants and the thousands of men and women acting at the grassroots throughout the region are demonstrating, resistance is also born from these economic and social policies. Liberalization policies have led peasants to feel that they are literally "on their own" and that they need to take charge. Land occupations throughout the continent and political upheaval of the kind seen in Central America and now in Mexico are expressions of an understanding that the state is there to protect the elites. The contrast between economic developments throughout Latin America with a detailed case study of a rural region of Western Guatemala provides an additional perspective of the interaction between external policies and people's agency.

Notes

1. For example, in Zunil, lots of less than 1 manzana represent 70 percent of all lots that cover 15 percent of the land; 78 percent of the lots in Cantel comprise 27 percent of the land; 80 percent of the lots in Salcajá comprise 29 percent of the land.

2. These conclusions were based on an in-depth analysis of a small number of individuals drawn from a random sample of the township who evidenced upward mobility. A survey of 10 percent of the households (N = 157) in Almolonga offers broader perspectives on the issue and allows exploration of other explanations of upward mobility and economic differentiation. Individuals who have explored trade as an alternative during this generation have reinforced their new practice by adopting new ideologies. Interestingly, the percentage of full-time traders has remained relatively constant for several generations (about 14 percent). Full-time traders have probably continued with traditional practices associated with long-distance trade, such as the "stepped" practice of transporting small amounts of produce that are exchanged in each town along the road by some commodity in which that town specializes (see Goldín 1988). While experiencing similar ideological changes to those combining trade and agriculture, professional traders probably continue economic practices inherited from parents and grandparents. So while in general it is known that diversification may bring a more stable but often lower income, in this case it seems that full-time traders have taken lower risks and derived lower economic status than the combined group. Full-time traders do not always trade in vegetables as the combined group does, and the trade of traditional merchandise would indeed also contribute to lower returns.

References

Adelman, Irma, and J. Edward Taylor. 1990. "Is Structural Adjustment with a Human Face Possible? The Case of Mexico." *Journal of Development Studies* 26(3):387-407.

AVANCSO/PACCA. 1992. "Growing Dilemmas: Guatemala, the Environment and the Global Economy." Asociación para el Avance de las Ciencias Sociales en Guatemala.

Barham, Bradford, Mary Clark, Elizabeth Katz, and Rachel Schurman. 1992. "Nontraditional Agricultural Exports in Latin America." *Latin American Research Review* 27(2):43-82.

Barham, Bradford, Michael Carter, and Wayne Sigelko. n.d. "Adoption and Accumulation Patterns in Guatemala's Latest Agro-export Boom." University of Wisconsin-Madison.

Binswanger, Hans P. 1991. "Brazilian Policies that Encourage Deforestation in the Amazon." *World Development* 19(7): 821-829.

Brockett, Charles D. 1989. "Power and Poverty: Agrarian Transformation and Political Conflict in Central America." Review Essay. *Journal of Latin American Studies* 21:173.

Brockett, Charles D. 1987. "Public Policy, Peasants and Rural Development in Honduras." *Journal of Latin American Studies* 19:69-86.

Burgos Debrais, Elisabeth, ed. 1985. *I, Rigoberta Menchu. An Indian Woman in Guatemala.* London: Verso.

Calí, Francisco. 1992. "Interview with Francisco Calí: 'We Must Join Hands...'" *Report on Guatemala* 13(3):2-4.

Cambranes, Julio C. 1985. *Coffee and Peasants in Guatemala.* South Woodstock: CIRMA.

Canak, William L. 1982. "Structural Transformation in Rural Social Relations." Review Essay. *Latin American Research Review* 17(1):223-234.

Collins, Jane L. 1993. "Gender, Contracts, and Wage Work: Agricultural Restructuring in Brazil's São Francisco Valley." *Development and Change* 21(1):53-82.

De Janvry, Alain. 1981. *The Agrarian Question and Reformism in Latin America.* Baltimore: Johns Hopkins University Press.

De Janvry, Alain, and L. Ground. 1978. "Types and Consequences of Land Reform in Latin America." *Latin American Perspectives* 19(5):4.

Deere, Carmen D., and Alain de Janvry. 1979. "A Conceptual Framework for the Empirical Analysis of Peasants." *American Journal of Agricultural Economics* 61(4):601-611.

Deere, Carmen D., and Magdalena León, eds. 1987. *Rural Women and State Policy. Feminist Perspectives on Latin American Agricultural Development.* Boulder, Colo.: Westview Press.

Edelman, Marc. 1991. "Shifting Legitimacies and Economic Change: The State and Contemporary Costa Rican Peasant Movements." *Peasant Studies* 18(4):221-249.

Edwards, Sebastian, and Simon Teitel. 1986. "Growth, Reform, and Adjustment: Latin America's Trade and Macroeconomic Policies in the 1970's and 1980's." *Economic Development and Cultural Change* 34(3):423-431.

Gates, Marilyn. 1988. "Codifying Marginality: The Evolution of Mexican Agricultural Policy and its Impact on the Peasantry." *Journal of Latin American Studies* 20: 277-311.

Glewwe, Paul, and Dennis de Tray. 1989. *The Poor in Latin America during Adjustment: A Case Study of Peru*. Living Standards Measurement Study Working Paper No. 56. Washington, D.C.: World Bank.

Goldín, Liliana. 1988. "Social and Symbolic Topography of the Traditional Trader of Western Guatemala." *Mesoamerica* 16: 287-310.

Goldín, Liliana. 1992. "Work and Ideology in the Maya Highlands of Guatemala: Economic Beliefs in the Context of Occupational Change." *Economic Development and Cultural Change* 41(1): 103-124.

Goldín, Liliana, and Brent Metz. 1991. "An Expression of Cultural Change: Invisible Converts to Protestantism among Highland Guatemala Mayas." *Ethnology* 30(4): 325-338.

Goldín, Liliana, and Brenda Rosenbaum. 1993. "Culture and History: Subregional Variation among the Maya." *Comparative Studies in Society and History* 35(1): 110-132.

Graham, Carol. 1992. "The Politics of Protecting the Poor During Adjustment: Bolivia's Emergency Social Fund." *World Development* 20(9): 1233-1251.

Handy, Jim. 1984. *Gift of the Devil*. Boston: South End Press.

Helwege, Ann. 1990. "Latin American Agricultural Performance in the Debt Crisis. Salvation or Stagnation?" *Latin American Perspectives* 67, 17(4): 57-75.

Hobsbawn, Eric. 1965. *Primitive Rebels: Studies in Archaic Forms of Social Movement in the 19th and 20th Centuries*. New York: Norton.

Hojman, David E. 1989. "Neoliberal Economic Policies and Infant and Child Mortality: Simulation Analysis of a Chilean Paradox." *World Development* 17(1): 93-108.

Hojman, David E., ed. 1992. "Neo-liberal Agriculture in Rural Chile." *Journal of Latin American Studies* 24: 215.

Immink, Maarten D. C., and Jorge A. Alarcón. 1993. "Household Income, Food Availability, and Commercial Crop Production by Smallholder Farmers in the Western Highlands of Guatemala." *Economic Development and Cultural Change* 41(2): 319-342.

Korovkin, Tanya. 1992. "Peasants, Grapes, and Corporations: The Growth of Contract Farming in a Chilean Community." *The Journal of Peasant Studies* 19(2): 228-254.

Kyle, Steven C., and Aercio S. Cunha. 1992. "National Factor Markets and the Macroeconomic Context for Environmental Destruction in the Brazilian Amazon." *Development and Change* 23(1): 7-34.

Lago, María Soledad. 1987. "Rural Women and the Neo-Liberal Model in Chile." In *Rural Women and State Policy. Feminist Perspectives on Latin American Agricultural Development,* eds. Carmen Deere and Magdalena León. Boulder, Colo.: Westview Press.

Lenin, Vladimir I. [1899 under Vladimir Ilyin] 1966. *The Development of Capitalism in Russia*. Moscow: Progress Publishers.

Llovet, Ignacio. 1987. "Estructura social y campesinado: Peculiaridad de la diferenciación campesina en el Ecuador." *Estudios Rurales Latinoamericanos* 10(2): 223-243.

Morrison, Andrew R. 1993. "Violence or Economics: What Drives Internal Migration in Guatemala?" *Economic Development and Cultural Change* 41:4.

Nash, June. 1993. *Crafts in the World Market*. Albany: State University of New York Press.

Paus, Eva, ed. 1988. *Struggle Against Dependence: Nontraditional Export Growth in Central America and the Caribbean*. Boulder and London: Westview Press.

Petras, James, and Steve Vieux. 1992. "Myths and Realities: Latin America's Free Markets." *Monthly Review* 44(1): 9-20.

Pfefferman, Guy P., and Charles C. Griffin. 1989. *Nutrition and Health Programs in Latin America: Targeting Social Expenditures*. Washington, D.C.: World Bank and Panama City: International Center for Economic Growth.

Phillips, Lynne. 1987. "Women, Development, and the State in Rural Ecuador." In *Rural Women and State Policy. Feminist Perspectives on Latin American Agricultural Development,* eds. Carmen Deere and Magdalena León. Boulder, Colo.: Westview Press.

Pino, Hugo Noé. 1993. "Structural Adjustment and Honduran Agriculture: Some Considerations." In *Recovery or Relapse in the Global Economy: Comparative Perspectives on Restructuring in Central America*, eds. Carlos Santiago and Alvin Magid. Westport, Conn.: Praeger.

Rosenbaum, Brenda, and Liliana Goldín. 1993. "New Exchange Processes and the Remaking of Maya Artisan Production in the World Economy." Paper presented at the Thirteenth International Congress of Anthropology and Ethnological Sciences. The Pre-Congress Conference: Artisan Production Through the Ages, San Cristóbal Las Casas, Mexico.

Scott, James. 1990. *Domination and the Arts of Resistance*. New Haven, Conn.: Yale University Press.

Shydlowsky, Daniel M. 1986. "The Macroeconomic Effect of Nontraditional Exports in Peru." *Economic Development and Cultural Change* 34(3): 491-509.

Stoll, David. 1990. *Is Latin America Turning Protestant?* Berkeley: University of California Press.

Tardanico, Richard. 1993. "Dimensions of Structural Adjustment: Gender and Age in the Costa Rican Labour Market." *Development and Change* 24(3): 511-540.

Thiesenhusen, William. 1982. "Land Reform in Latin America: Some Current Literature." Review Essay. *Latin American Research Review* 17(2): 199-211.

Thiesenhusen, William C., and Jolyne Melmed-Sanjak. 1990. "Brazil's Agrarian Structure: Changes from 1970 through 1980." *World Development* 18(3): 393-416.

Timossi Dolinsky, Gerardo T. 1990. "Debt and Structural Adjustment in Central America." *Latin American Perspectives* 67, 17(4): 76-90.

Wachtel, Nathan. 1994. *Gods and Vampires. Return to Chipaya*. Chicago: The University of Chicago Press.

Warren, Kay. 1989. *The Symbolism of Subordination*. Austin: University of Texas Press, Texas Panamerican Series.

Wise, Timothy. 1987. "The Current Food Crisis in Latin America. A Discussion of de Janvry's *The Agrarian Question.*" *Latin American Perspectives* 54, 14(3): 298-315.

Chapter 7

State, Society, and Dependent Neoliberalism in Mexico: The Case of the Chiapas Uprising

Sergio Zermeño

Introduction

This chapter examines the changes in civil society engendered by the new patterns of integration of Mexico into the global economy that have accompanied the signing of the North American Free Trade Agreement (NAFTA).[1] Latin America's experience with market-oriented reforms has shown that similar economic policies produce very different results depending on the sociohistorical matrix of the state, though neoliberal ideologues continue to underestimate the impact of this variable. As the initial shock of economic adjustment and restructuring subsides, it behooves analysts to return to the basic reference points of the social sciences and examine the social, human, and political effects of globalizing a national economy. Consequently, in the context of the globalization of the Mexican economy, this chapter addresses a key question: Where have the social movements gone? The Chiapas uprising offers a privileged vantage point from which to examine emerging realities as rooted in fundamental changes in the traditional patterns of participation, resistance, and organization of civil society in Mexico.[2]

The effects of social and economic restructuring vary widely within Latin America. Early modernizers, such as Chile, Argentina, and Uruguay, initiated their development trajectories as sparsely populated territories with high levels of immigration and urbanization and low miscegenation. These countries have been more successful in achieving neoliberal transformations. Societies that were modernized later, and somewhat less thoroughly, possessed stronger and more populous indigenous cultures. These differences partially explain why Mexico, Guatemala, Peru, Bolivia, and Ecuador, for example, are experiencing what one might call deficient neoliberal transformations.

This does not mean that only cultures of European origin or their immigrants can generate the strong social actors needed to promote industry, science, and technology. What is suggested, however, is that where modernizing processes are not based on, and do not promote, strong social actors, the resulting "modernity" may well lack elements of substance, resilience, and durability. In this sense, it takes more than a strongly interventionist or authoritarian state to implement neoliberal policy successfully: Strong social and economic actors are also essential.

The successful cases of transnational insertion — Japan, Korea, Chile, Taiwan, and Spain — and even the less spectacular cases of Uruguay, Colombia, Portugal, and Costa Rica were all characterized by the presence of strong social and economic actors. The cases of Venezuela and Ecuador serve to illustrate the opposite pattern. Despite huge public investments made possible by revenues from oil exploitation, neither country has generated strong or dynamic actors in the social sphere. Along similar lines, Mexico mercilessly is dismantling the very structures that support social actors — using "inescapable" global logic to justify its actions.[3]

Though they may be very efficient at integrating their economies into global markets, strong states with ancient origins, such as Mexico, often face enormous difficulties on the home front because globalization is further shredding the social fabric — a fabric that had already been tattered by the state's inability to provide Western standards of income, social justice, and civil rights to vast segments of society. In such states, the "politics of antipolitics" flourish, accompanied by a growing exclusion and a weakening of "the social." Few can deny that the problem goes well beyond just a transitory imbalance produced by the rapid shift from one model to another, as these changes are not exogenous, but endogenous to the neoliberal model. In this sense, when modernization is made subordinate to global markets, it tends to destroy modern actors in favor of a small, but very powerful, group of transnational associated with the highest political and bureaucratic echelons of state power.

For the past 15 years, globalization and transnational competitiveness (known in Mexico as modernization) have, in fact, waged a relentless siege against the actors of Mexican modernity. Between 1940 and 1980, industrialization in Mexico had developed in the classic manner, displacing the peasantry, swelling the ranks of the disorganized urban poor, and creating modern social actors: the bourgeoisie, the petit-bourgeoisie, the working class, and so on. The global integration of Mexico has radically dismantled these collective actors of civil society, systematically destroying the entrepreneurs of the import-substituting industries, middle-level bureaucrats, industrial workers, state employees, and also micro and middle sectors of the bourgeoisie. Moreover, the institutions and intermediaries that have traditionally inhabited the space between social actors and the state — the media, unions, corporations, political parties, universities, grassroots organizations, and social movements — also are being seriously undermined. Finally, although peasants are not generally considered modern actors, one should not overlook the ruthless assault on their identities and cultural traditions, as well as the elimination of their strongest institutional and organizational structures.

In Mexico, NAFTA and global integration are criticized for their powerful ability to dissolve the social — obliterating collective identities, spaces of communicative interaction, and the critical formation of the public sphere. Basically, the shrinkage and loss of the public sphere tend not to create an atomized individualistic consumer but rather undermine cultural traditions and massify poverty. The resurgence of personalized leadership in Latin America has been linked to this massification.[4]

What is meant by the "dissolving of the social?" This phrase refers to the impoverishment of the majority and the dismantling of the actors of civil society. Additionally, it implies the retreat to private life by consumers and other members of the modernized sectors (who hold the ideological position that the crisis was caused by state interventions, whether of the populist, socialist, or welfare-state variety) and the deliberate effort by the state to dismantle inconvenient collective identities. This process of disarticulation affects the most vulnerable sectors of urban Mexico but is particularly intense in peasant and indigenous communities, as the case of Chiapas will demonstrate.

Demography, Stagnation, and Globalization in Mexico

Massification and impoverishment are not new phenomena, nor are they exclusively the result of neoliberalism's globalizing project in Mexico and the rest of the Americas. Earlier in the 1960s and 1970s, rapid and chaotic urbanization, demographic explosion, and environmental devastation were associated with a boom in Latin American economic growth under the aegis of import-substitution industrialization. Thus, growth-related shocks have been a fundamental source of disorder and instability in Mexican society for many years.

The crisis of the 1980s — a second source of disorder — brutally engulfed Latin America precisely because the region had attempted to adapt to new global realities by entering international markets. Among the causes of the crisis are the transition from a traditional to an industrial society in Mexico, the global recession and international finance crisis, and deliberate, radical policies of petroleum-based development. Between 1980 and 1990, minimum salaries in Mexico fell precipitously by 40 percent (ILO 1993), and social spending in Mexico, as a portion of the gross domestic product (GDP), fell dramatically relative to other public expenditures.[5]

The trade opening, begun in Mexico in the early 1980s, was accelerated when Mexico joined the General Agreement on Tariffs and Trade (GATT) in 1985 and was institutionalized with the implementation of NAFTA. As sociologists have observed, acceleration, changes in rhythm, and severe disturbances to the public order undermine individuals' perceptions of shared social and moral limits and their senses of identity. This can be seen as a third disorganizing factor in Mexico.

The magnitude of this third destabilizing effect is staggering. Between 1980 and the year 2000, workers in the *maquila* industries of the border zone, primarily young women from the region, will have grown from 100,000 to

1,000,000 — one-third of the manufacturing labor force in the country (González Arréchiga and Ramírez 1990). Between three and 15 million Mexican farmers could be affected by end of the *ejido* system of collective land tenure, trade liberalization, drastic cuts in state subsidies, and the entry of lower-priced agricultural products (Calva 1991).

The working conditions and living standards in the *maquila* areas and among agroindustry laborers indicate that employment and poverty are not mutually exclusive categories. Similarly, a job with a multinational firm does not guarantee employment security or stability. To make matters worse, only a small minority of the great mass of internal migrants to the agroexporting or agro-*maquila* regions, the United States, and Mexico's large cities actually will find a formal job. Some analysts argue that only 1.3 million jobs were created between 1982 and 1990, against the 1.5 million youths who joined the ranks of the unemployed each year. These conditions have created a reserve of nine million people (perhaps one-half of this huge reserve may be in the United States witthout documents) who have not been absorbed by the labor market (*La Jornada* 1991).

The deindustrialization that parallels trade liberalization also provokes severe social dislocation. Without even considering the collapse of the large import-substituting firms, deindustrialization meant the closing of 70,000 medium and small-sized companies in less than eight years (50 percent of the total), and two out of five companies that survived into the 1990s in Mexico were on the verge of bankruptcy (de la Garza 1990).

How is the agrarian sector faring amidst this wholesale restructuring of the Mexican economy? Agribusiness is booming; the stagnant *ejido* is besieged; out-migration continues, and communities that are not attractive to investors are marginalized. Understanding this dynamic better than most academic analysts, the Zapatistas have become a potent political and ideological force in Mexican society, as shall be discussed below. First, a necessarily schematic overview of the fundamental concepts of identity, participation, and integration in the Mexican state is in order.

From Unity to Fragmentation

The conceptual categories with which Latin Americans have imagined and described their societies over the last 20 years have changed significantly. The popular social groups of the region — classes, masses, peasants, or *el pueblo*— who once gave Mexican history its "progressive" connotation, have become atomized, polarized, impoverished, and destructured. In some cases, the groups even have been swept into patterns of disorganized violence or defensive anomie.

Scholars close to government institutions, or those who focus on intermediate spaces (parties, parliaments, unions, corporations, institutions of culture and education, and mass media organizations), still hope for a "western" future for Latin America. Absorbed by the study of economic integration and democratic transition, many of these scholars maintain an almost schizophrenic separation of sociopolitical conceptions from their ethical implications. Implicit in this strand of theorizing is the assumption that the region is not heading toward disintegration, atomization, and anomie at all, and that this transition is marked instead by the integration of the excluded into the world of development and consumption, with democratic representation envisioned as heralding the emergence of new modal pattern of modernization. They have faith that modernization via globalization will integrate and reorganize society and consolidate the institutions and practices of democracy.[6]

Meanwhile, sociologists, anthropologists, and political scientists who focus their studies on the community, the neighborhood, or other grassroots phenomena continue to employ the negative images and conceptions of the "sociology of decadence" (Tironi 1986).[7] For these analysts, recognizing "the centrality of the marginalized," to speak of the "excluded" is to speak of the majority. This centrality, however, does not imply homogeneity. The poor in Latin America are a fragmented mass with many different characteristics, such as communitarianism, delinquency, anomie, populism, consumerism, and so on.

Convinced that they are observing disintegrated forms of "something," analysts who are critical of the neoliberal project attempt to find integrating and analytical principles to describe and comprehend marginal actors. This search is seen in the effort to reconstruct the world of the excluded in terms of social movements and the recreation of collective identities. The marginalized, according to Eugenio Tironi's surprising opinion, should not be reduced to an anomic mass, cut off from society:

> To the contrary, what one observes is an instrumental logic sharpened by the requirements of survival...the *pobladores* show a strong cultural adherence to the system and an irreversible incorporation into the urban world to which they have belonged for more than a generation. Therefore, they demand participation, not rupture; more support from the state, not more autonomy; access to industry, not self-subsistence workshops; a place in modern culture, not the reduction to folklore. (Tironi 1986, 78)

Poverty is not a folkloric element of traditional societies. It is part of modernity in Mexico, and that is why schizophrenic images appear so often in conceptualizations of the Latin American reality. According to Jean Chesneau,

> Modernization advances simultaneously in opposite directions around two antagonistic but inseparable ideas: There is modernity in prosperity and success, and there is modernity in failure, in the oceans of misery which surround pockets of prosperity. Both are as modern as each other, and the classical distinction between "traditional societies" and "modernizing societies" has lost all meaning. (Chesneau 1988, 65)

Dual modernity permits disorder, lack of identity, and anomie to exist side-by-side with the transition to democracy and the desire for society's integration. For many members of these societies hit by population growth, economic crisis and restructuring, and globalization, faith in the eventual democratic transition and integration of society is, at best, wishful thinking. At worst, it is a blatant deployment of the hegemonic ideas that reproduce domination.

Extenuation of the Basic Referents of Modernity

"The public" is weakened, not only by atomization and anomic disorder, but by the possessive individualism rooted in the personal consumption of the middle and upper classes. For these social strata, neoliberalism is more than a set of economic and political tools for addressing a crisis. It has become a moral instrument used to justify deepening social inequality, to assuage guilty consciences in the face of generalized poverty and dehumanizing conditions, and to displace blame for this state of affairs onto the state. The past hegemony of the state and its mistakes and corruption are held responsible for today's evils. The retreat into oneself, one's family, one's small professional group, or one's intellectual confraternity is justified in this manner.

Society's well-integrated sectors vote regularly and are quick to condemn the undemocratic methods sometimes employed by government officials in order to implement the neoliberal project. Yet they are similarly unsympathetic to eruptions of popular sentiment against neoliberalism, dismissing such protests as heralding the emergence of a new form of populism and patrimonialism or simply as unacceptable sources of instability in a very fragile internationalized economy. They are, after all, favored by current conditions.

There is also a fragmentation of political markets. Those that are better paid, educated, and integrated favor political trends toward amoral individualism and retreat into private life. The media and elitist cultural institutions diffuse and promote these preferences to the detriment of political parties, new social movements, and other modes of expression of mass sentiment. Conversely, society's less integrated sectors retreat into disorder, loss of identity, anomie, and apathy. Caught in a vicious circle, they participate even less in the new spaces opened by liberal-democratic reforms.

Dismantling Alternative Identities in Mexico

Given this segmentation of public spaces, the retreat into private life by society's better integrated sectors, and the disorder affecting most Mexicans, how can one speak of a strengthened social dimension, of democratic culture, or of the generalization of shared values? Where is the basis for creating a complex of stable institutions and procedures capable of encouraging the participation of the masses in public affairs?

This is the crux of the current Mexican social model. Electoral democracy does not necessarily bring broadened participation by society in public affairs as the party/government actually strives to deter participation in order to carry out neoliberal reforms. Proponents of the Mexican regimes' so-called transition to democracy openly assert that the neoliberal project consists of adjustment policies that rely on the exclusion and impoverishment of large sectors of the population over a long period of time (see Acuña and Smith 1994).

The transition regime braces for sustained periods of instability during which the survival of the neoliberal model is in jeopardy. Since waves of instability originate in certain constellations of social actors acutely affected by change, and since policymakers believe that growth is the necessary "end" to be achieved, various "means" are therefore justified. The regime may set out to prevent or dismantle all alternative sociopolitical identities and public spaces of communicative interaction.

Neutralizing potential challengers by either coopting or destroying them has long been one of the basic tenets of Mexican authoritarianism. Now that the procedural elements of democracy are demanded by powerful global actors (Vacs 1994), the elimination of collective spaces and identities must be accomplished by more subtle means to avoid the obvious use of violence. Thus, the seedlings of social democracy have to be uprooted and political democracy limited to spaces such as political parties, which can be controlled by fraud and cooptation. The "games" of party and parliament are used to divert attention, when necessary, and give the impression that there is someone "up there" protecting national interests.

Some specific illustrations of social dismantling in Mexico include but are not limited to the following:

1. The splintering of the National Action Party (Partido de Acción Nacional — PAN) over compromises made with the state to obtain recognition of the party's victories in state and local elections. In return, the PAN leadership sold out and opposed electoral reforms. In so doing, one of the few independent social organizations of Mexican political life was weakened like so many of its predecessors. As a consequence, leaders with a genuine popular following surrender their power in exchange for a place in the ruling clique. The price, of course, is to swear allegiance to the president, the modern-day *Tlatoani* (the maximum political and military authority in the Aztec empire).

2. Channeling massive quantities of resources into electoral engineering and fraud. A parliamentary majority must be maintained so that laws favorable to the governing elite can be enacted quickly and in an ad hoc fashion. Sophisticated computer-generated maps are used to track opposition parties' strongholds, and then these areas are targeted for the National Solidarity Program (Programa Nacional de Solidaridad — PRONASOL) investments and, more importantly, the manipulation of voter identity cards.[8] Finally, electoral engineering generates apathy and lowers participation because the electoral options for change are reduced to the "loyal" opposition of the PAN, which now shares the state apparatus with the Institutional Revolutionary Party (Partido Revolucionario Institucional — PRI), PRONASOL, the high clergy, other puppet parties, and the Televisa mass media empire.

3. Public universities, especially social science departments, are dismantled; funding is cut, and talented teachers are driven out of the profession. Private institutions are awarded all the prestige, even though their academic staffs come almost entirely from public

universities. Research institutions are kept separate from schools and faculties; factional in-fighting is encouraged, and perks and benefits are allocated on the basis of institutional loyalty. University budgets, once determined autonomously, are decided by the treasury department. No funding is allotted for "horizontal relationships" (a utopia of the 1970s) between university research and popular needs. The only horizontal links today are those between technology institutes and big business.

4. The mass media is controlled, even when it is privately owned. The selective use of government publicity contracts and tax policies or the deliberate veto of journalists and radio and television programs keeps the communications sector under strict vigilance.

5. Finally, as mentioned above, PRONASOL is the main tool for "emptying" intermediate levels. PRONASOL personalizes the presidency, linking the figure of the president directly with small, unorganized, and transitory associations of impoverished citizens at the lowest levels of society. It also confers prestige and channels funds via state-controlled organizations to the detriment of other groups that typically are more authentic and autonomous. Between the socially dispersed and the state, many diverse forms of social organization of the subaltern sectors suffer from PRONASOL's impact.

These telegraphic references suggest several observations regarding the dismantling of "the social" in Mexico. First, since the beginning of the 1980s, the entities and spaces of mediation in Mexican society have been weakened severely. Today, at the most basic social level can be seen a generalized crisis of social movements and popular struggles, the destruction of labor unions, and the restriction of strikes. Second, the pattern is repeated at the institutional level where fronts, assemblies, union confederations, agrarian coalitions, town and neighborhood organizations, and ecclesiastic communities are all in crisis. Third, in institutionalized public spaces, such as schools, universities, cultural organizations, and the mass media, collective participation is eschewed in the name of scientific and technical efficiency. A similar rationale is used to dismantle welfare, health, transportation, and housing systems. Even with regard to the political institutions of society (parties, parliament, labor, and entrepreneurial leadership), a weakening of social density probably is taking place.

The Mexican State Without a Hegemonic Project

When the intermediaries between state and society are historically weak — due to accelerated change, anomic disorder, the retreat into civic privatism, the segmentation of the political market, and deliberate state action to destroy identities — many individuals, especially the large majority living in poverty, feel isolated. Without leadership, they are unable to improve their lot. Precisely because the poor comprise the group with the least ability to defend themselves, they are hurt most by neoliberal reform and economic restructuring.

The poor are structurally prone to "populist" politics. Where systems of representation are fragmentary and weak, political actors create substitutes. Where parties have become liabilities, "movements" may emerge. Where intermediate organizations are fragile or hostile, they stimulate direct relationships with the people. When citizens distrust the system, politicians exploit the average person's readiness to invest trust in individual personalities. Without effective mediating institutions, telegenic populism may emerge to take their place.

In the context of market-oriented restructuring, the ascent of "the popular" and its accompanying leadership was observed first in Peru in the person of Alberto Fujimori and then in Mexico with Cuauhtémoc Cárdenas. Mexico, as well as the rest of Latin America, continues to be characterized by verticalism, the "politics of antipolitics," and populist relationships between leaders and followers.[9] Although the procedural elements of democracy may achieve a semblance of institutional consolidation, "the social" may not be strengthened at all and may experience accelerated atrophy. Even public expenditures and targeted social programs designed to address the dangers of extreme poverty and develop collective identities, such as the solidarity programs recommended by the World Bank and the International Monetary Fund, may actually reinforce cults of personality.

In Mexico, precarious intermediate levels of the social order are being weakened as a more direct relationship between the leadership and the masses crystallizes. As corporatist mechanisms of state tutelage erode, the masses come to resemble inorganic aggregates of individuals, and their atomized manifestations are integrated in a weak, contradictory, and discontinuous manner. It is increasingly difficult to construct and maintain communitarian and associational bonds in neighborhoods, *ejidos*, cooperatives, or other groups organized to improve the quality of life. Furthermore, those concerted efforts by political parties and cultural groups that do exist are aimed at the neediest sectors of the population and produce few results. These efforts have to contend with a widespread faith in the strongman, the belief that the leader is able to find a solution, and that "betting on" him is the best option.

This strange affinity between neopopulism and neoliberalism defines the dilemma of state elites, who find themselves obliged to globalize the country as quickly as possible, imposing on Mexico the sacrifices that Western countries, with established liberal traditions embedded in mature modernizations, have endured only with great hardship. With regard to the social realm, unexpected changes and sudden disruptions almost invariably lead to anomie. Whenever profound changes engulf a society, actors with a certain degree of autonomy — the state, political parties, corporate or religious organizations, or intellectuals — may attempt to mitigate the impact of the shocks. In Mexico, this response has failed to materialize. On the contrary, those very forces are helping actively and uncritically to hasten change. The Mexican state seeks neither to moderate nor to mitigate the consequences of globalization and restructuring; instead, it champions the dismantling forces and proclaims that it is "refounding" Mexican history.

In this context of pervasive crisis, is it possible that a return to populism and the rebirth of the national-popular relationship might represent the only rational form of sociopolitical integration? Although no one would have thought so 15 years ago, populist solutions today may not be so unrealistic. In contemporary Mexican society, beset by atomization, restricted identities, middle-class consumerism and privatism, and the threat of explosive violence (a generalization of Zapatismo beyond the boundaries of Chiapas?), perhaps the viability of some variant of state-led mobilization is less far-fetched than is commonly assumed.

The possible initiation of a new cycle of authoritarian-paternalism responds to a very real need. Obsessed with halting inflation, restructuring industry, servicing the foreign debt, and making the economy globally competitive, the exclusionary neoliberal project has abandoned any attempt at reintegrating the splintered Mexican social panorama. Given this alternative, is it really so implausible to suggest that an *aggiornamento* of Mexico's tradition of national-populism might stand a reasonable chance of addressing the problems of national cohesion and identity reconstruction?

Most Mexicans, as well as many other Latin Americans, would benefit from the strengthening of intermediary organizations linked to a class compromise centered in strong state institutions. The interactions of individuals at the highest level of rationality for the collective interest of the polity would make socioeconomic aggregates correspond to political parties and to ideologies or projects of future societies. This would allow for the cultivation of stable social and political institutions. However, Mexico does not appear to be moving toward a variant of democracy rooted in civil society, nor is it evolving into a neocorporatist democracy governed by political society, with political parties, legislatures, and the large bureaucratic organizations of business and labor. Rather, developments are tilting in favor of what might be called a statist-popular or national-popular logic.

The Emergence of Chiapas:
Order and Disorder at the End of the Millennium

Collective disorder and lack of social identity are central to understanding what is happening in Mexico today. However, there also are significant instances of collective actors organizing to challenge these destructive developments. Social movements are constituted in extraordinary situations in which a group defines an opponent, fights against said opponent, and articulates objectives giving cohesion and a collective identity to the group. Frequently, however, the homogeneity of the group's members and their interests often is more apparent than real. The Chiapas uprising is one of the most significant exceptions to this chronic "emptying" of the social in Mexico.[10]

The presence of a well-defined collective identity in the southwestern region of the country has had a much greater impact on Mexican society as a whole than any of the other movements. The call to arms by the Zapatista

National Liberation Army (Ejército Zapatista de Liberación Nacional — EZLN) caused many politicians, intellectuals, journalists, and citizens to express surprise and incredulity, to condemn the violence, and to commiserate with the poor. More importantly, the nation's perception of the Zapatista movement has vacillated between seeing it as simply a local conflict and viewing it as the unintended flashpoint for all the discontent felt by the enormous majority of Mexicans, many of whom are convinced that their role in neoliberal reform will never amount to more than endless sacrifice and permanent frustration of hopes and aspirations.

When social and political order breaks down, Mexicans tend to behave in ways that make it meaningless to try to separate the local from the national. No matter how different the situation of the Chiapas Indians is from that of Mexicans in the north, the fact remains that immediately after the Zapatista uprising, indigenous and campesino groups in the north took control of 50,000 hectares of disputed land and recognized the EZLN as a belligerent force. Posing serious threats to national stability, these actions found an echo and spread to states, such as Guerrero, Michoacán, San Luis Potosí, Guanajuato, Yucatán, México, and Veracruz, where the election of politicians of the PRI via blatant fraud had long been the norm.[11]

What binds rebels together in Mexican society is not a shared identity but rather a common adversary. Beyond that, the rest is disorder. The unifying principle of Mexican society is the state, not civil society; again, this is part of the Mexican heritage of not having constructed powerful social actors and intermediaries between the state and dispersed citizens or the masses. The Mexican upper classes as well as workers and middle classes have been buffeted repeatedly by revolts, wars, and incursions by foreign capital. Most of all, however, the Mexican state and Mexican culture have little notion of how to coexist in tolerance and mutual respect. As a result, Mexico continues to be a petri dish for popular uprisings against the common enemy — the state — especially when it appears to be an accomplice in transnational projects perceived as antinationalist in orientation.

These are not problems of Mexico's campesino history, although these manifestations of resistance and potential rupture clearly draw upon the practices and symbols of Mexico's past. Moreover, fundamentally, some Mexicans are realizing that their country's capitalist modernization has been not only extraordinarily savage but also incomplete. What would bring Mexico closest to modernity is not for every member of the upper class to have a cellular telephone, VCR, and personal computer but rather for there to be 1) a fairly robust entrepreneurial class (today in shreds); 2) groups of workers with a certain capacity to negotiate (like the Koreans); 3) a peasantry and rural proletariat sufficiently organized to influence the pace of trade opening, the level of subsidies, and protective social legislation (like the French farmer); 4) networks of information and opinion that are autonomous from the state; and finally 5) an electoral system with some degree of transparency and credibility.

In an interview just prior to the fateful first days of early 1994, President Carlos Salinas de Gortari was asked if neoliberal reform did not destroy deliberately and systematically all spaces of intermediation and balkanize the party system. Did this not, went the query, contradict Jesus Reyes Heroles' wise observation, "*lo que resiste apoya*" (that which resists, strengthens), understood to mean that alternative spaces for criticism, collective identity, and opposition provide an indispensable source of support for any healthy political system? Given all this, Salinas was asked, was there not a risk that his government's implementation of neoliberal reforms might sink the foundations of the state into a kind of quicksand?

President Salinas responded that the ill-conceived, poorly designed intermediate institutions of Mexico's post-revolutionary political system (unions, peasant organizations, universities, public schools, and parties) were being replaced by more modern forms. He offered by way of example non-governmental organizations (NGOs) and solidarity committees. There was no opportunity for a follow-up question about whether those groups were not too small, poorly organized, and transient to fill the enormous void that was being generated in Mexican society in the wake of neoliberal reform.

This brings up a key question: How did the Chiapas rupture occur? The regime was accustomed to governing by controlling the media and eliminating actors, groups, and spaces of collective identity. However, the regime was distracted by its dismantling task and took for granted that, in the destitute regions, the predominantly indigenous campesinos could be counted on to see to their own destruction. It was assumed that "Deep" Mexico would continue to be cowed by alcoholism, religious schisms, and a *caciquismo* of white guards and periodic military repression. Mexico's rulers overlooked the fact that when communities maintain structures of cohesion firmly anchored in ancestral cultural and religious values, they may respond to the threat of dislocation by manifesting a seemingly reckless willingness to confront the overwhelming coercive power of local propertied classes and the state in a fundamentalist defense of their way of life.

Therefore, the Chiapas rupture is imminently national, not local, in both scope and consequences. Who would have imagined that "Deep" Mexico would activate "Broken" Mexico (the waste products of savage modernization)? Or that "Rough" Mexico (the plebeian masses) might awake from its slumber and threaten to derail the "Citizen" Mexico comprised of those who are integrated into modernization, the children of the "victors" of free trade and the proclaimed transition to democracy?

Many Mexicos

Peace talks between the Zapatistas and Manuel Camacho Solís, President Carlos Salinas' representative, began in the Cathedral de San Cristóbal in March 1994. These talks resulted in a document called *Compromisos para una Paz Digna en Chiapas* (Bases for a Dignified Peace in Chiapas). In point number eight of this document, the government accepted some of the EZLN demands as legitimate but claimed that they were strictly local in nature.

Restricting the issue to the "indigenous question," the government proposed to solve these "grave agrarian problems" with a *Ley General de las Comunidades Indígenas* (General Law of the Indigenous Communities). The proposed law left intact the recent reforms to Article 27 of the Constitution that declared the end of the land reform program and converted the *ejido* lands into a transferable commodity, thereby legalizing and stimulating the concentration of land in the hands of modern capitalist farms and agribusiness firms.

The EZLN, for its part, returned to the jungle to carry out a consultation on the accords. They returned to public visibility in mid-1994 with a resounding "no" to the government's 32 proposals.

The Mexican state meanwhile designated enormous sums of money via PRONASOL to shore up the much-questioned structure of political representation in Chiapas and tried to inject some legitimacy into the thoroughly repudiated *presidencias municipales* (municipal mayors). This was a desperate attempt to reconstruct a system of domination based on 1) the existing landholding class, which received government compensation for its properties under occupation; 2) existing political institutions such as PRONASOL-funded *presidencias municipales*; and 3) the campesino organizations and the so-called producers organizations that had been trying for more than a decade to modernize the region's agriculture via coffee-for-export cultivation.

Naturally, the EZLN had to compete with the state to win over local forces. In the process the EZLN created the conditions leading to a peasant invasion of 50 million hectares. Later, an additional 100 million hectares also came under peasant control in the zone of Altos de Chiapas and de Las Cañadas, in territories not militarily controlled by the Zapatistas. The EZLN had sufficient influence to keep the 200-odd organizations of the CEOIC (Coordinadora Estatal de Organizaciones Indígenas y Campesinas or State Coordinating Council of Indigenous and Campesino Organizations) from being controlled by official channels like the government-affiliated National Peasant Confederation (Confederacíon Nacional Campesina — CNC) and the ARIC-Unión de Uniones, even though the CEOIC was initially created and run by President Salinas himself. Pro-government organizations were losing popular support, especially among young people, to groups championing *la vía armada*. Campesino and indigenous organizations increasingly identified with the Zapatistas, and many advanced beyond the status of sympathizer to become full-fledged EZLN participants.

The Zapatistas must have calculated that the prospects for reaching a peace plan with the outgoing Salinas government in 1994 were slim. After the assassination of the PRI presidential candidate, Luis Donaldo Colosio, the Zapatistas assumed a wait-and-see stance. If Cuauhtémoc Cárdenas of the Democratic Revolutionary Party (Partido de la Revolución Democrática — PRD) won, it would strengthen and legitimate the Zapatistas. Even in the event of a close election won by the PRI, the Zapatistas would have found themselves well positioned, in conditions very favorable to their consolidation and cooperation with other opposition forces. The EZLN's *Segunda Declaración de la Selva* (Second Declaration of the Jungle) of mid-1994 was issued in this context. The Zapatistas' rejection of the PRONASOL-administered reforms proposed by Salinas' representative surprised no one. Regardless of whether Camacho's mediation was weak, uneven, and poorly backed by President Salinas and the PRI, the exchange provides insight into why social conflicts and movements in Mexico are inherently dynamic and seldom remain purely local. Such conflicts are frequently propelled onto the national scene because of the weakness or absence of legitimate channels of political intermediation. When this occurs, movements tend to unravel in an uncontrollable chain reaction of malaise, or the movement annihilates itself against the wall of the state. Or worse yet, movements enter into a dynamic of slow attrition due to internal schisms aggravated by the selective elimination tactics orchestrated by the *Tlatoani*-cum-state.

In Mexico, a suicidal actor (social movements and their leadership) and a homicidal actor (the state) historically have confronted each other, inevitably converting moments of direct action by society into catastrophe.[12] The *guerrilla chiapaneca* was, therefore, hurtled onto the national stage, compelled to join with other forces on the national level.

Contrary to the wishes of the Mexican government, the Chiapas uprising simply could not be contained in the category of a local-indigenous conflict. Delaying tactics on the part of the government did not work, and it became an agrarian-campesino problem, generalizable to vast regions of the country. With the August 1994 presidential elections nearing and the number of land invasions climbing, Chiapas witnessed the transmutation of a war between armies (one in the mestizo cities, the other in Lacandonia) into a war between social groups — the landowners, backed by government institutions, versus the campesino and indigenous squatters, backed by the Zapatistas.

The presence of the Zapatista guerrillas in the jungle ceased to be the most important point, and as a result the Mexican army and internal security apparatus began focusing on the struggle for land. The Zapatistas appeared anew all over the region and beyond as invading campesinos. They seized both farms and municipal governments, declaring independence and autonomy for their localities. During the first hours of December 19, 1995, the Zapatistas took control of close to 40 towns. The EZLN made it clear that the essence of their movement was not military but rather social and cultural. Less than 24 hours later, the financial system collapsed as international capital fled Mexico, thereby halving the value of the peso and virtually depleting the nation's currency reserves.

For the Mexican army, the transmutation would be even more costly. Since the beginning of the conflict, human rights violations against the civilian, indigenous population of Chiapas had been intolerably high and, what was worse, visible to the world via CNN and other international media. In the new scenario, it quickly became obvious that the army sided blatantly with the landowning class. Once the conflict burst out of its indigenous-local origins, the regime's strategy required more than merely containing the Zapatistas. Campesino organizations had to be divided; PRONASOL-style solutions had to be devised, and the surrounded interlocutor (the EZLN) had to be silenced.

The neoliberal government wanted desperately to depict the conflict in Chiapas as an exception; yet it could not be confined to a part of *México Profundo* (Deep Mexico, inhabited by the indigenous people of an atypical state like Chiapas). The conflict threatened to spread to other indigenous areas of the country and also to *México Maicero* (the large, impoverished, uncompetitive peasantry that subsists on beans and corn tortillas). People began to question whether the EZLN and its allies constituted an exception, or if the problem was the devaluation, the balance of payments deficit, the dismantling of national industries, or the foreign debt and the impossibility of its ever being repaid. The globalization model itself was soon subjected to close scrutiny.

The Mexican state hoped to make the "Indians" in Chiapas into an exceptional case by removing their communities from the free play of market forces, by means of the *Ley General de las Comunidades Indígenas* (General Law of the Indigenous Communities). Fewer than one million people (1 percent of Mexico's total population) would be affected. Deep Mexico, with its strong cultural ties organically anchored in indigenous traditions, touches some 10 million Mexicans. Thus, Traditional Mexico — the sum of Deep Mexico and Mexico Maicero — encompassed around 20 million Mexicans.

At the other extreme, a Transnational Mexico is made up of those who have been able to connect competitively with global markets. Strictly speaking, one out of 10 Mexicans can be considered part of this group. Another 20 percent of the population constitutes Modern Mexico, whose imperiled living standards are the product of the period of urbanization and import-substitution industrialization from the end of World War II until the debt crisis and global recession of the 1980s.

By combining Transnational Mexico with Modern Mexico, an Integrated Mexico encompasses three out of every 10 Mexicans. Some are competitive and successful business owners, but many linger on the edge. This group includes students, whose level of academic preparation is inversely proportional to their future employment prospects, employees pauperized and stripped of the rights of their predecessors, and legions of minimum-skill, minimum-wage, and minimally organized workers.

Between the 20 percent of Traditional Mexico and the 30 percent of Integrated Mexico lies the raw disorder of Broken Mexico, fragmented and scattered by savage modernization including people from social groups that the previous economic model disrupted but had never been capable of integrating into the postrevolutionary state or the emerging market economy. Broken Mexico's ranks swelled during the "lost decade" and the later shocks of neoliberal reform to include the masses of urban marginals and the informal sector — perhaps one out of four Mexicans — who are no longer campesinos and have little hope of securing regular jobs. Many are migrants or live in regions condemned as "uncompetitive." One final group that must be considered part of Broken Mexico are *maquila* workers and their families (5 percent of all Mexicans by the year 2000) and most of the workers in export agriculture whose very low incomes preclude their being considered legitimate participants in the dominant model.

Chiapas: The Local and the National

Chiapas has shown that Deep Mexico is no more exceptional than Transnational Mexico and that it is illusory to attempt to depict all of Mexico as belonging to the latter category, as many advocates of the neoliberal model would like to do. As PRI presidential candidate Luis Donaldo Colosio said on the last day of his life:

> I do not believe that the play of market supply and demand will resolve the problems of misery that exist, for example, among Oaxacan Mixtec. There has to be there a deliberate policy by the government [to address this problem]. (*La Jornada*, March 22, 1994)

By making an exception of Chiapas, as the regime tries to, one-half of all Mexicans are relegated to the status of exceptionally condemned, revealing that neoliberalism is a catastrophe. The situation in Chiapas thus obliges a rethinking of the development model that realizes Deep Mexico cannot be considered apart from Traditional Mexico and Broken Mexico.

Trying to be competitive in the global marketplace is acceptable within reason, keeping in mind the sacrifices involved for *maquila* and agribusiness workers and services related to these enterprises. Yet indiscriminately flinging open the border to imports of corn, beans, meat, milk, and services and manufactured goods produced on a global scale (converting their own entrepreneurs into smugglers or franchise operators) is another story. Remember, every time Mexico has managed to be competitive in a particular product — cement, steel, beer, tomato, tuna — domestic legislation in the United States has been used to limit that success.

Korea, Japan, Taiwan, and Malaysia never opened their borders to cheap imported rice while they integrated into global markets, and trade policies that threaten to put their well-fed peasantries out of work are strictly opposed. Moreover, Korea and Japan closed their borders to more competitive manufactures for crucial intervals, encouraging research and technical development in national universities and corporations.

In Chiapas, excellent-quality beef from abroad costs half, before the December 1995 currency devaluation, of the price of locally produced beef of moderate quality. When the Zapatistas took up arms, coffee, long promoted locally as a potential export, was no longer worth the effort to plant because world prices were so low and competition from other producing nations was so intense. It is true that in regions like southeastern Mexico, there is no alternative to modernizing the traditional economy. Yet it also is equally imperative that the social dimension be respected and strengthened. Thus, any economic project for the region must be centered on the people who live there, even if this means closing the border to products of superior quality and lower price. Carefully calibrated moves in the direction of limited autarky should not be ruled out if, as the environmentalists say, this would promote genuine sustainable development.

However, the problem of the national development model and the question of state control remain. From the beginning, the EZLN had no other option than to raise, as they did in the *Primera Declaración de la Selva* (First Declaration of the Jungle), the subject of elections and democracy. The Zapatistas could not ignore these larger issues of democracy and political transition, even though engaging these issues would inexorably thrust them into the center of the Mexican political stage and signify that "technical" solutions for the region (Los Altos and Las Cañadas in Chiapas) had to be rejected in favor of national demands.

Seen from this perspective, Chiapas is a dramatic example of the way social struggles in Mexico become part of over-arching conflicts over the development model and the desired political regime and the appropriate form for state supervision of the economy. The most deeply rooted indigenous groups rose up with the autonomy of ethnic groups as their main objective. The Chiapas conflict was soon caught up in the dynamic forces that drive the entire country, forces that are thrust into the struggle against the state and its promotion of neoliberal restructuring. The option was a stark choice: to be converted into a national actor of great stature or to be cornered, belittled, and forgotten in the jungle.

The EZLN: From Social Movement to Guerrilla War

On February 9, 1995, President Ernesto Zedillo announced the startling decision to break off the truce with the EZLN. This decision was fundamental because Mexico's sociopolitical panorama may have been altered as a result. With the benefit of hindsight, one can reassemble the pieces and comprehend why Zedillo risked radicalizing society and jeopardizing the accords (addressing the crisis unleashed in December 1994 when the peso's value fell 100 percent) just signed with all of the national political parties.

Seventy-two hours after the arrest orders for the EZLN leadership were circulated, the situation was clear: Dialogue and political negotiations with the Zapatistas, which left the territorial gains of the Zapatista army intact, were not acceptable to President Zedillo or the armed forces (nor to the region's dominant classes, national entrepreneurs, or the national and international banking sectors). Allowing the accords to move forward would have meant at least tacit acceptance that one-half of Chiapas would remain effectively under the autonomous control of indigenous groups. Indicative of this danger was the fact that the Zapatistas and allied groups already had begun to collect taxes for the parallel government of Amado Avendaño, the Democratic Revolutionary Party (Partido de la Revolución Democrática — PRD) gubernatorial candidate for the state of Chiapas.

Less than 100 hours after the truce was broken, the tide had turned: The EZLN retreated deep into the Lacandonia jungle, and the Mexican army established military control over the autonomous municipalities. With the Zapatistas cornered in the jungle like outlaws and with the prelate Samuel Ruíz maligned by government and media, Zedillo's call to recommence peace talks sounded less than sincere. The call, widely diffused in the media, was calculated to be rejected by the EZLN, thus portraying the Zapatistas as renegade proponents of violence. From this perspective, the operation looked like a complete success, although at the cost of part of Mexican territory being militarized. The military presence in the area may become permanent to prevent popular-campesino-indigenous groups from regaining control of city halls and municipal offices. The Mexican army has become the conspicuous guarantor of the status quo in Chiapas (Kruijt 1994).

Following Zedillo's initial decision to break off peace talks in early 1995, Zapatismo continued to evolve as a local-regional, national, and international social movement. The local-regional level is strongly indigenous, heavily religious, characterized by agrarian injustice, *caciques* and white guards. Poverty, sickness, discrimination, the destruction of nature and environment, the struggle for survival, and threats to the autonomy of the Indian villages constitute the reality of everyday life. The objective of the Mexican army's invasion of Chiapas was to destroy everything, and it made Zapatismo's project for community reconstruction difficult if not impossible. With some clear exceptions, the Mexican army did not violate the physical integrity of civilians directly as it advanced toward the Lacandonia. Nevertheless, the army did ruthlessly destroy the means of material reproduction in every home suspected of sympathizing with the Zapatista movement (the great majority) and attacked all the communities where inhabitants had fled. The army did not loot but rather smashed, burned, and dismantled household utensils, farming tools, harnesses, saddles, machetes, hatchets, radios, ovens, and mills. Most importantly, seed grain for the next planting was destroyed; tubing was slit, and water receptacles dumped (Martínez 1995). The military presence thus deliberately prevented the peasantry from reforming the local coffee economy along more profitable, market-oriented lines or from carrying out the planting phase of the agricultural cycle for other crops, leaving the region today without food reserves.

Under the pretext of destroying drug-producing plots, the army comes and goes as it pleases in Chiapas. In the town of La Realidad, Zapatismo's sanctuary, armed columns of 30 or 50 motorized units (jeeps, tanks, military trucks, and so on) pass through slowly once or twice a day, coming and going along the road that divides the town in half, threatening and occasionally detaining the local inhabitants. In regions not under strong Zapatista control, police and white guards controlled by local landed elites and supported by the military have driven out refugees frightened by the degree of violence and the number of dead and wounded.

At the same time, the money provided by PRONASOL, PROCAMPO (the rural component of the National Solidarity program), and other ad hoc programs further divides the population and saps their morale. These social programs divide communities by creating organizations willing to accept these funds in exchange for their support against the Zapatistas and their peasant sympathizers, who then find it impossible to maintain their occupation of lands or local municipal governments. Under such conditions, how can peasants seek to improve their lot by sowing a hectare of fruit or vegetables or by using the crystalline waters of the river of La Realidad to raise fish? How can they better their diet of beans and rice? Such efforts are, according to some, impossible, given the presence of the army and its determination to destroy everything. Where such conditions prevail, the idea of working on behalf of the community is an illusion that only outsiders could entertain. In fact, Zapatismo always has been very respectful of the indigenous communities of Chiapas by not attempting to impose upon them foreign forms of organization. And so Aguascalientes always has been constructed at a certain distance from Guadalupe Tepeyac, from La Realidad, from San Miguel....

To this vision of its control and dismantlement, there is another vision of Zapatismo that insists that the consciousness of the members of this movement has deep roots, whose coherence extends far beyond the comings-and-goings of *soldaditos* and opportunistic attempts at cooptation via governmental social programs. To support this view, one need look no further than the sudden mobilization (out of nowhere) of hundreds of women from the Zapatista communities in the center of San Cristóbal de las Casas in early 1996 for the National Indigenous Forum. One can only confess bewilderment when confronted with these two scenarios, the positive and the negative.

Zapatismo also has demonstrated its prominence at the national level. This was clearly seen in the successful realization of the National Democratic Convention in the Lacadona jungle and then in the *rapprochement* and subsequent distancing of the EZLN with respect to *perredismo* and its presidential candidate Cuauhtémoc Cárdenas in the high-spirited 1994 election. The rapid unfolding of events with national repercussions continued in 1995 and 1996, with the Zapatista-sponsored national referendum, followed by the Fourth Declaration of the Jungle, the creation of the Zapatista National Front, the formation of a Broad Opposition Front, and, finally, in October 1996, with Zapatista participation in a nationwide conference of indigenous peoples in Mexico City.

The strengthening of a Zapatista organization with national ramifications, together with the reaccommodation and greater unity on the part of progressive forces and the beginnings of a shift from a state-centric political culture to greater autonomy and initiative for civil society, are all very welcome. However, these positive developments have yet to feel the full brunt of the deployment of the *ingeniería desmanteladora* ("dismantling engineering") of a state bent on their destruction. Regardless, as the new millennium approaches and the terrifying dimensions of Mexico's crisis become more evident, this project's momentum may continue to accelerate unless disorder and unorganized violence gain the upper hand.

The third and perhaps the most clearly triumphant dimension of the Zapatismo of the 1990s has come on the international stage. What is it that the Spanish, Italian, Belgian, and German youth see in Zapatismo? An indigenous cultural force capable of "defeating" the overwhelming power of U.S. military, institutional, and cybernetic imperialism and its neoliberal, looter puppet governments claiming to favor a democratic opening? An enigmatic leadership that has had the power to force the puppet Salinas into exile and to expose his corrupt circle of friends? Do these youth see a "force" (made more potent by the same global media of the information age) that, incredibly, has proven itself capable of holding the line (quite literally, the line marked by the road running through the village of La Realidad) against all the destructive paraphernalia of the state and its army? Do these youth see an extraordinary leader with great legitimacy among the Indian communities, a leader capable of overcoming the errors of the artificial *foquismo* (guerrilla "focos" inspired by the Cuban revolution) of the 1970s? A leader who expresses the cultural extremes of the indigenous movement of the jungle and the most sophisticated society of the most important metropolises of the world? That people are dying of hunger, of sickness, that they have no work, that their culture is being destroyed, that we cannot continue to tie our fate to the craziness of globalization?

While the local and national manifestations of Zapatismo continue to be shaped by the passage of time, occasionally pretty stars appear on the horizon (Oliver Stone, Danielle Mitterand, Regis Debray, Carlos Monsiváis, Fernando del Paso, and others) who attract the attention of the cameras in their visits to Las Cañadas. As they get lost in the jungle, they reveal to all the world that Zapatismo is alive. How many more such media events will be tolerated in the face of the hostility of the cynical and imperturbable *Tlatoani*, in the face of the silence, the *desmemoria*, and the charlatanism of the government's lackeys at San Andrés Sacamchen, whose only demand in the negotiations is the surrender of the Indians?

The harsh reality is that the official culture of the Mexican state cannot tolerate the existence and liberty of the "other." In fact, in the case of Chiapas, it seems that if a region is not under the control of an envoy from the center (a PRI *chiapaneco* municipal leader, organizer of submission, and destroyer of collective identity), national sovereignty is believed to be in imminent danger. The sovereign Mexican state does not know how to coexist alongside a sovereign society. What a political system this is that mortgages revenues from petroleum exports to the U.S. Treasury practically in perpetuity (as a guarantee of repayment for a $20 billion bailout) but is so frightened by a group of Indians (with access to the information superhighway) that it sends tanks and helicopter gunships to snatch the national flag from their hands.

Conclusions

A final question about Mexican social movements and civil society remains. There is no denying a great activism exists in Mexican society today. Small and medium-sized social organizations — NGOs, civic, Christian, human rights, ecology, and electoral watchdog groups — have proliferated. People are taking to the streets — in Mexico City in 1994, there were 100 marches a day, and three marches, with close to 100 thousand participants in each, took place the week after Zedillo broke the truce. Political participation among campesinos and indigenous peoples is overcoming apathy, disorganization, and manipulation. In central and northern Mexico, indebted farmers organized in the El Barzón protest movement are rebelling against NAFTA and the trade opening. The PAN has won important elections in Jalisco (which includes Guadalajara, the country's second largest city), in powerful northern states (including Monterey, the third largest city), and in the populous farming, and very Catholic, center of the country (in Puebla, for example). The Civil Alliance for Electoral Observation (La Alianza Cívica de Observación Electoral) organizes public consultations and plebiscites. These plebiscites, with unexpectedly high participation despite the media blackouts, broach topics such as whether former President Salinas should be prosecuted for his economic policies, whether the Mexican army should cease its punitive actions in Chiapas, and whether Mexicans should accept the terms of the Clinton administration's bailout plan to stabilize the economy and forestall the risks of international financial disorder. The uproar caused by the discovery of Raúl Salinas de Gortari's drug connections and secret bank accounts, plus strong suspicions of his involvement in the political assassination of a top PRI official, add insult to injury. Are these not clear examples of collective mobilization and vigorous social movements?

Again, it is a question of whether Mexican society is being disorganized or reorganized. The image of hundreds of marches and demonstrations in Mexico City and elsewhere should not be confused with the strengthening of civil society. Institutional or organizational intermediation is not being constructed or reinforced in Mexico nor, at least for the time being, are social actors being strengthened or demonstrating greater staying power. The most regrettable outcome of the current politico-economic crisis, though not the least likely, would be for an explosion of unstructured popular participation to drive coercive forces to intervene and suppress public space.

The organizations restricted to the sphere of civil society (NGOs, Catholic ecclesiastical base communications, and so on) also require a closer look. Societies take refuge in more restricted and defensive organizational arenas when public space is monopolized by a powerful force or when it is suppressed by a repressive force. In this regard, one must inquire whether the proliferation of small defensive identities in Mexico, under the guise of neoliberalism, may not signal a growing monopoly of the public by the Mexican state and the defeat of society.

Regardless of the answers to these queries, none of the preceding arguments negates the presence of those forces with stronger identity-based constituencies and greater survival prospects. These forces include the small agricultural producers movement in El Barzón, PAN voters, navistas,[13] Christians, farmers from the center and north of the country, and resurgent indigenous peoples' organizations that forcefully assert a cultural fundamentalism (the Zapotecs of the Isthmus of Tehuantepec having the greatest potential). Nor, finally, should one doubt the significance of organizations whose culture has deep historical roots such as the *Asamblea de Barrios* (Assembly of neighborhoods) and the first widely popular anti-neoliberal personality: *Superbarrio*. Can one add to this list small and medium-sized entrepreneurs and the middle class homeowners who, dispirited by the debt resulting from soaring interest rates, massively joined the *Barzón* debtors protest movement? Probably not yet, at least not by late 1996.

Mexico's history of savage modernization has resulted in a segmented and unfinished modernity. Mexican society in socioeconomic, political, and cultural terms has granted an inordinate amount of power to the state. The actors that dynamize civil society have been perceived and dealt with by the state as threats, essentially because of the presence of a powerful neighbor and adversary to the north and an unavoidable and relentless growth of the popular sectors. Weakened intermediate actors and the lack of a secure social order perpetuate the problem in a vicious cycle of a strong state towering over a weak and disorganized civil society.

Notes

1. The thesis advanced in this chapter is meant to go beyond, rather than to refute, Carlos Monsiváis' (1987) essay analyzing the ascent of the most prominent social movements of the past decade, such as the groups that organized in the wake of Mexico City's 1985 earthquake, the Coalición Obrero Campesino Estudiantil del Istmo (COCEI) in Juchitán, Oaxaca, and the student movement at UNAM.

2. Acuña and Smith (1994) have presented a typology of probable outcomes of neoliberal reform. Two of their four scenarios are particularly relevant to my argument. In the first scenario they term "inclusionary democracy," social actors are strengthened, marginalized groups are actively incorporated, democratic practices are institutionalized, and an activist role for the state (purged of its authoritarian vestiges) is preserved. Economic policies are negotiated by the state with the leadership of associations of workers and capitalists. Basing democratic stability on this type of sociopolitical pact requires making assurances to key collective actors that their interests will not be hurt by future neoliberal policies. Moreover, the pacts need to be monitored by the national legislature to minimize the shifting of costs onto particular groups who are not party to the tripartite negotiations (ethnic minorities, consumers, students, or women, for example) or onto the public interest (the environment or future generations). In the second scenario Acuña and Smith label "fragmented and exclusionary democracy," the neoliberal economic model is implemented by excluding vast segments of the population from democratic spaces and institutions. Here the maintenance of majority political coalitions is necessary, but it is not sufficient to accomplish the neoliberal project's goals. Neutralizing opposition also requires that the institutions created to facilitate strategic behavior by social and economic actors be dismantled. Social networks must be disrupted and collective identities and political solidarity eroded. In other words, the democratic regime's capacity to carry out political domination relies on "the silence of civil society," made possible by the fragmentation of social actors and by exclusionary politics embodied in the socioeconomic model.

3. Even among these cases, however, the state's role varies both qualitatively and quantitatively, as does the degree and density of collective social actors. Similar outcomes may be arrived at by a variety of historical paths.

4. For excellent theoretical discussion, see the chapter by Alvaro Díaz in this volume and the essay by Kenneth Roberts (1995).

5. During the 1980s, spending on health fell from 2.5 percent to 1.4 percent of GDP and from 6.2 percent to 2.5 percent of total expenditures on public services. Comparison with Mexico's NAFTA partners is instructive: In 1990, Mexico spent 2.4 percent of GDP on social welfare, while the United States spent 12 percent, and Canada spent 19 percent. See Asa Cristina 1987 and ILO 1993.

6. Smith and Acuña (1994) offer compelling reasons to think that this combination of successful neoliberal reform and consolidation of the procedural aspects of democratic rule represent the least probable scenario for most Latin American countries.

7. Apart from overly optimistic theorizing about the "transition to democracy," some recent proposals coming from Latin America suggest the need for a sociology of disintegration or a "sociology of decadence" (Tironi 1986) to replace the sociology of modernization. From this perspective, the current Latin American reality can perhaps best be understood using concepts inspired by Durkheim, de Tocqueville, or Gramsci. The dissolution of social cohesion, the disintegration of intermediary identities, the atomization of society, particularization, and the retreat into the individual are key concepts. They contemplate a panorama of anomie, generalized disaffection with the social order, and the weakening, fusion, or disappearance of basic social units. Classes, groups, and strata are seen as giving way to delinquent and individual forms of adaptation.

8. The National Solidarity Program (PRONASOL) was the Salinas government's strategy to combat poverty through targeted social spending along the lines advocated by the World Bank. By folding most of previous social programs into PRONASOL, Salinas created a powerful instrument to promote his government's neoliberal policies, and his own image, among the urban and rural poor who bore the brunt of structural adjusmtent. Approximately 150,000 Solidarity Committees were created nationwide, with spending rising from US$2 billion in 1989 to about US$10 billion in 1992.

9. There are indications that it is a phenomenon touching all of Latin America: Raúl Alfonsín was overtaken by a new style of Peronism in Argentina; Carlos Andrés Pérez of Venezuela was soundly rejected by a disorderly and atomized mass as he put his first neoliberal measures into effect; Lula and the Partido dos Trabalhores (PT) in Brazil appeared as though they might win the presidential elections. Massive demonstrations in Brazil and Venezuela built and destroyed leaders' popularity like castles of sand. The flashing apparition of leaders, and their instability, can be explained by the disorder and atomization of society.

10. There are, of course, many other exceptions, both historical and more contemporary, to this chronic emptying of the social in Mexico. From Cosijopi, COCEI fought against the epicenter of Aztec power and managed to retain its regional identity, even after becoming involved with PRONASOL. The *sinarquistas* in El Bajío since the *Cristiada* have struggled against a central state obsessed with destroying small landholders (see Monsiváis 1987 for a description of these movements). Similarly, the organizations that emerged in the aftermath of the great 1985 earthquake — the *Asamblea de Barrios*, the CEU, and the *Cardenistas* — all had high visibility in the capital, thereby creating the impression of a great deal of social participation. This impression turned out to be a smoke-screen impeding the ability of observers to gauge the dismantling of Mexican collective actors. Many failed to differentiate between short-term activation (with its enormous potential for defining an adversary and constructing an identity for mobilized individuals, which in its moment appears so powerful) and what could be called the "normal" behavior of Mexican society.

11. The numerous plebeian revolts that occurred in 1994, 1995, and 1996 should not be overlooked either. These riots typify another category of Mexican social behavior in periods when order breaks down or appears to be weakening. This behavior unfolds in a haphazard fashion beginning with laziness, street parties, insubordination, and menacing gestures that escalate into disorganized violence and destruction.

12. The 1968 Olympic Massacre is the most spectacular example of this.

13. *Navismo* emerged in the 1950s in the state of San Luis de Potosí. In 1958, the opposition *Unión Cívica Potosina,* led by Dr. Salvador Nava, defeated the PRI candidate in the state capital. *Navismo* became an important independent political force in the 1960s and 1970s. In 1983, Dr. Nava was elected mayor of San Luis Potosí with the support of President Miguel de la Madrid, who wanted to liquidate the *cacicazgo* of the Jongitud Barrios, the local Prista head of the teacher's union. In the early 1990s, the *navistas* organized a broad anti-PRI coalition with the PAN, the PRD, and smaller groupings to compete with the PRI. In protest of the disputed victory of the PRI candidate in the 1991 local elections, Dr. Nava led a peaceful march of resistance to Mexico City. Although Dr. Nava died in 1992, the *navista* movement remained a significant regional political force. See Calvillo Unna 1994.

References

Acuña, Carlos H., and William C. Smith. 1994. "The Political Economy of Structural Adjustment: The Logic of Support and Opposition to Neoliberal Reform." In *Latin American Political Economy in the Age of Neoliberal Reform*, eds. William C. Smith, Carlos Acuña, and Eduardo Gamarra. Coral Gables, Fla.: University of Miami North-South Center.

Aguilar Camín, Héctor. 1991. *La Guerra de Galio*. México, D.F.: Cal y Arena.

Calvillo Unna, Tomás. 1994. "San Luis Potosí." In *La República Mexicana: Modernización y democracia de Aguascalientes a Zacateca*, eds. Pablo González Casanova and Jorge Cadena Roa. México, D.F.: Universidad Nacional Autónoma de México and La Jornada Ediciones.

Asa Cristina, Laurel. 1987. "Reestructuración productiva y salud obrera." *El Cotidiano* 20.

Bennett, Vivianne. 1993. "Orígenes del movimiento urbano-popular mexicano: Pensamiento político y organizaciones políticas clandestinas (1960-1980)." *Revista Mexicana de Sociología* 3.

Boucher, Josiane. 1990. "La Coordinadora Nacional del Movimiento Urbano Popular (CONAMUP)." In *Movimientos sociales, democracia emergente y sistema político en México*, eds. S. Zermeño and A. Cuevas. Mexico: Centro de Investigaciones Interdiciplinarias en Humanidades, UNAM.

Calva, José Luis. 1991. "Posibles efectos de un Acuerdo de Libre Comercio México-Estados Unidos sobre el sector agropecuario mexicano." *Revista Mexicana de Sociología* 3.

Cardoso, Fernando Henrique, and Enzo Faletto. 1969. *Dependencia y desarrollo en América Latina*. México: Siglo XXI.

Chesneau, Jean. 1988. "La Modernité Monde." *Les Temps Moderns* (June).

de la Garza, Enrique. 1990. "Reconversión industrial y polarización del aparato productivo." In *México en la década de los ochenta*, eds. Garavito and Bolívar. Mexico: UAM-Azcapotzalco/El Cotidiano.

González Arréchiga, Bernardo, and José Carlos Ramírez. 1990. "Definición y perspectiva de la región fronteriza." *Estudios Sociológicos* 7.

ILO. 1993. *El trabajo en el mundo*. Geneva: International Labor Organization.

Kruijt, Dirk. 1994. "Guerras étnicas y cogobierno militar." *La Jornada Semanal*.

Labastida, Julio, ed. 1980. *Hegemonía y alternativas de cambio en América Latina, 1980*. Mexico: Siglo XXI.

La Jornada. 1991. November 16.

La Jornada. 1994. March 22.

Martínez, Carlos. 1995. "Tlacuilco." Video Trópico Sur. México, D.F.

Monsiváis, Carlos. 1987. *La sociedad que se organiza*. México, D.F.: Ediciones ERA.

Montemayor, Carlos. 1991. *La guerra en el paraíso*. México, D.F.: Editorial Diana.

Moore, Barrington. 1973. *Los orígenes sociales de la dictadura y de la democracia. El señor y el campesino en la formación del mundo moderno.* Barcelona: Ediciones Península.

Nuñez, Oscar. 1990. *Innovaciones democrático-culturales del movimiento urbanopopular.* México, D.F.: Universidad Autónoma Metropolitana.

Roberts, Kenneth M. 1995. "Neoliberalism and the Transformation of Populism in Latin America: The Peruvian Case." *World Politics* 48: 82-116.

Smith, William C., and Carlos H. Acuña. 1994. "Future Politico-Economic Scenarios for Latin America." In *Democracy, Markets, and Structural Reform in Latin America: Argentina, Bolivia, Brazil, Chile, and Mexico,* eds. William C. Smith, Carlos H. Acuña, and Eduardo A. Gamarra. Coral Gables, Fla.: University of Miami North-South Center.

Tironi, Eugenio. 1986. "Para una sociología de la decadencia." *Proposiciones* 12. Santiago de Chile: Instituto SUR.

Tokman, Victor. 1987. "El imperativo de actuar. El sector informal hoy." *Nueva Sociedad* 90, Caracas.

Touraine, Alain. 1988. *La Parole et le Sang, Politique et Societé en Amerique Latine.* Paris: Editions Odile Jacob.

Vacs, Aldo C. 1994. "Convergence and Dissension: Democracy, Markets, and Structural Reform in World Perspective." In *Latin American Political Economy in the Age of Neoliberal Reform: Theoretical and Comparative Perspectives for the 1990s,* eds. William C. Smith, Carlos H. Acuña, and Eduardo A. Gamarra. Coral Gables, Fla.: University of Miami North-South Center.

Warman, Arturo. 1989. "Presencia de la Pobreza." *Cuadernos de Nexos* 8 (March).

Zermeño, Sergio. 1989. "El regreso del lider: Crisis, neoliberalismo y desorden." *Revista Mexicana de Sociología* 4.

Zermeño, Sergio. 1993. "La derrota de la sociedad." *Revista Mexicana de Sociología* 2.

Chapter 8

New Social Movements, Old Party Structures: Discursive and Organizational Transformations in Mexican and Brazilian Party Politics

Diane E. Davis

Tracking the Future with a Focus on Parties

S cholars generally have studied the recent political and economic changes in Latin America by focusing directly on social movements and their roles in democratizing the state and civil society[1] or analyzing domestic and global pressures on the state to eliminate protectionism or establish administrative efficiency.[2] Scant attention has been paid to the activities of political parties in the current transition, except to hold them responsible for the economic bottlenecks and political crises that spur social movement support for democracy and markets in the first place. This is a mistake because Latin American parties, by mediating between the state and civil society and responding to the contradictory pressures of political and economic liberalization, have proven to be key actors in the politics of emerging democracies.

However, do all political parties confront the dual challenge of social movements and economic liberalization in the same fashion, or do their unique organizational or ideological profiles lead them to respond differently, and why? The intent here is to consider such questions using a comparative analysis of two parties that differ dramatically in organization, ideology, ties to their grassroots, and commitment to democracy: Mexico's semi-authoritarian governing party, the Institutional Revolutionary Party (Partido Revolucionario Institucional — PRI), and Brazil's socialist and democratic opposition party, the Workers' Party (Partido dos Trabalhadores — PT). A "most different systems" comparison — where virtually everything about the parties is different while the challenge to them is very similar — should reveal how the new context of social movements and economic liberalization has affected party activities, perhaps independently of their individual natures, and with what implications for Latin America's future.

In taking this perspective, this chapter departs from most current scholarship on Latin America, which assumes that by definition parties and social movements hold contradictory objectives or that party dynamics work to fragment or undermine social movement claims, impeding democratization.[3] This chapter begins from the premise that there can be some articulation of social movement and party goals. Research shows that owing to the high value movements accord autonomy, parties generally have been active partners in attempting to explore the possibilities of this relationship. From the vantage point of parties, one may better understand party-movement relationships: why they develop as they do in neoliberal economic conditions and what their impact is on society and politics.

Mexico and Brazil: The Logic of Comparison

At first glance, one could hardly think of two more different parties than Mexico's PRI and Brazil's PT. The PT is a relatively new and avowedly socialist party, comprised of active cadres of social movements struggling against corrupt and antidemocratic state practices. Mexico's PRI is perhaps the mirror image of the PT, embodying many of the practices the PT is committed to eradicating. Divorced from the people and bureaucratically entrenched in the state, the PRI has a history of corruption and authoritarianism that spans more than half a century. While the PRI is reluctant to implement democratizing reforms that jeopardize its grip on national power, these are precisely the reforms the PT promotes in its efforts to acquire power at the national level.

Despite these stark differences, however, the PRI and the PT face very similar social, political, and economic conditions within their respective countries, thereby justifying a comparative analysis. Both the PRI and the PT are old-style parties that in the past used class as a basis for organization, yet both now are scrambling to accommodate the demands of a growing array of social movements and their so-called new way of doing politics. Both parties also face the constraints of economic liberalization, which limits state capacity to redress (via social policies and expenditures) social movement demands.

Several questions guide analysis of these two parties and their dilemmas in responding to social movements in a neoliberal context. First, what organizational strategies and discursive rhetorics have they used to appeal to the grassroots? Second, to what extent have social movements or their demands been incorporated into party practices, how and why, and with what implications for the structure and rhetoric of the parties or their capacity to further either democratization or economic liberalization objectives? Third, how have the parties' strategic responses contributed to the construction of new social and political identities and the consolidation of competitive party politics, and how might these new developments affect the political prospects and economic solvency of each country? Last, have the parties' efforts reproduced the same problems that turned people off to party politics in the first place, or will they generate enough citizen loyalty and confidence to strengthen the party system and democratically guide their respective countries to a more promising political and economic future?

In considering these questions, the focus will be on the parties, their strategies and discourses, and the similarities and differences between them. Despite their obvious importance, the complexities of the social movements' structures, ideologies, or histories, and how these influence party responses will not be addressed here. A comprehensive analysis of this topic would scrutinize the subtle interplay of parties and specific movements — and their specific demands — within each country. However, space considerations limit the present discussion to a focus on the parties themselves, supplemented by references to secondary accounts of general social movement conditions in Mexico and Brazil.

Mexico: One-Party Rule and Social Movements

Over the years, the PRI has shown a remarkable ability to coopt social movements and prevent mobilized citizens from curtailing the party's power. Yet a new challenge has arisen: how to continue using clientelist practices that undermine or accommodate social movements while at the same time advancing a project of economic liberalization. The PRI leadership publicly backed President Carlos Salinas de Gortari as he worked to eliminate protectionism and promote economic opening, but pent-up demand from the poor and disenfranchised populations who suffered a decade of economic crisis limits the party's ability to shed fully its social spending responsibilities. Making this balancing act even more difficult, the party leaders are split over how to meet social and economic goals and still keep opposition parties like the leftist Democratic Revolutionary Party (Partido de la Revolución Democrática — PRD) or the right-wing National Action Party (Partido de Acción Nacional — PAN) from capturing the electorate.

The PRI has been concerned especially about losing support from four critical groups: participants in social movements who have long fought for greater democracy, political participation, or party reform and many of whom seek increased public spending on housing, infrastructure, and other urban services (Hernández 1987, Perlo and Schteingart 1984, Ramírez Saiz 1986) or democratization in general (Hellman 1994, Foweraker and Craig 1991); organized public sector workers, most of whom are active in the party and many of whom support its *corriente democrática* but fear losing their political power and jobs in the government's latest round of privatization and austerity measures (NOTIMEX 1990, 35); the lower middle classes (including urban informal sector workers and the petty self-employed, in Mexico often referred to as microindustrialists), who are not covered by many government programs or its recent wage pact with labor and whose political influence within the party has declined steadily since the mid-1960s, despite their organization (Davis 1990, Dresser 1991); and the middle classes (including intellectuals and some professionals), whose incomes have been ravaged by the 1980s economic crisis and who include former party loyalists as well as those who have long viewed the PRI as a corrupt machine dominated by backward-looking "dinosaurs" (Davis 1994, Loaeza 1985).

To bring these four groups to its side, the PRI employed a two-pronged strategy. First, it introduced a massive public relations campaign to convince citizens that the party and state finally were going to be "modernized," by promoting internal democracy and creating the conditions for economic recovery (PRI 1990).[4]

Second, party leaders sought to put meat on these claims with a major institutional restructuring of the PRI, to be carried out first within the National Confederation of Popular Organizations (Confederación Nacional de Organizaciones Populares — CNOP) or so-called "popular sector," one of the party's three main corporatist institutions and the sector that in the past had accommodated many from the four dissatisfied groups.[5] A stunning announcement was made in early 1990: The old CNOP was to be replaced by a new organization, the UNE, an acronym that stood for absolutely nothing. The popular sector was selected for reorganization because its constituents — especially social movements and associations of *colonos* — were seen as the party's biggest present challenge (in contrast to legitimacy crises of past decades, when the labor and peasant sectors had been most problematic). This change was the first modification of the PRI's national corporatist structure since 1943.

How was this new sector to be organized, and how did party leaders expect to accommodate unhappy class forces or new social movements within a party-led organization that obviously intended to legitimize PRI rule? In characteristic fashion, the party revamped its principles of political participation in such a way as to accommodate — some would say preempt — various opposition forces that had emerged over the decade. At a CNOP meeting in 1990, President Salinas said the party must break from its past and recognize that "diversity of interests and ideas in society [was] conducive to a more open and competitive system," for which the principal logic of organization should be plurality (Osorio Marbán 1994, 331-332). Openness, competition, and pluralism were to occur within the party, however, not within the larger context of Mexican society, and the UNE was to house the new organizations and the party's newfound plurality.

The new UNE had an entirely different structure than the old CNOP. Rather than acting as a confederation of the popular middle class, comprised of various groups, unlimited in number and unrelated to each other in action or organization, the reconstituted popular sector had a more coherent internal logic. It consisted of five different *movimientos* (listed below), each of which would form part of the UNE's governing structure. The new sector's slogan was *Ciudadanos en Movimiento* (Citizens in Movement), and its documents extol the principles of (movement) autonomy, plurality, representation, and active militancy (PRI 1991, 37-39). By emphasizing citizenship and other principles that permeated the discourse of Mexico's new social movements (NSMs), the PRI hoped to demonstrate its responsiveness to the concerns and political culture of movements.

The new organization and its rhetoric were intended to accommodate a wide variety of social and class forces, however, not just the new social movements. Of the UNE's five constituent "movements," three held groups of workers that long had been organized and active within the party's popular sector: The Movimiento Gremial included small *comerciantes*, street vendors, informal sector workers, *transportistas*, *cooperativistas*, microindustrialists, and rural property owners; the Movimiento Sindical encompassed workers from a variety of governmental agencies, including service workers affiliated with the Syndicate of Public Sector Functionaries (FSTSE), the Social Security Institute, state and municipal government, and banks; and the Movimiento Profesional included so-called technical and professional personnel. It was only the remaining two movements, the Movimiento Urbano Popular and the Movimiento Ciudadano that were intended to bring together what the PRI called "new social bases": mainly neighborhood groups with demands for infrastructure and services or new social movement and citizen activists in causes such as the environment, public safety, human rights, and consumer rights, among others.

The UNE's organizational and political logic suggests several things. First and foremost, the PRI still was unwilling to allow real popular participation, preferring instead to use time-tested corporatist tactics for collectively bringing the dissatisfied and mobilized into the party through one of its sectors in order to control, coopt, or preempt challenges to its legitimacy and power. Yet the reforms also reveal the party's attempt to respond — albeit in an institutional manner that was consistent with a strong party apparatus — to current ideas and prevailing citizen support for movement autonomy and plurality.[6]

Second, in seeking to balance control and participation, the party hoped to create room for all, holding on to its old constituent base in the CNOP (public sector employees, shopkeepers, informal sector workers, *transportistas*) while also incorporating new forces, such as human rights and ecology groups. Third, the PRI hoped to cultivate a rhetoric of unity that would give organizational coherence to the UNE's broadly cast, pluralist structure. The sector's new name, loosely translated as "unite," and its slogan, "UNITE! Citizens in Movement," typify the party's efforts in this regard. In speeches inaugurating the UNE, its Secretary General, Silvia Hernández, continually repeated the unity theme as the new sector's most important feature, along the way paying lip service to the UNE's diversity and NSM constituency:

> We are united by a great country...and a grand and marvelous party that changes once again for the better. We are united by a force that competes and wins and knows that what triumphed for us was the unity, respect, and maturity of a great organization that once again puts itself forward. We are united in an agreement with the new generations of youth, with women, and with public workers who create wealth, build streets, and construct houses by hand. We are united by care and protection of the environment, the land, and resources. We are united by a new struggle for the human rights of children, the aged, and the handicapped. We are united by the battle for security in cities and for land in the countryside; we are united by the necessity to produce with better tools and in better conditions. We are united by the desire to defend the consumer and by the challenge of supporting a global economic project, a democratic project of Mexican stature, and a social project that will be just and immediate. (PRI 1991, n.p.)

Last, the UNE's structure and principles of organization made clear the PRI's efforts to distance itself from class rhetoric or class-based organization. These omissions are striking for a party historically structured around class identities and for a sector that until this time had been defined in class terms, even if they were rather ambiguous (the "popular middle" classes). Nowhere in the UNE's founding documents were constituents identified in class terms of any kind.

Of course, eliminating languages of class was perfectly consistent with a post-1989 world and with the orientations of the NSMs that the PRI wished to incorporate within the UNE, many of which also shunned class rhetoric and organized themselves around non-workplace concerns. Yet even references to *sindicato* and *gremio* constituents, whose self-identification undeniably was based on their status as workers and union members, were purged of their class content. For example, the stated objective of the Movimiento Sindical was to "defend its rights, the administration of its interests, its posture of solidarity with the community, and party political action" (PRI 1990, 17). In short, rights in the new UNE never were discussed as class rights, despite the fact that several of its constituent federations were organized and juridically treated as such.

Beyond Movements

The PRI's use of *movimientos* as the organizational and discursive basis for restructuring the so-called popular sector was a bold move, and if rhetoric were enough to guarantee citizen support, the party well might have solved many of its problems. Yet something remained amiss, and scarcely two years after the establishment of the UNE in 1990, the PRI renamed and restructured the popular sector again. In early 1993, the party replaced the UNE with the FNOC (Frente Nacional de Organizaciones y Ciudadanos) or National Front of Organizations and Citizens, a new entity comprised of three distinct and autonomous organizations: the Coalición Nacional de Agrupaciones Productivas y de Servicios, which replaced the UNE's Movimiento Gremial; the Movimiento Nacional Sindical, which was to replace the Movimiento Sindical; and the Foro Nacional de Profesionales y Técnicos, which replaced the Movimiento Profesional. In doing so, the party abandoned its efforts to construct a unified and coherent party sector around a discourse of movements and sought a new organizational identity as a front for different groups with openly divergent constituencies and demands.

The PRI's departure from the organizational rhetoric of and commitment to movements was clear from the fate of the two UNE *movimientos* that originally had been created to hold the "newest" social movement forces: the Movimiento Urbano Popular and the Movimiento Ciudadano, both of which were eliminated. To replace the former, the party created the Alianza Urbana, which was to be part of an altogether distinct organization, also newly created, called the Movimiento Territorial del Partido Revolucionario Institucional. The Movimiento Ciudadano, for its part, was all but abolished, though not without controversy. Initially, the Frente Nacional de Organizaciones y Ciudadanos inaugural documents mentioned a fourth organization, the Red Ciudadana (Citizen Network), which was to replace this Movimiento Ciudadano and act as a fourth network of organizations in the UNE (PRI 1993, 7). However, within a month, both the FNOC's Red Ciudadana and its precursor in the UNE had vanished completely.

These changes and the UNE's short-lived fate not only show the difficulties of transforming the popular sector into an organization of movements where rhetorics of citizenship prevailed, even for a highly institutionalized, hierarchical, and powerful party like the PRI. They also highlight the contradictions embodied in the UNE's attempt as an institution to accommodate disparate and dissenting forces by including all collectively organized Mexicans. Indeed, joining the UNE had been possible via partici-pation in a movement at one's place of employment or residence or on the basis of other "temas con que mas se identifiquen," that is, one's allegiance to practically anything anywhere (PRI 1990, 15). Individuals, organizations, neighborhoods, municipalities, even states could affiliate. And by seeking to embrace people organized around an impossibly diverse range of identities — citizen, neighborhood, occupation, class, gender, age, and, of course, party loyalty — the UNE was filled with tensions obvious to all.

In its efforts to operationalize the popular Mexican phrase, "todo cabe en un jarrito" (everything fits in a mug), the UNE undermined the party with conflicts in three areas: unity versus plurality, participation versus control, and identity based on class versus movement or citizenship-based identities. Despite its rhetoric of unity, then, the UNE was a grab-bag with little internal coherence, and not surprisingly, it generated very little enthusiasm. These tensions forced the party leadership to stop trying to impose unity and once again to reform the sector, this time into a much narrower front.

Of course, the PRI's history of manipulation in the domain of symbolic and rhetorical reforms leads most scholars to discount institutional changes such as shift from the CNOP to the UNE to the FNOC. Such tinkering is seen as exemplifying the PRI's tactical efforts to avoid substantive change and maintain power in the face of demands for greater popular participation. However, if the PRI's institutional accommodations were just rhetorical in this case, existing only in the realm of discourse, or if they really had nothing to do with how the popular sector functioned as a mechanism for participation and governance, then one would not expect such fundamental changes in so short a period of time. The UNE's complete restructuring within two years of its founding, however, suggests that its creation was more than a symbolic maneuver and that there was internal party dissent about its nature and underlying principles. Real issues were at stake.

The Problem of Eliminating Class Identity

Two factors inspired the PRI to abandon the UNE and create the FNOC, which embodied an entirely different organizational and discursive rationale for the popular sector. First, the UNE had not achieved the party's objective of appealing to social movements while maintaining plurality and unity. With its constituents organizationally divided on the basis of competing identities, the UNE lacked a common project around which to unite its various constituent movements — except, of course, support for the PRI, a theme that alienated rather than inspired many. Without this unity, the party was weaker and in less of a position to advance economic liberalization, a goal written right into the UNE's founding principles (PRI 1991, 19-20). As such, rather than helping ease the contradictions of democratic participation and liberalization, the changes embodied in the UNE's establishment called into question the party's capacity to accomplish either one of these objectives. Second, the new UNE exacerbated rather than solved problems in an equally difficult terrain the party was trying to negotiate: the class-citizenship-movement problematic. Indeed, in its attempt to replace class concerns with an emphasis on movements and citizens, the UNE was a disaster. The PRI's shift to a more general language of movements and citizenship for organizing the popular sector alienated many of its oldest constituents, who at one time had embraced class rhetoric and did not consider themselves necessarily as free-floating citizens or anti-statist new social movements that rejected the PRI or party politics. Moreover, it also angered other class-oriented members of the party, especially those in the labor and peasant federations, who interpreted the reform as the first frontal challenge to the party's larger logic of class-based sectoral organization.

The PRI was caught in this bind because it had good reasons for abandoning class rhetoric when founding the UNE: It actually wanted to accommodate issue-oriented new social movements and other organizations that explicitly rejected class identities, since they were developing such high political profiles. Also, since the CNOP was a sector for the "popular middle" classes, many of its constituents long had faced problems of self-definition, and these class ambiguities intensified throughout the 1980s. Economic crisis impoverished many members of the middle class and often pushed workers into irregular and low-paying informal sector work, but sometimes it also increased worker autonomy. With even previously loyal constituents increasingly unsure whether they were working, popular, or middle class, the PRI's shift to participation based on a discourse of citizens and movements rather than class made even more sense.

Furthermore, the PRI leadership's abandonment of class-based organization and rhetoric in the popular sector was part of a larger strategy for the party as a whole. The PRI was grappling with the fact that its industrial labor (Confederation of Mexican Workers or Confederación de Trabajadores Mexicanos — CTM) and peasant (National Peasant Confederation or Confederación Nacional de Campesinos — CNC) sectors threatened to thwart neoliberal economic plans to open industry and agriculture to foreign investment and free-market competition, and thus party leaders sought to undermine the organization and power of the class-based sectors.[7] By choosing the least class-coherent sector, the CNOP, to chip away at the use of class identities for defining party concerns and organizing its institutions, the PRI hoped to build the political space for eventually eliminating the other two class-based party sectors, the CTM and CNC. The structuring of the UNE around a language of movements and citizenship, and not class, was thus a calculated move that the PRI hoped would create the maneuvering room within the party and with new social movements in society at large to allow it to carry out its larger political and economic objectives.

However, it appears the PRI miscalculated, if ever so slightly, when it introduced the UNE and shifted from a discourse of class to movements. While eliminating class as the basis for sectoral organization no doubt helped undermine the strength of industrial laborers and peasants in the CTM and CNC, it also alienated the national federation of state workers and other producers of goods and services who had been the party's principal constituents and who were supposed to be the bulwarks of the popular sector. The UNE's foundation antagonized these erstwhile constituents by ignoring their principal basis of self-identity: class or, at least, workplace concerns. These groups were not very willing to accept an ambiguous class status or the organizational fragmentation generated by the UNE's five distinct movements. Moreover, these groups — especially organized state workers with their long history of party primacy — were anxious to maintain their power within the popular sector and hence party politics. The movement autonomy that the new discourse presupposed and that the UNE's structure formalized held little appeal to those who defined themselves in terms of class identity and saw the new structure as eroding their influence.

Many neighborhood associations, also long active in the CNOP, were equally unwilling to abandon class discourse, since they saw urban neglect and poverty as part of larger class inequalities.[8] Adding to the PRI's troubles, the UNE had even failed to elicit enthusiasm in many of the NSMs that were to be its new constituents. Those involved in ecology, human rights, or other issue-specific causes may have applauded the rhetorical and organizational move from class to citizenship or movement identities, but they also resented being grouped into a sector with "dinosaurs" who still pledged allegiance to class conflict, embraced some form of one-party rule, and thus represented the PRI's non-democratic past. As such, something had to be done, and the UNE's swift replacement by the FNOC helped reverse the damage.

First, the FNOC dispelled from its ranks urban movements whose demands for services and decentralized urban policymaking both challenged Salinas' liberalization agenda and underscored the paucity of party mechanisms for neighborhood-level participation. Second, by failing to include the so-called citizens' movements as one of the three principal organizations in the new FNOC (although rhetorical references to citizenship, democracy, autonomy, and human rights remained), the PRI marginalized more of its vocal opponents. In this manner, the party eliminated from within its sectoral ranks the two sets of forces with the strongest positions on the class issue and the weakest support for the PRI: urban social movements, many of which were sympathetic to working class or progressive opposition parties like the PRD, and citizen movements for human rights, democracy, and ecology that shunned class concerns and increasingly were casting their support to other parties, including the right-wing PAN.

This new, pared-down version of the popular sector, or Frente as the FNOC often was called, now was comprised of groups organized principally according to work-based identities, many of which were longstanding supporters of the party. These groups, as organized in the FNOC's three new "fronts" — *sindicatos, agrupaciones productivas y de servicios,* and *profesionales y técnicos* —were less strident about class languages, despite being proud of their occupational status as service providers, technicians, professionals, or unionized state employees. As such, they provided the party with an easily malleable social base, lacking any clear commitment to either movement or class discourse but loyal to the new popular sector and party nonetheless.

Capturing the Middle Class

Does this mean the new FNOC, organized as a front of different occupations, avoided any rhetoric or logic of identity, organization, or affiliation? Not quite. The FNOC adopted a territorial rationale: incorporating individuals or organizations on the basis of their locale, be it workplace, neighborhood, or whatever, apparently in the hope that spatially defined participation would be easier both to justify democratically and to control. The switch away from movement-based to territorial organization underscores the hypocrisy of the PRI's embrace of the discourse of the NSMs. There was never much intention of letting movements share power in directing the party's agenda, least of all those movements agitating for autonomy and an end to one-party rule. In contrast, the use of territory as a language and basis for participation would not carry with it a particular menu of demands, yet it would be inclusive enough to let the party incorporate whomever it wanted, including pro-PRI federations of state workers and professional bureaucrats. This new rationale also allowed the PRI to appeal to women's and youth groups and other social forces that lost the special representation they had in the CNOP and the UNE. Most important, encouraging participation in politics on the basis of territorial location rather than some type of collective social identity allowed the party to appeal rhetorically to the unorganized middle classes whose electoral support could counterbalance the participation of activist social movements or other organized cadres.

Yet once the PRI moved beyond corporate or collective identity and embraced territoriality as the basis for political organization and party appeals, it also rather paradoxically resumed its use of class rhetoric to appeal to potential constituents — but this time it was a discourse that stressed middle and not popular class participation and identity, along with political liberalism. The FNOC's receptivity to middle class concerns and its discourse of liberalism may arise from the fact that many of the occupational groups within the new FNOC — government employees, professionals, and service producers ranging from shopkeepers to small industrialists to self-employed vendors — preferred to be identified in explicitly middle class terms, especially now that the PRI was "modernizing" and dismantling its working class and peasant institutions and rhetorics. This shift in class emphasis also allowed the PRI to target unorganized individuals of the middle classes, who increasingly were influenced by Western liberal values and acted as swing votes capable of supporting the PAN, the PRI, and even the PRD. These people, in particular, were seen as potential allies in the struggle to reform both the economy and the party.

The new middle class rhetoric of the FNOC was acknowledged by its Secretary General, Miguel Angel Barberena Vega, who proclaimed, "one of the principal problems of [the party] is that...the emergent middle classes...lack adequate organization to defend their interests and obtain representation that corresponds to their social profile" (Osorio Marbán 1994, 339-347). In its constant references to liberalism and the concerns of the middle class, the FNOC differed sharply from the UNE, which shunned all class languages and cultivated movement identities. The discourse of the middle classes also broke with the practices established in the original popular sector or CNOP. While the CNOP leadership frequently appealed to middle classes, such appeals always were coupled with the recognition that the CNOP represented primarily the poor and popular classes. Indeed, CNOP constituents generally were referred to as "the popular middle classes," a term that acknowledged their marginal economic position and elective affinity with the working class, granting only lip service to constituents' middle class status. Not so with the new FNOC now in place. Shortly after its creation, sector leaders announced that "the middle classes of the country [would] find in the Frente a new mechanism of representation committed to the intransigent defense of their rights and to working with them so change will be to their benefit" (PRI 1984, 342).

In sum, the changes to the party structure embodied in the creation of the FNOC greatly diminished the threat of strong working class activism within the party, allowing the PRI leadership to begin courting the middle classes in earnest, a shift that attested to the party's eleventh-hour recognition that winning truly competitive elections would be impossible without the support of the middle classes. Of course, the importance of the middle classes long may have been recognized by party leaders. It was only after movement organization and general citizenship rhetoric produced insurmountable problems that the popular sector was transformed and the party had the will and institutional capacity to target middle classes apart from the popular and working classes. With the FNOC in place, the PRI appears successfully to have circumvented many of the tensions that plagued the original popular sector, regarding unity and diversity as well as identity. Equally as important, by replacing a working or popular class with a middle class discourse, the party is now able to use this third sector to target a political base more likely to support its economic liberalization measures and the austerity wage cuts they most likely will imply.

This is not to say that Mexicans will be receptive enough to the party's new language and organization to support the PRI and its policies at all costs, since the political franchise it now heralds is much narrower than earlier ones that afforded popular, working, and middle classes a formal, if not substantive, place in party organization and rhetoric. However, with the PRI's most serious rival, the PAN, also appealing to the nation's middle classes, the emphasis on middle class liberalism and its cousin, economic liberalism, may make the PRI competitive enough to win elections, especially if low income and working class votes split across the many competing parties now on the scene. These trends not only may mean that future electoral competitions and the nature of democratization in Mexico may be negotiated primarily in the domain of middle class politics but also may suggest a further marginalization of social movements and working class or popular languages and identities.

Brazil's PT: Class Party or Party of Movements?

These findings about transformations in the PRI and Mexican politics could be due to the country's unique political system of one-party rule and not necessarily the more general challenge posed by an emergent political culture of social movements. If so, one hardly would expect the PRI's reduced commitment to industrial laborers and peasants and its neoliberal turn to the middle classes after its appropriation and subsequent elimination of movement and citizenship discourses to be replicated by other parties in a similar situation, least of all Brazil's PT. The PT long has identified itself as a workers' party committed to socialism and has eschewed use of the antidemocratic tactics associated with parties such as the PRI. However, Brazil's political culture, like Mexico's, is characterized by the growing visibility and moral authority of social movements. Brazil also is undergoing a process of economic liberalization, and thus the PT, like the PRI, similarly is faced with the dilemma of accommodating social movements within the restrictive context of economic austerity. Indeed, the data indicate that the Brazilian PT, like the PRI, has modified its rhetoric over the last decade in order to broaden its support among the middle classes. Last, as the PT becomes more popular and achieves electoral success — despite a sincere commitment to the grassroots that the PRI can claim only in rhetoric — the PT also faces tensions between unity and plurality and gropes for a common purpose consistent with a diverse constituency. The concern here, then, is the extent to which the PT has responded to these challenges in ways similar to the PRI or whether its unique organizational and ideological profile has led it to respond differently.

To address these questions, it is helpful to examine the PT's foundation. Discussions about the formation of a workers' party that eventually became the PT began in 1978-1979 among São Paulo union leaders who sought an institutional mechanism for gaining political power in a democratizing Brazil.[9] The workers were adamant that the union movement and new party must be kept separate and autonomous,[10] although members saw themselves in terms of a "double militancy;" that is, most of the founders of the PT were leaders of social movements or involved in the union movement (Keck 1992, Sader and Silverstein 1991, Tavares de Almeida 1987). This dual mandate led the PT leadership to open its arms to movements or groups as diverse as "industrial workers, salaried workers in commerce and services, public functionaries, inhabitants of the periphery, autonomous workers, peasants, rural workers, women, blacks, students, Indians, and other exploited sectors" (Gadotti and Pereira 1989, 54). Thus, from its inception, the PT reached out to social movements and truly sought to make them a key base in the party, in contrast to the PRI, that, after decades of distancing itself from its popular origins, aimed to restore legitimacy by opportunistically accommodating social movements.

Still, what is striking about the early PT is similarity in terms of composition to the PRI's popular sector. Both organizations held movements of residents from poor neighborhoods (Mexico's *colonos* were "members of the periphery" for the PT), self-employed and informal sectors' workers (the PRI's microindustrialists were the PT's "autonomous workers"), and women's and students' organizations. Of course, the PT also aimed to include peasants, rural workers, and industrial workers, forces that Mexico's PRI had incorporated but in separate sectoral institutions. Yet it was precisely this organizational difference that complicated the PT's efforts to transform itself from a "movement of social movements," with a genuine commitment to the grassroots, into a broad-based institutionalized party that could win elections and govern nationally. While both the PT and the PRI rhetorically embraced the same spectrum of class and social forces, the PRI could count on distinct party sectors, using the CTM to appeal to industrial workers and its popular sector to accommodate the rest, while the PT sought to do so within one organization. Thus, finding a common language to unify its social bases was more difficult for the PT than the PRI, a task complicated further by the PT's sincere — rather than symbolic — commitment to participation by social movements and the working class.

Of course, one might suppose that the PT would find it easier to use class languages[11] or identities as its organizing principle, with so many from the PT's founding ranks seeing themselves part of the working class[12] and with those from the union movement having high visibility and a powerful voice in party deliberations. The PT's efforts to use a broad conception of workers as the party's defining identity were made problematic by the diversity of its social and class bases and by a changing political culture in which social movements — not class concerns — were capturing the moral high ground. Indeed, the inclusion of social movement forces that did not see themselves in class terms alongside industrial laborers and peasants that did created organizational problems for the PT that Mexico's more narrowly cast popular sector avoided.

In Mexico, the potential challenge of social movements was met by restructuring the CNOP, shedding languages of class, and adopting the discourse of "movements of citizens" and later of territorality. The absence of industrial workers or peasants in the popular sector's ranks made these transformations relatively easy, as did the party's authoritarian style of implementing change from above. For the PT, however, such facile machinations were difficult, given its organizational commitment to workers and the inclusion of such intermediate class forces as the self-employed and salaried workers in commerce and services. As such, the party walked a fine discursive line between recognizing its identity as a class party and attempting to transcend its class language and concerns.

The Dilemma of Democratic Participation: Unity versus Diversity

Conflicts over how to find a unifying language amid constituent diversity and a political culture of social movements first rose to the surface in the early 1980s in response to the ascension of middle class and professional unions and the growing visibility of NSMs. With both "old" and "new" social movements[13] under the PT umbrella, room for maneuver was limited, though the conflicts between these two types of social movements were much less intense in Brazil than in Mexico. Many Brazilians — the PT included — sought to link the two types of movements to each other and to a larger political project. The PT's tradition of double militancy assured this, as did founding members' contentions that diversity in social movement bases should not be a problem for the PT. However, it was easier said than done.

Despite their commitment to the party, even NSMs themselves disagreed on whether a discourse of class identity or any other common language could or should be used to unify the party. Complicating matters, in these early stages many of the social movements and community organizations that formed the political base of the PT "were unable to draw the line between party militancy and movement militancy," owing to their limited prior experience in elections (Alvarez 1990, 156). This meant that "the local PT, the would-be conduit of grassroots demands, also assumed for itself many of the organizational and mobilizational functions previously performed by social movement groups," which in turn caused many grassroots organizations to complain about the party's breach of movement autonomy (Alvarez 1990, 157). Tensions over these issues accelerated since some felt that the direct connection between the movements and the party as an institution was withering away. Although the party originally had conceived of itself as being the voice of social movements, by the early 1980s, many of the PT's leaders feared

> the opposite was occurring: The PT was on the receiving end of a laundry list which expressed the concerns of a whole variety of groups that were not organically integrated into any coherent form of party practice. The cement that held all of the elements together, to the extent that this was at all possible, was their common condition of exclusion from the Brazilian political agenda. (Keck 1992, 27)

Despite similar tensions in Mexico caused by internal diversity and an organizational commitment to movement involvement and autonomy, the PT's response was the opposite of the PRI's: to assert that it was not a front of various opposition groups but rather a political body with a unified program constructed democratically in internal discussions among its bases. To put it in the discourse of the left, the PT saw itself as a strategic rather than a tactical party, providing the means of educating workers for alternative forms of democratic participation as it worked toward its long-term goal of construct-ing socialism. As such, a discourse of popular mobilization and direct democracy was thus the PT's solution to the problems of constituent diversity

(Sader and Silverstein 1991, 92). This discourse appealed to many social movements; yet it also held the potential to please radical working class constituents by linking the nature of the party to the achievement of socialism, through which their class concerns eventually would be addressed.

Unfortunately for the PT, however, this discourse was no panacea. First, it provoked heated debate within the party about how democracy and socialism should be defined (Weffort 1992, 1984) and over the costs of building a mass-based popular movement with socialism as the ultimate goal but which also sought to become a forceful actor in local and national political institutions. These debates continued to divide the party rather than unify it, accentuating ideological and organizational differences between the party's different "tendencies." The so-called tendencies, which varied greatly in internal structure and discipline, cross-cut local and national levels of party organization and often hindered the party's efforts to present a unified face to the electorate, to reach consensus on party discourse, and to develop parliamentary strategy and public policy.[14]

Second, contrary to its intended purpose, the new discourse of popular participation and internal party democracy brought to the surface the uneasy relationship between the NSMs and the party leadership. At stake were two issues: the extent to which the new strategy prevented party leaders from harnessing the power of social movements for electoral purposes and the extent to which the discourse of mobilization and direct democracy could be a substitute for larger struggles over the democratization of Brazilian politics. By focusing on intraparty dynamics and failing to find a practical issue or identity with major resonance among the general public, many felt that the party was relinquishing its struggle for electoral victory.

At first, not everyone associated with the party saw this as a problem. Many in the social movements were so wedded to the notion of movement autonomy that they were content to pursue an independent struggle, focusing on their own organizational problems and constituent demands while avoiding the "impure" domain of electoral politics or difficult questions about the meaning of socialism and how to achieve it via democratic elections (Krischke 1984). Some of the PT's militants on the left felt similarly, though for different reasons: They were not convinced that socialism could be achieved through electoral means and so saw little reason to rebuild the party or adopt identities or issues just to enter the trenches of institutional politics. As a result, many in the party simply rejected PT involvement in the state and the formal political establishment (Tavares de Almeida 1987, 153, 166). When the party barely made a mark in the 1982 elections, however, its leadership began a reassessment. Could the PT balance its commitment to social movement autonomy and grassroots democracy with the more class-specific concerns of constituents and the larger objectives of socialist transformation and still win elections?

In an effort to do so, the PT adopted a new language and strategy to unite its disparate constituents: the notion of class formation. According to Margaret Keck (1992, 140), this entailed a shift in emphasis from that of an already formed working class to the notion of "class in formation." While still affirming the ideal of direct democratic participation by the masses, the PT replaced a descriptive, straightforward view of class representation with a more constructionist view of class formation, which was to occur by means of the pedagogic involvement of party activists in social movements and the involvement of movement leaders in local and regional party debates (Novaes 1993). This new project was consistent with the PT's founding principles, which linked movements to the party in a two-way relationship. Now the party had a new mechanism for giving life to these principles and at the same time holding its diverse bases together. Class now could be an active process of self-organization, not only to win elections but also to unite the party, build democracy, and encourage grassroots activism. Moreover, class concerns were no longer to be defined narrowly as the domain of industrial laborers and union activists; they consciously were recast to include the increasingly well-organized rural and white-collar workers, as well as other social movement forces also struggling to self-organize as collective agents with a larger purpose.

From Class Formation to Citizenship and Beyond

The new discourse of class formation, though it may have solved the problem of party-movement articulation and helped broaden the party's bases beyond industrial workers, did not translate into electoral success or ameliorate problems posed by class diversity in the party. As a result, between 1984 and 1988, the PT endeavored once again to construct a wider base for the party, this time by altering its discourse to emphasize citizenship and democracy as much as class formation. The PT did not eliminate completely the discourse of class, which remained an important, though much debated, point of departure for many in the party. Nor was this new language intended as a liberal, "middle class" discourse of citizenship that, by nature, would be inconsistent with a militant class focus. Many in the party considered the new discourse of citizenship and democracy to conform with the broadened notion of class formation and the centrality of class and socialist politics, and in fact, party leaders worked hard to convince skeptics within and outside party ranks that references to citizenship and democracy were intended to denote the social and economic as well as political participation of previously marginalized sectors of society.[15] Still, the new discourse of citizenship and democracy, even when couched in languages of class, represented an essential shift, insofar as it helped the PT broaden its base and advance the effort to win electoral power.[16]

Margaret Keck (1992, 191) notes that the new discourses of citizenship, democracy, and access to power that emerged after 1984 were in many ways a byproduct of the changing character of the organized labor movement, especially the rise of white collar unions. Associations of white collar workers and other class-ambiguous professionals employed by the state had become some of the most powerful organizations on the scene, so the PT's exchange of old conceptions of class for ones of citizenship was not surprising. Yet the new languages can also be traced to two other factors: first, the PT's ongoing internal debates over how to balance its electoral objectives with its commitment to expressing the interests of its grassroots membership and, second, the nature and organization of the NSMs on which the PT counted for support.

Before 1984, when more orthodox class discourses prevailed in the PT, groups that organized around women's and ecology issues, housing and neighborhood concerns, and Catholic community groups often were marginalized by party deliberations that highlighted class identity above any other and class concerns over all other problems. In the early 1980s, many of these movements began pushing for the inclusion of different forms of identity and new demands on the party agenda. Sonia Alvárez's study (1990, 171-172) of women's and neighborhood movements in São Paulo shows, for example, how strains emerged in their relationship to the party as they tended to become more concerned with gender inequalities and urban service scarcities than with working class struggle. When the PT appropriated a discourse that emphasized citizenship rather than class, the party was responding to such pressures from NSMs.

Yet the shift to languages of citizenship also solved another equally important organizational problem for the PT leadership: that more radical, working class factions generally were privileged within party debates. Once traditional class allegiance was reformulated to include other forms of solidarity, social movements that had stressed consensual, dialogic, and non-hierarchical methods of organization and participation — among the most prominent in this regard were women's movements (Alvarez 1990) — were able to gain new power and visibility within the party, which further cemented their commitment to the PT and its electoral struggle.

With a new discourse of citizenship and democracy, employed after 1984, the party further enhanced its popularity by appealing explicitly to the concerns and frustrations of the middle class (Sader and Silverstsein 1991, 94). The middle classes were far more receptive to these issues than those of class formation or class struggle, and many of the NSMs counted among their cadres members of the middle class (Boschi 1987, 191). Still, the PT's appropriation of languages of citizenship and democracy and its newfound receptivity to middle classes during this period were aided equally by its involvement in the national campaign for direct elections that swept the country in 1984. While this campaign was spearheaded by the Party of the Brazilian Democratic Movement (Partido do Movimento Democrático Brasileiro — PMDB), the PT played an important role in mobilizing grassroots support around the idea of democratic participation for the larger democratic good of the country. The PT garnered both criticism and credibility in the aftermath of the defeated campaign, when negotiations between the PMDB and the Democratic Social Party (Partido Democrático Social — PDS) refused to take part in the electoral college, and thus in the long run was able to wear the oppositional mantle with greater credibility. Most important, perhaps, participation in the campaign for direct elections forged PT-middle class alliances and demonstrated the benefits of infusing the party's rhetoric with support for citizenship and procedural democracy.

For all these reasons, after the 1984 election the PT turned more frequently to middle classes for support. As such, the 1985 elections were marked by the predominance of middle class and liberal professionals as PT candidates, a departure from the 1982 theme of *trabalhador vota em trabalhador*, (worker voting for worker) and this broader-based profile gave the PT a surprisingly strong showing in local elections that year. The PT's success in 1985 (and again in 1986) showed the party it had a serious shot at winning elections, particularly local ones, if it continued to cultivate its citizenship and democracy rhetoric and its links to the middle class. PT leaders also understood, however, that the newfound emphasis on citizenship, democracy, and the middle classes, while aiding in the electoral arena, could also create tension between working class and middle class party constituents and privilege the party's more moderate social movement factions. This realization prodded the party leadership actively to coordinate the disparate demands of social movements and different classes so as to present a more unified position to the electorate.

The subtle shift in strategy was clear in the party's fifth national convention in 1987, when the PT acknowledged that in the past, it had "confused the autonomy and independence of the social movements with the absence of political proposals and direction" and thus had been unprepared to compete in the electoral domain (PT 1987, n.p.). Now, it was going to

> have to turn itself into the political director of the workers...this means that, while respecting the democracy of the movements and their particular characteristics, [the PT must] dispute the leadership of the movements with proposals previously debated within the PT, articulating our popular and union struggles with the construction of the party and our strategy in the struggle for power. (PT 1987, n.p.)

During the party conference, the class problematic also arose once again, this time in renewed discussion over the trade-offs between maintaining a working class emphasis in organization or rhetoric and the newfound prospects for electoral success in the upcoming 1988 local elections and the 1989 presidential race. Still, it was acknowledged that there was no historical precedent for a class transforming society without placing the state at its service (Sader and Silverstein 1991, 94; Gadotti and Pereira 1989, 132-138); and in pondering this dilemma, many party delegates called for continued alliance-building with the middle classes (especially rural and urban small business owners), as well as acknowledgment of the different political needs of different classes and social groups that could be accommodated by the PT if it recognized that all were struggling against forms of oppression (Sader and Silverstein 1991, 94-95).

After 1986, then, the PT trod carefully in its efforts to widen its class bases of support, preserve autonomy, and meet the institutional and electoral objectives of the party. This balancing act was apparent particularly in the positions taken during the 1987 Brazilian constitutional assembly. The PT declared that "it based its conception of a truly democratic society upon two fundamental pillars: the restoration of individual rights and guarantees and popular control over public power" (Sader and Silverstein 1991, 89). During the deliberations on the new constitution, the party did not abandon necessarily its socialist vision or working class orientation, maintaining that it spoke for society as a whole "based upon the wishes and demands that arise from those who constitute our reason for existence: the rural and city workers" (Sader and Silverstein 1991, 89). Yet again, much of the language the PT employed emphasized democracy, citizenship, individual rights, and popular participation. This time, too, the strategy brought remarkable gains in the elections of 1988 and 1989, particularly at the local level.

The Dilemma of Public Administration

Following its electoral gains in 1988 and 1989, however, the PT faced yet another serious problem that produced still a third shift in rhetorical emphasis and organizational strategy. Once the PT assumed office, particularly in major cities like São Paulo but also in smaller municipalities around the country, the challenges of public administration threatened the party's relationship to social movements and produced new tensions between middle and working classes. As a result, intraparty conflict flared over the competing goals of providing effective government for all constituents, pursuing direct democracy and economic redistribution, and maintaining a still-present but rhetorically deemphasized working class and socialist orientation. As Emir Sader and Ken Silverstein (1991, 99) put it, once the PT successfully came to power, its "own classism collided with the public nature of [its] administrations" so that "incoming [PT] mayors had difficulties administering the cities they controlled."

Because the party's ideological mandate made it most responsive to the demands of its poorest constituents, usually organized at the neighborhood level, PT administrators allotted much of their time and resources to highly localized services and projects that catered to only one segment of the population. Many municipal services that affected "the city as a whole — such as highway construction or central market renovation — were overlooked" (Abers 1994, 15). In consequence, members of the middle classes, who owned cars and whose other demands were also more likely to transcend locale, grew alienated. Complicating matters, the party's ideological commitment to popular participation and its social movement bases caused serious administrative problems (Sader and Silverstein 1991, 108), as PT elected officials found themselves on the receiving end of the particularistic (and often corporatist) demands of social movements unaccustomed to having their interests weighed against other social priorities. Moreover, it became obvious to many PT administrators that running a city required working relationships with the business community, service providers, and other sectors.

The practical exigencies of government soon tempered the party's plans to govern through the use of "popular councils" directly linking local movements and PT elected officials. By and large, local PT administrators ended movement participation in policymaking and instead began "implementing policies favoring the poor *before* meaningful participation in these programs could take place" (Abers 1994, 11). Yet these changes elicited an interminable debate within the party over the desired proportion of institutionalization (from above) relative to local legitimacy (from below). That is, efforts to modify the radical participatory conception of government — the *modo petista de governar* (Bitar 1992) — by delegating authority to administrators or negotiating with a wide range of conflicting interests generated dissatisfaction among the party's movement bases.[17]

PT administrators soon found it necessary to assert autonomy from both party and social movements in order to mediate effectively between all the competing demands and interests and formulate policy for their whole jurisdiction (Kowarick and Singer 1993, 205). Administrators' independence, however, further alienated the movements and also some party leaders, who decried what they called *administratismo* and the party's abandonment of the grassroots and larger socialist objectives. Moreover, the issue of party control that was so linked to these new problems of administration produced even more serious tensions among the different social bases of the party, as grassroots organizations found themselves shut out of decisionmaking and pitted against each other for scarce resources or political access.

The experience of Luiza Erundina, mayor of São Paulo, is revealing. Erundina opted for a managed-negotiation style of governance, directing an administration that sought autonomy from the popular councils and delegated political power to institutional mediators. In so doing, she generated widespread opposition from both public employee unions, affiliated with the militant PT-affiliated workers union (CUT), and women's and neighborhood organizations, linked to the semiautonomous popular movement wing of the party. When the public employee unions challenged Erundina's policies for giving priority to the consumption of public services over their production, the resulting strikes threw urban services into chaos. In the end, Mayor Erundina's popularity waned permanently, and her capacity to govern was questioned by working class militants, middle class groups, and social movements alike.

As spiraling intraparty tensions over the correct way to govern eroded party support, concern among PT leaders coalesced during the 1989 presidential campaign (Sader and Silverstein 1991, 137). The PT presidential candidate, Luis Inácio "Lula" da Silva, sought to reverse the damage by structuring campaign speeches around a popular-democratic project and virtually eliminating his public calls for socialism. He also used class-neutral language such as "the permanent participation of organized civil society" (Sader and Silverstein 1991, 134, 130), a discourse that allowed the party to continue couching its calls for the increased participation of excluded sectors in more universal and inclusive terms while avoiding some of the social movement-class tensions of earlier periods and keeping the specter of working class-middle class conflict at bay. This strategy, combined with the PT's reputation as an alternative party with a nontraditional political ethic, allowed it to garner enough votes to qualify for the run-off. In the second round, however, Lula lost to the conservative Fernando Collor de Mello, whose anti-communist rhetoric drew middle class support away from the PT. With Lula's defeat also attributed to the PT's electoral losses in São Paulo, a previous PT stronghold debilitated by intraparty conflict over Mayor Erundina's style of administration, the PT went back to the drawing board to plan its strategy for the next decade.

Where to Now?

Faced with intraparty conflict and a recent electoral defeat, in 1990 the PT ended its formal commitment to double militancy. To address further the growing split between the party's radical and reformist factions that had been exacerbated by efforts to balance ideology and grassroots participation with administrative pragmatism, it also reversed its earlier practice of allowing the various tendencies to "maintain separate internal discipline, newspapers, and finances while using the PT as a vehicle for mass organization and ideological struggle" (Sader and Silverstein 1991, 106). These changes allowed Lula and other reformist factions to prevail over the party's far-left, class struggle-oriented factions, and a centrist rhetorical line emerged at the next party congress in 1991. In articulating a strategy for the upcoming local elections and the 1994 presidential bid, PT congress delegates called for greater unity among the different social movements, a language and political project that would treat *workers as citizens* [author's emphasis], and a self-conscious "correction of errors" in popular democratic administrations that would allow elected PT officials to "combine the achievement of popular aspirations with a workers' struggle for the construction of socialism" (PT 1991, 10; Fernándes 1991, 13).

Nevertheless, an ambiguous mix of support for both new and old social movements persisted and so did internal conflicts within the party. The electoral consequences were disastrous. The party lost the city of São Paulo when Mayor Erundina lost her bid for reelection in 1992, despite her undeniable success in cleaning up public finances and dramatically improving health, education, and transportation services. Other significant defeats in São Paulo and elsewhere led the PT to try again to address the administrative and ideological tensions that were pitting new social movements against old and the party's militants against its elected officials.

With an eye to the 1994 presidential election, and a desire to stem intraparty conflicts, from 1993 on, PT discourse stressed ethics and public morality and linked them to questions of democracy. Party leaders calculated that this theme, which appeared at the 1991 party congress, would offer the PT the hope of capturing the moral high ground, since its officials generally earn clean reputations as administrators. This discourse, tied to action and not identity for the first time, tapped into public disgust with one of the most pressing problems in Brazilian party politics.

In addition to these ethical concerns, the PT also continued to emphasize the centrist and popular-democratic character of its program. This tone was evident in Lula's 1989 presidential campaign and now reappears in some of the party's social and economic policy positions. In the 1994 presidential campaign, Lula worked to "combat an image of leftist radicalism and to woo new supporters to his cause" through guarded support for partial privatization and prioritization of social service concerns such as transportation, housing, education, and health (de la Dehesa 1994b, 1). Lula even went on record claiming "the PT program never had a socialist approach," although this statement was followed by a qualification that stated that "since the meeting of February 1993, we managed to separate the Socialist utopia from the strategic program and from the government program" (de la Dehesa 1994b, 9). Clearly, Lula and the PT have staked a claim to a new cross-section of social and class groups, modifying rhetoric and objectives in the process.

So where will these discursive and policy shifts lead the PT, and what will be their impact on Brazilian politics and society? In mid-1994, Lula remained the front-runner in polls gauging support for presidential candidates, and surveys indicated his party as the first choice of 36 percent of Brazil's low-income populations and 41 percent of the nation's lower middle classes (*Latin America Monitor* 1994b, 2). However, a corruption scandal in the CUT, the PT-affiliated labor federation, tainted Lula specifically and the party in general (*Latin America Monitor* 1994a, 2; de la Dehesa 1994a, 7), casting a mortal blow to the theme of ethics and moral authority with which the PT replaced discourses of class and socialism.

Most important, despite — or perhaps because of — Lula's centrist campaign discourse, the PT remains deeply divided. According to press accounts (Veja 1994), almost 54 percent of the party has remained affiliated with factions — Opção de Esquerda (Left Option) and Na Luta PT (PT in the Struggle) — that represent the militant left and continue to push for a stronger commitment to socialism and class struggle. As of 1994, only 40 percent identified with the reformist factions (Unidade e Luta and Democracia Radical, which include Lula, ex-Mayor Erundina, and most members of Congress and municipal administrators) that make governance and electoral success their priorities. Not only have these two groups continued to disagree on discursive, organizational, administrative, and policy strategies, their existence exacerbated tensions between the new and old social movement bases of the party. The radicals relied heavily on working class *nucleos* of support and opposed economic liberalization, while the reformers cultivated ties with social movements in the locales they administer and were open to limited forms of economic liberalization. So, despite the shifting organizational strategies and party rhetorics, internal conflicts remain.

Of course, the PT has come far despite the conflict over languages of class and citizenship, party-social movement tensions, and administrative versus ideological priorities. Nonetheless, as Brazilian political culture evolves, other parties have not stood still. They too have successfully adopted the PT's strategies for dealing with social movements, while avoiding internal contention. Lula's most serious challenger, Fernando Henrique Cardoso of the PSDB, appealed effectively to the country's social movement constituents, couching his successful 1994 presidential campaign in languages of popular democracy and introducing his own "Caravan for citizenship" campaign, both of which hold the potential to eat into the PT's electoral bases. Moreover, by focusing his campaign almost exclusively on practical agencies of governance and on specific policy issues — especially those relating to the economy and its liberalization — Cardoso avoided controversial identity issues and class versus social movement tensions and thus generated widespread electoral support. The PT under Lula, while hoping to do the same, could not so easily transcend these issues and, therefore, still remains saddled with internal disagreements that limit its electoral appeal and its discursive and administrative capacity to manage the economy to the majority's liking.

The PT, in short, is still handicapped by its dual legacy of class militancy and social class accommodation, a paradoxical fate for a party that was among the most sincere and democratic in facing the challenges of new social movements, new identities, and new ways of doing politics. When considered next to the PRI, which has turned its capacity to sidestep these issues to its electoral and policy-making advantage, the PT's fate appears somehow unfair.

When New Social Movements Confront Old Party Structures

This comparison of the PRI and the PT reveals several common discursive and organizational transformations in party politics in contemporary Mexico and Brazil, each of which can be 'raced to the recent emergence of social movements as a key political force and to the parties' subsequent strategies to accommodate these movements while securing electoral power and maintaining administrative legitimacy. Regardless of each party's ideology, level of institutionalization, or commitment to internal democracy, and independent of the national political context (waning one-party rule versus nascent democratic competition), both parties responded similarly to social movements and the challenge of elections and governance. If only temporarily, they both publicly dropped "old" languages of class and began to target a wider variety of constituents using more universal languages of citizenship and other organizational and discursive strategies.

Much of the shift in emphasis can be traced largely to the nature and organization of social movements. Though they all have not necessarily abandoned class identities and concerns, many organize around single-issue concerns that by nature generate support from myriad class forces. Many have shunned class languages explicitly or at least consciously have avoided rhetorical or programmatic vestiges of corporatist party politics that use class-based organization or languages to co-opt and control. Many of the NSMs, moreover, have heralded the call for democracy, autonomy, popular participation, and citizenship rights, which further motivated both political parties to find new languages and new organizational bases for participation. As such, the PRI and the PT have distanced themselves from class discourses, especially to the extent that they seek a broader social and political basis for organization and action.

To win votes among increasingly influential groups that were neither organized nor self-identified in class terms, both parties introduced rhetorical and institutional reforms. In trying to tap into new, social movement constituencies, both parties also found themselves constrained or inspired by similar strategic objectives. They struggled to balance unity with diversity and participation with control and were forced to negotiate a complicated terrain of competing languages and identities. Moreover, both parties attempted continually to reform or reorganize themselves until they "got it right," so to speak; in this regard, NSM intransigence, especially when it came to insistence on autonomy or unwillingness to compromise with forces organized around class concerns, made both parties' jobs extraordinarily difficult.

Yet there are some very important differences in the two cases, especially in each party's willingness and capacity to accommodate both new and old social movements, and in the political impact of their actions. For example, the reforms undertaken by the PT and the PRI were historically bounded — that is, organizational and discursive transformations were fashioned as much by the success or failure of earlier reforms as by the exigencies of the time — so that each party's path unfolded, in a somewhat different fashion, according to its unique ideological and organizational starting point. Although in the first stages of reform both the PT and the PRI distanced themselves from languages of class and moved through a discourse of movements toward a preoccupation with citizenship, subsequent reforms took different paths. The sequence and content of these ensuing shifts reflected each party's peculiar history, ideology, and internal class or movement dynamics. Moreover, though both parties initially moved away from class and toward citizenship discourses, those citizenship discourses had different purposes.

In Brazil, languages of citizenship were motivated by electoral ambitions yet tempered by a commitment to class politics and society's most exploited populations. Hence, the rhetoric of citizenship always was infused with vocabularies of equality, access to power, social justice, and democracy. In Mexico, languages of citizenship were intended to extend the party's organizational tentacles while diffusing class politics and stifling popular power. Therefore, the PRI's citizenship rhetoric was infused with vocabularies of movement autonomy or participation in movements, not effective party participation or citizen involvement in a larger political project.

All of this suggests that the common appropriation of languages of citizenship in response to the challenge of social movements means little unless it is placed in context because similar terms can be imbued with different content, character, and purpose. Furthermore, it is important to consider the extent to which this language lasts or simply serves as a transitional or mediating discourse until the party recoordinates the discursive projects with the organizational structures and political objectives of its constituent bases. Rather than signaling a new political culture along the lines of Western liberal democracies, then, or a fundamental break from corporatist or neopatrimonialist past, as some are wont to claim, these cases may merely indicate the organizational limits of introducing languages of citizenship into social, political, and class contexts that require a much more coherent discourse or well thought-out political project.

To claim that languages of citizenship are transitional or mediating is not to say that they cannot last. In Brazil, even with the recent shift to languages of ethics, morality, and popular democracy, the discourse of citizenship still appears. And in Mexico, despite the PRI's newfound discursive appeals to the middle classes, public rhetoric is still often built around languages of citizenship. The point is that in both countries other more encompassing discourses are now salient. Citizenship rhetorics have shown themselves to be either partial or transitory, appropriated, dropped, or combined with other languages. In short, even though a language of citizenship may be a common party response to the rise of social movements, it is a generalized and fluid discourse used for many different purposes. Without an understanding of its historical roots or embeddedness in a political party's larger project, the emergence of citizenship discourses — just like democratic discourses, perhaps — tells little about society and politics. Indeed, while the proliferation of social movements may contribute to a shift toward citizenship in political discourses, whether or not such transformations are accompanied by greater democratization and social justice, whether they hurt or help movements themselves, whether they aid or hinder competitive party politics, or whether they signal inclusive or exclusive party structures will depend on the conditions under which parties construct and employ these languages.

That context and party objectives are crucial in determining the significance of citizenship and other movement-inspired discourses is illustrated by what followed each party's use of such languages. Mexico's PRI toyed with languages and organizational reforms emphasizing citizens and movements, then backtracked on the institutional incorporation of these forces. By resuming an emphasis on workplace identities, they organizationally isolated urban movements and citizen movements from other classes or social sectors, and by introducing a territorial base for political organization, which technically allowed almost anyone to participate without having to appropriate a common social or political identity, they pre-empted working-middle class tensions that could call into question the party's larger political project. As a result, the PRI was able to reduce its organizational and ideological commitment to working classes, urban movements, and other disenfranchised groups and focus on the middle classes instead. Mexico's PRI, in short, used discourses of citizenship to narrow its institutional and ideological contours, a move that has allowed it to achieve not only more middle class coherence in structure and rhetoric but also a stronger mandate to pursue to economic liberalization.

Though it also increased its electoral gains using languages of citizenship and an appeal to the middle classes, Brazil's PT took a different and more difficult path. After diminishing the rhetorics of class and socialism, at least publicly, and using citizenship as a common rallying cry for a time, the PT turned to a popular-democratic project and other discourses. The shift aimed to accommodate both working and middle classes without privileging one over the other. Thus, while in Mexico the shift to a focus on the middle classes was to substitute for a language and organization based on movements, in Brazil it was a byproduct of a linguistic and organizational shift that was intended to appeal to social movements, both citizen- and class-oriented. Rather than narrowing its discursive and organizational project, the PT widened its franchise by incorporating languages of citizenship along with a focus on popular power, popular identity, and the democratization of state and civil society. And while popular power and democratization were exactly what the PRI was trying to avoid when it eliminated the CNOP with its popular and inclusive character, in Brazil popular rhetorics were introduced precisely because they allowed the PT to appeal to middle classes while still maintaining a commitment to the working and lower classes.

How can one explain these differences and understand their larger implications? The depth of each party's commitment to internal party democracy is one obvious explanation. The PT was dedicated to developing democratic channels for party participation. Even when plagued with the difficulties of trying to balance substantive participation with efficient administration, the PT never abandoned its commitment to the grassroots. And even though its popular-democratic rhetoric brought in so many disparate forces as to make political participation unwieldy and the task of administration difficult, the party's links to the grassroots and its commitment to alternative politics were always as important as acquiring electoral power. Mexico's PRI, in contrast, has been concerned almost exclusively with maintaining control, either through electoral results or, when that fails, by sustaining enough legitimacy among strategic social forces to make a claim to power without overwhelming public reprisal. Internal party democracy, in any meaningful form, has been very low on the agenda of the PRI leadership. It is not that no one in the party cares about links to the grassroots, but the goal is generally legitimacy not popular participation or direct democracy. As a result, most of the reforms introduced by the PRI were created from the top down in order to target certain difficult populations, and this usually entailed narrowing the political bases for participation both rhetorically and organizationally.

Finally, the difference in commitment to internal democracy also helps explain why, after dispensing with citizenship and movement discourses, the PRI shunned languages of popular democracy, unlike the PT, and gravitated toward territorial political identities that fueled a middle class discourse.

However, it is not merely variations in commitment to democracy that explain the differences between Mexico's PRI and Brazil's PT, because in many ways these variations should be considered the product as much as the cause of differences. One also must take into account the parties' distinct institutional histories and the economic and political contexts in which they operate. The PT is still new; it has never held national power, and it is free of the corruption and self-serving practices that plague incumbent and overly institutionalized parties such as the PRI. Moreover, the PT derives its ideological stances — and its popularity in a tight, competitive political arena — from its commitment to balancing party, movement, and class concerns with progressive and egalitarian political projects and discourses. Without this commitment, it would lose much of what makes it distinctive and appealing.

The PRI, on the other hand, holds national power and for various reasons has invested its political capital in the successful liberalization of the economy, an objective more consistent with a narrow, middle class rhetoric. The PRI is not vying for a spot in power but rather trying to carry out past policy commitments without being thrown out of power. Each of these factors provided different incentives and constraints for the party's institutional and rhetorical responses to social movements. So too did the fact that the PRI had in place a three-tiered party structure that allowed it organizationally to separate its working class and social movement constituents and thus appeal to them independently. As such, it could avoid many of the problems the PT faced in finding a common discourse that could accommodate working classes, social movements, and middle classes equally.

Yet there is one final difference between the two parties that may lie at the heart of their divergent projects and organizational strategies, despite the common rhetoric. The PRI is and always has been a national party; its structures of organization and participation are geared toward maintaining national power, and its legitimacy always has been greater in national than local elections. This profile persists today, and although opposition parties of both the right and left have won numerous municipalities and some states, the PRI has remained a visible and surprisingly popular party on the national level, at least until recently.[18] Unlike the PRI, however, the PT has achieved some of its greatest successes on the local level. Having built its reputation as a locally based party of the grassroots, the PT made its way into national politics by slowly building its base in communities and municipalities. Thus, the PT is strong where the PRI is weak, and vice versa. Indeed, the PT has made great strides on the local level, and over the years, it has proved itself capable of connecting to the concerns of local constituencies well enough to help stake its claim to national power. In contrast, after years of bureaucratic centralization and armed with constituent sectors nationally organized around class identities that increasingly are unable to accommodate urban or other local problems and concerns, the PRI has found itself hard pressed to compete for power on the local level. Yet it is in these local — not national — domains where social movements in Mexico have made their greatest impact — hence, the party's actions to limit their involvement.

That the PRI has been preoccupied first with national power and the PT first with local politics also explains why the administrative objectives and ideological contours of the parties' shifting discourses have been so different. Because in Mexico the party-state has worried primarily about the national project of economic liberalization, it is particularly inclined to limit the participation of localized groups, urban social movements with community demands and other citizen groups with issue-specific concerns. The organizational and discursive transformations of the PRI were intended precisely to reduce the participation of locally based movements opposing the PRI's economic development objectives or public spending priorities. In appealing to the middle class and establishing a territorial basis for national politics, the PRI's objectives in this regard are met more easily. The PT, in contrast, because it sees itself as a locally based party, has worked hard to introduce organizational strategies, structures, and rhetorics that are responsive to its grassroots constituencies, particularly in the communities and cities where it is building power. For this reason, it is concerned with cultivating broad-based internal party democracy and keeping social movements involved. Yet because of these commitments, the PT has suffered through debilitating internal disputes over how to balance movement with party objectives and how to use elections and public administration to broaden its class bases of support.

In short, the PT's organizational and discursive path has differed from that of the PRI because of differences in their local and national objectives. Many of the PT's internal transformations have been motivated by its desire to accommodate the demands of local, community-based constituents (many of them NSMs), even if it cannot do so fully. The PRI's shifts, however, have been motivated by an attempt to distance itself from or control such local forces that the party increasingly finds institutionally and ideologically incapable of incorporating into its national political projects. The democratic limits and prospects for each party, then, are tied intricately to the capacity of each to accommodate locally based populations institutionally and discursively in larger party objectives, as well as to oversee local and national politics simultaneously.

Of course, parties should not take all of the credit or blame for the principal differences between the cases. One other key factor is that in Brazil, social movements have been more willing to work with parties for the larger political objective of institutionalizing democracy, while in Mexico, many social movements completely shunned negotiations with the party. This state of affairs helps explain why it was so easy for the PRI to dispense with a language and organization of movements and turn its focus to the middle classes.

There are obvious reasons why social movements in Mexico have avoided bargains with the PRI, most of them etched in the party's institutional history of co-optation and semi-authoritarian rule. Yet in Mexico, many social movements have shunned lasting alliances with all parties, even the left-leaning PRD, and this has been true at times even for class-based urban movements not just citizen-oriented ones. A principled position on autonomy, however, has not stopped some social movements from opportunistically using either the PRI or the PRD for achieving movement objectives (Bruhn 1994), and if anything, it played into the PRI's narrowing scope. Thus, social movements' diehard rejection of party collaboration may need a second look by both scholars and movement activists. Does it really serve the cause of social justice or democratization? Is it possible that such a stance may even facilitate a narrower political franchise focused on the more privileged to the exclusion of working classes and other disenfranchised forces?

The advantages and disadvantages of shunning party linkages and emphasizing movement autonomy could be reexamined in light of the Brazilian case, in particular, which shows that the difficult tasks of connecting movements to political parties and finding a place for rhetorics of class equality and movement autonomy can sometimes produce positive results, at least if the PT's greater popularity and widened social bases are any indicators. The key is for parties and movements to construct linkages and a common project together, as equal participants in a process. Granted, compromises are in order for all: Movements must soften their commitment to autonomy and not be entirely closed to class politics, just as party leaders must accept the fact that their capacities to govern, win elections, or make policy are diminished when their organizations become inclusive and participatory. However, such give-and-take is fundamental to a functioning democracy in a heterogeneous society. As parties accept some loss of ideological purity, administrative efficiency, or electoral security in order to keep themselves connected to the grassroots, new and old social movements have to work toward a "cooperative autonomy" (Sanyal 1994, 1991) that permits both antagonism and engagement with each other and with parties.

The debilitating divisions within the PT, especially as compared to the PRI's triumph in the 1994 elections, show that this is by no means an easy road. Indeed, the ascendance of social movement politics can test the patience of any political party, even one committed to the grassroots. But without conscientious efforts to coordinate or mediate their impact, social movements can all too easily — although inadvertently, perhaps — push parties away from a concern with the country's poorest and least privileged. The PT, to its credit, tried to work with movements to prevent this from happening. It is hoped that its and other parties' efforts in this regard will pay off, since it is in the trade-offs and the organizational and discursive underpinnings of social movement-party negotiations — not merely in the coherence of either's political and ideological projects or in capacities to achieve electoral or policy success — that democratic cultures and democratic politics are constructed.

Notes

1. For some of the most compelling work on the role of social movements in political development or democratization in Latin America, see Oxhorn 1995; Slater 1994; Jelin 1994, 1987, 1985; Assies 1994; Schild 1994; Kowarick 1993; Escobar and Alvarez 1992; Hellman 1994, 1992; Foweraker and Craig 1991; Eckstein 1989; Cardoso 1987; Lechner 1987; Mainwaring 1987; Touraine 1987; Scherer-Warren and Krischke 1987; Offe 1985; and Castells 1984.

2. Those who see economic dynamics as central in driving political and economic transitions include Sachs 1993, Przeworski 1991, Kaufman 1988, Nelson 1989, Singer 1989, and Smith 1989.

3. O'Donnell, Schmitter, and Whitehead (1986) have proposed that the resurgence of political party activity frequently corresponds with the *demobilization* of mass actors, and Philip Oxhorn, for example, argues that "the concepts of representation, participation, and interest aggregation upon which political parties are based are often at odds with the emphasis of popular movements on solidarity, direct participation, and consensus" (1994, 49). See also Alvarez 1990 and Cardoso 1992.

4. During his sexenio, President Salinas and the president of the PRI's Executive Committee, Luis Donaldo Colosio, gave speech after speech highlighting the new era into which Mexico was entering and the party's efforts to guarantee democracy, social justice, human rights, the "democratic associationalism" of citizen movements, and the fundamental reform of the state and its economic activities (PRI 1990, 7-9, 46).

5. The CNOP was founded in 1943 in order to incorporate dissatisfied public employees and urban social movements of the lower and middle classes (Davis 1994, 91-99).

6. Perhaps in acknowledgment of the recent literature on new social movements, UNE documents call associations of *colonos* "new social forces," despite the fact that they have been key members of the CNOP since its founding in 1943. On past incorporation of groups into the CNOP, on reforms in the sector's platform, or its recent internal restructurings, see Miguel Osorio Marbán 1994.

7. Party boss and CTM leader Fidel Velázquez did control the labor sector, preventing its internal democratization or opposition to neoliberal policies, but he was not going to live forever. More important, industrial workers had been leaving the CTM in droves for independent union movements that demanded internal democratization of unions and stridently opposed liberalization, while peasant mobilization against marketization was on the rise owing to the PRI leadership's intention to eliminate *ejidos*.

8. Many of the NSMs took on a working class orientation or closely allied themselves with workers' organizations or the leftist PRD, especially when Cuauhtémoc Cárdenas was a contender for the presidency (Bruhn 1994).

9. When the party was being formed, discussions among union leaders were opened to include dissident intellectuals, opposition politicians, representatives of social movements, activists from the Catholic Church, and members of clandestine leftist groups. There were sharp differences over the would-be party's identity. Some wanted to renovate the old Movimento Democrático Brasileiro (MDB); others urged a new "popular" party, and still others wanted to create a workers' party along explicit class lines. When forces supporting the third project prevailed, some of the more moderate participants left to form the Brazilian Democratic Movement Party (Partido do Movimento Democrático Brasileiro — PMDB) and the Democratic Workers' Party (Partido Democrático Trabalhista — PDT). These defections reinforced the PT's identity as a party with a narrower, more explicitly "classist" basis of organization, even though it was committed to grassroots organization and movement autonomy and the party itself "more closely resemble[d] a social movement" (Sader and Silverstein 1991, 3).

10. The founders of the PT struggled to differentiate the party both from traditional communist parties of the vanguardist left and from so-called populist labor parties (like the Brazilian Labour Party — PTB) that were tied to the patrimonialist and corporatist politics of the Brazilian state. Thus, the PT institutionally distanced itself from the two prevailing tendencies in the labor movement: the far, sectarian left bent on rigid class struggle and the more right-leaning, collaborationist labor movement that used populist rather than class rhetoric. One notable exception to this split was the Central Única De Trabalhadores [Central Union of Workers (CUT)], which at this early stage was also cultivating a third path apart from these extremes. Not surprisingly, the CUT and its debates played a central role in the foundation and organization of the PT, as they continue to do today.

11. One should make a distinction between internal and external languages, especially with respect to the tension between class and electorally oriented politics, though space prevents the adequate development of this distinction here. In the case of Brazil's PT, as with Mexico's PRI, I focus much more on so-called "external" languages: discourses of the party floated in the public domain after internal deliberation. While obviously linked to internal discourses, the public discourse generally down-played the tensions associated with different "tendencies" within the PT, in no small part because the party's most charismatic leader and high-profile spokesman, Lula, came from the tendency that emphasized unity and a national political project.

12. As Maria Herminia Tavares de Almeida (1987, 164) puts it, "the PT's stance on class was ambiguous, because its notion of what constituted the working class tended to be ambiguous. If some preferred a narrower definition of workers as blue collar workers, others pressed for a version that was broad enough to include all wage- and salary-earning employees. Not surprisingly, a compromise version emerged in which 'workers' were synonymous with the 'popular masses.'"

13. These are not neat dichotomies. Many of the PT's union bases were as concerned about the issue of autonomy as class identity, just as many of the "new" social movements viewed social phenomena through the lens of class. Nevertheless, there were two competing tendencies that played themselves out within particular movements and the party as a whole.

14. As noted by Sader and Silverstein (1991, 106), "competing forces inside the party make the PT's internal decision-making process extremely hectic. Public battles between factions and a large number of policy proposals sometimes project an image of organizational chaos." For further discussion of these various tendencies, sometimes called "basism" or referred to as factions, see Novaes (1993, 220) or Sader and Silverstein (1991, 104-107).

15. Again, the rhetorical shift to themes of popular democracy and citizenship did not mean that the party had abandoned its profile as an explicitly socialist party nor its allegiance to workers and the exploited masses. Socialism remained very much "on the horizon," and whether it required a rupture with the bourgeois state and classic forms of revolutionary confrontation or could be constructed "from within" through tactical negotiation and alliance-building with progressive and moderate sectors was now an even more critical point of debate. It was precisely discussion of the latter possibility that allowed the PT to use languages of democracy and citizenship while still retaining its commitment to socialism and its original working class supporters.

16. As noted in the text and corroborated by Sader and Silverstein (1991, 95-99, 105-106), the new language was not intended as a break from either movements or class, but rather signaled a shift in emphasis toward certain tendencies that had always been present in the party rhetoric.

17. The movements cared primarily about local services and community-level problems, while PT administrators, tied to the national party leadership, had a larger vision of the party's purpose and future and furthermore were severely restrained by fiscal difficulties. The rhetoric and organization of the PT pushed its elected officials to encourage social movement participation in municipal decisionmaking, leaving PT administrators to face "thousands of demands for public works and services, only a fraction of which could be accounted for with the funds available" (Abers 1994, 10). When only a handful of the movements could be accommodated, disillusionment and suspicion spread among those who were left out, and grassroots support declined dramatically.

18. Electoral fraud offers only a partial explanation for the PRI's continued strength at the national level. For various reasons, including the sectoral structure of the party, the nature of its development policies, and its revolutionary heritage, the PRI has been better able to maintain national legitimacy than local support. However, opposition on the local level has now reached such heights that the PRI's national legitimacy is fully under question (Davis 1994).

References

Abers, Rebecca. 1994. "The Partido dos Trabalhadores and Participatory Governance in Brazil." Unpublished manuscript, Department of Urban Planning, UCLA.

Alvarez, Sonia E. 1990. *Engendering Democracy in Brazil: Women's Movements in Transition Politics.* Princeton, N.J.: Princeton University Press.

Assies, Willem. 1994. "Urban Social Movements in Brazil." *Latin American Perspectives* 21, 2: 81-106.

Bitar, Jorge, ed. 1992. *O Modo Petista de Governar.* São Paulo: PT, Secretaria Nacional de Assuntos Institucionais.

Boschi, Renato. 1987. "Social Movements and the New Political Order in Brazil." In *State and Society in Brazil: Continuity and Change,* eds. John Wirth, et al. Boulder, Colo.: Westview Press.

Bruhn, Kathleen. 1994. "The Seven Month Itch. Neoliberal Politics, Popular Movements, and the Left in Mexico." Paper presented at the Columbia University Conference on Inequality and New Forms of Popular Representation in Latin America, March 3-5.

Cardoso, Fernando Henrique. 1987. "Democracy in Latin America." *Politics and Society* 15: 23-43.

Cardoso, Ruth Correa Leite. 1992. "Popular Movements in the Context of the Consolidation of Democracy." In *The Making of Social Movements in Latin America: Identity, Strategy and Democracy,* eds. Arturo Escobar and Sonia Alvárez. Boulder, Colo.: Westview Press.

Castells, Manuel. 1984. *The City and the Grassroots: A Cross-cultural Theory of Urban Social Movements.* Berkeley: University of California Press.

Confederación Nacional de Organizaciones Populares (CNOP). 1990. *Construyendo una nueva organización política.* México, D.F.: PRI.

Davis, Diane E. 1994. *Urban Leviathan: Mexico City in the Twentieth Century.* Philadelphia: Temple University Press.

Davis, Diane E. 1990. "Urban Social Movements, Intra-state Conflict over Urban Policy, and Political Change in Contemporary Mexico." In *Breaking Chains: Social Movements and Collective Action,* ed. Michael Peter Smith. Beverly Hills and London: Sage Publications.

De la Dehesa, Rafael. 1994a. "Workers Party Under Scrutiny: CPI to Investigate Illegal Financing by Union." *INFOBRAZIL* 15, 2: 7.

De la Dehesa, Rafael. 1994b. "Workers Party Finds its Center: But as Lula Faces New Challenger, Will He Miss the Mark?" *INFOBRAZIL* 15, 3: 1-9.

Dresser, Denise. 1991. *Neopopulist Solutions to Neoliberal Problems: Mexico's National Solidarity Program.* La Jolla, Calif.: Center for U.S.-Mexican Studies.

Eckstein, Susan, ed. 1989. *Power and Popular Protest: Latin American Social Movements.* Berkeley: University of California Press.

Escobar, Arturo, and Sonia Alvarez, eds. 1992. *The Making of Social Movements in Latin America: Identity, Strategy, and Democracy*. Boulder, Colo.: Westview Press.

Fernándes, Florestan. 1991. *O PT em Movimiento*. São Paulo: Cortéz Editora.

Foweraker, Joe, and Ann Craig, eds. 1991. *Popular Movements and Political Change in Mexico*. Boulder, Colo.: Westview Press.

Gadotti, Moacir, and Otaviano Pereira. 1989. *Pra que PT: Origem, Projeto e Consolodição do Partido dos Trabalhadores*. São Paulo: Cortéz Editora.

Hellman, Judith Adler. 1994. "Mexican Popular Movements, Clientelism, and the Process of Democratization." *Latin American Perspectives* 21, 2: 124-139.

Hellman, Judith Adler. 1992. "The Study of New Social Movements in Latin America and the Question of Autonomy." In *The Making of Social Movements in Latin America: Identity, Strategy, and Democracy*, eds. Arturo Escobar and Sonia Alvarez. Boulder, Colo.: Westview Press.

Hernández, S. Ricardo. 1987. *La Coordinadora Nacional del Movimiento Urbano Popular (CONAMUP): Su historia, 1980-1986*. México, D.F.: Equipo Pueblo.

Jelin, Elizabeth. 1994. "The Politics of Memory: The Human Rights Movement and the Construction of Democracy in Argentina." *Latin American Perspectives* 21, 2: 38-59.

Jelin, Elizabeth. 1987. *Movimentos sociales y democracia emergente*. Buenos Aires: Centro Editor de América Latina.

Jelin, Elizabeth. 1985. *Los nuevos movimientos sociales*. Buenos Aires: Centro Editor de América Latina.

Kaufman, Robert R. 1988. *The Politics of Debt in Argentina, Brazil, and Mexico: Economic Stabilization in the 1980s*. Berkeley: Institute of International Studies, University of California.

Keck, Margaret. 1992. *The Workers Party and Democratization in Brazil*. New Haven, Conn.: Yale University Press.

Kowarick, Lúcio. 1993. *Social Struggles and the City*. New York: Monthly Review Press.

Kowarick, Lúcio, and Andre Singer. 1993. "A Experiência do Partido dos Trabalhadores na Prefeitura de São Paulo." *Novos Estudos CEBRAP* 35: 195-216.

Krischke, Paulo J. 1984. "Os Loteamentos Clandestinos e os Dilemas e Alternativas Democráticas dos Movimentos de Bairro." In *Terra de Habitação, Terra de Espoliação*, ed. Paulo J. Krischke. São Paulo: Cortéz Editora.

Latin America Monitor-Brazil. 1994a. "PMDB Candidate May Gain Ground," 2, 7 (July): 2.

Latin America Monitor-Brazil. 1994b. "LULA consolidates lead," 2, 6 (June): 2.

Lechner, Norbert, ed. 1987. *Cultura política y democratización*. Buenos Aires: Consejo Latinoamericana de Ciencias Sociales.

Loaeza, Soledad. 1985. "Las clases medias mexicanas y la coyuntura económica actual." In *México ante la crisis: El impacto social/las alternativas*, ed. Pablo González Casanova. México, D.F.: Siglo Veintiuno Editores.

Mainwaring, Scott. 1987. "Urban Popular Movements, Identity, and Democratization in Brazil." *Comparative Political Studies* 20, 20: 131.

Nelson, Joan. 1989. "Crisis Management, Economic Reform, and Costa Rican Democracy." In *Debt and Democracy in Latin America*, eds. Barbara Stallings and Robert Kaufman. Boulder, Colo.: Westview Press.

NOTIMEX Mexican News Service. 1990. August 29.

Novaes, Carlos Alberto. 1993. "PT: Dilemas da Burocratização." *Novos Estudos CEBRAP* 35.

O'Donnell, Guillermo, Philippe Schmitter, and Laurence Whitehead, eds. 1986. *Transitions from Authoritarian Rule.* Baltimore: Johns Hopkins University Press.

Offe, Claus. 1985. "New Social Movements: Challenging the Boundaries of Institutional Politics." *Social Research* 52, 4: 817-869.

Osorio Marbán, Miguel. 1994. *El sector popular del PRI.* México, D.F: Coordinación Nacional de Estudios Históricos, Políticos y Sociales del CEN del PRI.

Oxhorn, Philip. 1994. "Where Did all the Protestors Go? Popular Mobilization and the Transition to Democracy in Chile?" *Latin American Perspectives* 21, 3: 49-69.

Oxhorn, Philip. 1995. *Organizing Civil Society: The Popular Sectors and the Struggle for Democracy in Chile.* University Park, Pa.: Penn State Press.

PT (Partido dos Trabalhadores). 1991. *Resoluções do I Congreso do PT.* São Paulo: PT.

PT (Partido dos Trabalhadores). 1987. *Resoluções do VI Encontro Nacional.* São Paulo: PT.

PRI (Partido Revolucionario Institucional). 1990. *UNE, Ciudadanos en Movimiento: Estatutos.* México, D.F.: PRI.

PRI. 1991. *UNE, Ciudadanos en Movimiento: Documentos básicos.* México, D.F.: PRI.

PRI. 1984. *Historia documental de la CNOP.* Vols. I, II, III. México, D.F.: Edicap.

PRI. 1993. *Frente Nacional de Organizaciones y Ciudadanos UNE: XII Asamblea Nacional, Documentos de Trabajo.* México, D.F.: PRI.

Perlo, Manuel, and Marta Schteingart. 1984. "Movimientos sociales urbanos en México." *Revista Mexicana de Sociología* 46: 105-127.

Przeworski, Adam. 1991. *Democracy and the Market: Political and Economic Reforms in Eastern Europe and Latin America.* Cambridge: Cambridge University Press.

Ramírez Saiz, Juan Manuel. 1986. *El movimiento urbano popular en México.* México City: Siglo Veintiuno Editores.

Sachs, Jeffrey. 1993. *Poland's Jump to the Market Economy.* Cambridge, Mass.: MIT Press.

Sader, Emir, and Ken Silverstein. 1991. *Without Fear of Being Happy: Lula, the Workers Party, and Brazil.* London: Verso Press.

Sanyal, Bish. 1994. *Cooperative Autonomy: The Dialectic of State-NGO Relations in Developing Countries.* Geneva: International Institute of Labor Studies.

Sanyal, Bish. 1991. "Antagonistic Cooperation." *World Development* 19, 10: 1367-1379.

Scherer-Warren, Ilse, and Paulo J. Krischke, eds. 1987. *Uma Revolução no Cotidiano? Os Novos Movimentos Sociais na América do Sul.* São Paulo: Brasilense.

Schild, Veronica. 1994. "Recasting 'Popular' Movements: Gender and Political Learning in Neighborhood Organizations in Chile." *Latin American Perspectives* 21, 2: 59-81.

Singer, Paul. 1989. "Democracy and Inflation, in the Light of the Brazilian Experience." In *Lost Promises: Debt, Austerity, and Development in Latin America,* ed. William Canak. Boulder, Colo.: Westview Press.

Slater, David. 1994. "Power and Social Movements in the Other Occident: Latin America in an International Context." *Latin American Perspectives* 21, 2: 11-38.

Smith, William C. 1989. "Heterodox Shocks and the Political Economy of Democratic Transition in Argentina and Brazil." In *Lost Promises: Debt, Austerity, and Development in Latin America*, ed. William Canak. Boulder, Colo.: Westview Press.

Tavares de Almeida, Maria Herminia. 1987. "Novo Sindicalismo and Politics in Brazil." In *State and Society in Brazil: Continuity and Change*, eds. John Wirth, et al. Boulder, Colo.: Westview Press.

Touraine, Alain. 1987. *Actores sociales y sistemas políticos en América Latina.* Santiago, Chile: PREALC/OIT.

Veja. 1994. "O PT Brilha e Tambêm Mete Medo: Como é o Partido que Empurra a Caravana de Lula, Promova Agitação e Está na Frente nas Pesquisas." June 15, 38-45.

Weffort, Francisco. 1992. "The Future of Socialism." *Journal of Democracy* 2: 90-100.

Weffort, Francisco. 1984. *Por que Democracia?* São Paulo: Brasiliense.

Chapter 9

The Party or the Grassroots: A Comparative Analysis of Urban Political Participation in the Caribbean Basin[1]

Alejandro Portes and José Itzigsohn

Introduction

The purpose of this study is to examine the patterns of political participation and attitudes toward different forms of participation of urban low-income groups in five Caribbean Basin capital cities. Contemporary forms of popular participation in the Caribbean and, more generally, in Latin America represent major departures from the political experiences of this region in the past. These patterns are also at variance with the ways in which popular political participation is conceptualized in the advanced countries. The analysis of these novel trends and their determinants can cast light on processes so far unexplored in the contemporary literature on social movements.

The emergence of what are known in Latin America as the "new social actors" took established political parties in the region, as well as political analysts, by surprise. These "new actors" comprise a wide variety of community and grassroots popular organizations that have emerged spontaneously out of the needs of their respective constituencies and that, for the most part, have avoided entanglement with the traditional political organizations. Despite their dislike of "politics as usual," these grassroots organizations have come to play an increasingly important role in both local and national affairs through their organized demand-making, mass protests, and electoral support of like-minded figures (Jelin 1985). In Peru, for example, community organizations have eclipsed traditional political parties during the last two national elections, and in Colombia, a number of grassroots human rights organizations have appeared to provide a measure of protection for human rights and against widespread violence (Fals Borda 1992).

This chapter will examine the extent of actual community grassroots participation among the populations of five Caribbean capital cities as well as the attitudes held toward them. It will explicitly contrast this mode of participation with traditional political parties and will analyze the factors leading to different forms of participation. The analysis will highlight the significance of different political systems and state policies in promoting or deactivating popular mobilization, a factor commonly neglected in studies of the topic in the First World. In the advanced democracies, the overarching institutional framework within which participation takes place is generally taken for granted. Since Seymour Lipset's *Political Man* (1963), the analytic focus of studies of popular participation has concentrated on variables at the individual level such as class membership, level of education, gender, and family status that are theorized as key determinants of participation. Under the influence of rational choice theory, recent empirical work in this area has focused on the "free-rider" problem of collective movements and more generally on the individualistic calculus of rewards and costs that is assumed to underlie participatory decisions (Hechter 1987, Przeworski 1985, Nielsen 1986).

Quite different is the situation of Third World countries where a range of political regimes — from relatively stable democracies to repressive dictatorships — plays a decisive role in the character and extent of popular political participation. The constraints imposed by the polity, allied to the hardships of economies of scarcity, often have led to innovative and vigorous forms of grassroots organization where the "problem" of free-riding and others of a similar bent, prominent in the research literature of the advanced democracies, are moot (Portes and Johns 1989). The principal contribution of the following analysis is to bring into play both individualistic and national-level (political system) variables as potential determinants of the observed differences in actual participation and sympathy for community-based organizations. In order to accomplish this, it is necessary to examine such processes in a comparative framework involving a number of political systems.

Theoretical Background

The literature on Latin American urban movements has undergone a remarkable transformation since the days in which most writings on the topic emphasized the "urban explosion" and the widespread revolutionary fervor of the impoverished masses (Beyer 1967, Ward 1964). These theories were prompted less by direct observation of the behavior of the alleged radical groups than by the expectations of middle-class observers as to the political behavior appropriate for people living under such abysmal economic conditions. The vicarious imputation of seething fury to the "marginal mass," as urban popular groups were then labeled, found ample resonance in the printed media but precious few instances of empirical support. To the contrary, study after study weighed in with a very different portrayal of political behavior among urban low-income sectors.

According to these studies, shantytown dwellers in Latin America were not about to lay siege to the cities that they surrounded in part because they were so preoccupied with their own survival. Instead of the dramatic instances of popular radicalism anticipated by journalistic and scholarly publications, researchers in the field found diverse and creative adaptations to the existing social order. These adaptations did include popular mobilizations and demand-making but always within the bounds of established political parameters and always focused on specific goals (Leeds 1969, Mangin 1967, Eckstein 1977). This syndrome of "rational adaptation" to existing social and political conditions (Portes and Walton 1976, 109-110) included participation in traditional parties and effective manipulation of electoral politics for community advantage.

The research literature that put to rest the myth of mass radicalism did not anticipate, however, that the adaptability of popular groups would go beyond taking part in existing political organizations. The shift toward new innovative forms of participation started in the 1970s and gathered momentum in the 1980s, in response to the rise of highly repressive authoritarian regimes, followed by a severe economic downturn. In Latin America, the debt-induced economic crisis led to a halt and then a reversal of economic development, as country after country registered negative growth rates during the early 1980s. This decline, the worst since the Great Depression, was experienced with particular force among the low-income sectors (Iglesias 1985, Lagos and Tokman 1983, CEPAL 1990, PREALC 1990). During the 1970s and early 1980s, the situation was made worse by military dictatorships in many countries that blocked all institutionalized channels for the expression of grievances (Lehman 1990, Tironi 1986).

In response, shantytown dwellers and other working class groups began to create their own community-based organizations for survival and for the gradual expansion of alternative spaces for making demands. To avoid repression, they resolutely shunned contact with the existing political parties and rallied instead around unimpeachable values: children's health and education, mothers' need for care, access to basic food staples, shelter, and protection from crime (Cardoso 1983). Unlike trade unions, community organizations did not coalesce around workplaces as many of their members were jobless, but rather organized on the basis of common places of residence (Razeto 1985, Schkolnik 1986, Friedmann 1989). These neighborhood-based groups — mothers' associations, youth centers, self-help housing coopera-tives, communal kitchens, and so forth — proved so successful that not only did they endure the military dictatorships of the 1970s, but they contributed effectively to their demise and then proceeded to expand to city-wide and national levels (Campero 1987, Hardy 1987, Matos Mar 1985).

At this point, however, the literature on the "new social actors" became bifurcated into those authors who saw their growth as a sign of a qualitative shift in the relationship between civil society and the state and those who perceived them as no more than an innovative popular response to unusually difficult political conditions. Manuel Castells (1983), David Slater (1985), and John Friedmann and Mauricio Salguero (1988) echoed the optimism of local social scientists, particularly in Chile, who regarded these new self-reliant community groups as the building blocks for the emergence of a truly democratic society. Others like Susan Eckstein (1989), Alejandro Portes and Michael Johns (1989), and Ruth Cardoso (1992) were less sanguine about the transformative capacity of grassroots movements and viewed their growth as dependent on the spaces of opportunity created by the dominant political system. Contrary to the most enthusiastic exponents of the first position, who portrayed community-based movements as a new global wave transcending national differences, this second school regarded popular participation in these new movements as contingent on both individual-level variables and the national polity.

The literature on the new social movements encompasses different types of social phenomena. Two types of social movements are broadly distinguishable. On one hand, there are those social movements that organize poor communities around collective consumption demands such as housing or health. On the other hand, there are those movements engaged in politics of identity or the fight for human rights and the rights of particular groups, such as feminism, gay rights movements, and others. The latter movements tend to have a larger, although not exclusive, middle class character (Jelin 1994, Melucci 1991). This work focuses on the attitudes about political participation of the popular sectors, hence it deals mainly with the first type of social movement.

The Latin American literature on the new social actors and the theoretical controversies surrounding it provide the context for this analysis of popular political participation. Instead of formal hypotheses, key points of the above discussion are summarized in the following four questions:

1. What is the real extent of participation of urban popular sectors (defined below) in grassroots organizations versus traditional political parties?

2. What are the attitudes of these popular sectors toward both forms of participation?

3. To what extent are political attitudes and participation influenced by individual-level variables, such as those emphasized by the collective movement literature in the advanced countries?

4. To what extent are political attitudes and participation influenced by cross-national differences in political systems and, in particular, the character of the state?

Data and Method

The data for this study come from surveys conducted simultaneously in the capital cities of five Caribbean Basin countries during 1992. The countries selected were Costa Rica, Guatemala, the Dominican Republic, Haiti, and Jamaica. They comprise the largest island-nations of the Caribbean (with the exception of Cuba), the largest Central American nation, and encompass the most diverse political systems in both subregions. The five countries share a number of characteristics as part of the same broadly defined geographical area. These include their uniformly small size, the high concentration of the urban population in a single city, their proximity to the United States, and the profound dependence of their economies on the U.S. market. They are all members and beneficiaries of the Caribbean Basin Initiative (CBI).[2]

The Caribbean Basin was targeted for this study because of its geopolitical and economic importance as part of the immediate southern periphery of the United States and because of the extraordinary variety of political and economical systems encompassed in a relatively small area. The region includes the poorest and most politically unstable country in the hemisphere (Haiti) and the most stable democracy south of the U.S. border (Costa Rica). It also includes democratic parliamentary systems in the British model (exemplified by Jamaica) and military-dominated autocracies in the traditional Latin American mold (represented by Guatemala). These vast differences are directly relevant to the topic of study because they will allow a direct examination of the extent to which popular political participation in its alternative forms is affected by the national political system, controlling for individual-level variables. Table 1 presents a brief sociopolitical profile of the five countries included in the analysis. Although space precludes a detailed discussion of their histories, a brief outline of their respective political systems is necessary to clarify the character of their potential influence on popular participation:

- Costa Rica ranks as one of the most democratic countries on the continent in which the state guarantees human and civil rights and encourages citizen participation in electoral politics through the established parties. Although not actively encouraged by the state, community-based organizations are flourishing and, as legal groups, are granted ready access to the authorities (Lungo, Perez, and Piedra 1991; Vargas 1992).

- Guatemala is at the other extreme with a history of repression of popular organizations dating back to the CIA-sponsored overthrow of the elected Jácobo Arbenz government in 1954. Since that time, political life has been dominated by an alliance between the armed forces and an entrenched economic elite. Paramilitary death squads have been used liberally to intimidate and eliminate opponents of the existing order. Although two successively elected presidents provided a semblance of democracy during the 1980s, the country is still politically unstable and continues to be dominated by the same elite/ military alliance. Violations of human and civil rights are still widespread (Jonas 1991, Pérez-Sáinz 1991).

- The Dominican Republic is an incipient democracy with a strong presidentialist regime. Since the U.S.-led invasion of the country to thwart a leftist takeover in 1964, the country has been governed by democratically elected presidents. Dominican political life has been dominated during the last two decades by the figure of Joaquin Balaguer, elected repeatedly as president. Under his administrations, political parties have been allowed to compete openly, and the influence of the military on the government has waned. Although civil rights violations are still common, the situation has improved significantly. Community-based organizations are legal and are seldom interfered with (Lozano and Duarte 1991, Dore-Cabral 1985).

- Neighboring Haiti continues its turbulent political life with a brief hiatus of democracy under President Jean Bertrand Aristide. As in Guatemala, an alliance of the armed forces with an entrenched economic elite has made use of any means to preserve its power. Death squads, known locally as Tonton Macoutes, have been systematically used to intimidate and do away with opponents. The Aristide electoral campaign gained widespread popular support, and his election further stimulated popular mobilizations in hopes of transforming the old political order. After the coup that ousted Aristide, there was a sustained campaign by the military to deactivate community organizations and repress opposition parties (Manigat 1992, Trouillot 1990). At the time of this writing, international pressure has forced the military and traditional elites to acquiesce to Aristide's return, but the future of his U.N.-backed government is quite uncertain.
- The Jamaican parliamentary system is a legacy of the British colonial period. There has been an uninterrupted succession of democratically elected administrations, but elections are frequently marred by fraud and widespread violence. The two parties that alternate in power — the Jamaican Labor Party (JLP) and the People's National Party (PNP) — have large popular followings. However, armed gangs belonging to the two parties frequently stage violent confrontations in Kingston's shantytowns and other urban areas, leading to a climate of widespread fear and instability (Gordon and Dixon 1991, Pinkow 1993).

Data collection for this study was conducted by local research teams under senior social scientists in each of the five selected cities. "Popular sectors" were defined operationally as those living in low-income areas of each city. To provide enough socioeconomic variation in the sample, sampled neighborhoods ranged from government housing projects and other areas with a population composed primarily of lower middle-income government employees and formal workers to peripheral shantytowns, where most inhabitants survive through work in the informal economy. Budgetary limitations prevented the organization of city-wide surveys; instead, neighborhoods deemed representative of the lower-middle to poor sectors in each city were selected for the study. Within each neighborhood, dwellings were selected with a probability proportional to total size, and in each dwelling the household head was interviewed.

Four hundred interviews in three or four popular neighborhoods were conducted in San José (Costa Rica), Santo Domingo (Dominican Republic), and Guatemala City. In Kingston, the final sample reached 800 because it was necessary to cover the low-income population of the city itself and of the vast suburbs in the adjacent St. Catherine's Plain. In Port-au-Prince, a planned survey of three low-income areas was cut short by the coup that ousted President Aristide. The local research team managed, however, to complete a total of 300 interviews in these areas, mostly before the coup. The full sample thus consists of 2,300 cases in five cities. The same questionnaire — translated

Table 1.
Characteristics of Countries Selected for Study in 1991-1992

	Total Population¹ (000s)	Urban Population² %	Gross Domestic Product (Million constant 1980 US$)	Gross Domestic Product per Capita (constant 1980 US$)	Total Exports (Million US$)	Principal Sources of Foreign Exchange 1989 %	Political Regime 1991
Costa Rica	3,191	53.6	4,488.1	1,442	1,974.0	Coffee (15.5) Bananas (15.4) Tourism (11.5)	Stable Democracy
Dominican Republic	7,471	60.4	7,731.6	1,056	1,980.4	Tourism (41.7) Ferronickel (17.3) Sugar (9.0)	Incipient Stable Democracy
Guatemala	9,745	42.0	8,762.0	925	1,687.2	Coffee (26.7) Tourism (7.6) Sugar (6.5)	Unstable Restricted Democracy
Haiti	6,754	30.3	1,317.3	199	249.6	Assembled Goods (46.2) Tourism (29.5) Coffee (14.6)	Military Dictatorship
Jamaica	2,469	52.3	3,204.0	1,311	2,225.7	Alumina and Bauxite (31.1) Tourism (31.5) Assembled Goods (9.1)	Stable Parliamentary Democracy

Sources: Economic Commission for Latin America and the Caribbean 1992. Tables 5, 103, 112, 182, 184, 233, 244, 248, 251, 254. *Encyclopaedia Britannica* 1991. Britannica World Data, Nations of the World.

1 = Estimates.

2 = Urban population is defined according to national criteria.

into Spanish, English, and Haitian Creole — was applied in all city surveys to insure the comparability of results.[3] The questionnaire included items on sex, marital status, migratory status, education, occupation, income, and class self-identification. Also included were membership in political parties, participation in community-based organizations, and attitudes toward both forms of political action. The last set of items comprises the dependent variables in the following analysis; the first set comprises the individual-level predictors whose effects vis-à-vis national political systems will be evaluated below.

Preliminary Results

Preliminary tabulations of survey results reveal an interesting pattern of variation both across dependent variables and across countries. The emphasis placed on grassroots organizations as the favored form of popular political expression by the recent Latin American literature is not borne out by these results. As Table 2 shows, reported membership in any kind of community organization represents a tiny minority, hovering around 10 percent in most countries and in the full sample. On the other hand, participation in established political parties reaches almost half (47 percent) of the combined sample. This figure is inflated by results for Kingston, Jamaica, where almost all respondents are members of one of the two main parties. However, in the other two democracies — Costa Rica and the Dominican Republic — participation in party politics far exceeds that in community-based associations.[4]

There are notable differences between these countries and the remaining two. In Guatemala and Haiti, both long governed by military dictatorships or military-controlled civilian regimes, party membership among popular groups is minimal. This absence of participation is not compensated by grassroots organizations since participation in them is also very low. This general pattern of popular demobilization and apathy is also apparent in the attitudinal questions, especially in the Guatemalan sample.

There is a significant reversal between political behavior and attitudes toward parties and grassroots organizations. As shown in the next rows of Table 2, majorities in all countries support community organizations as "true representatives of the popular will" and believe that more power should be vested in them.[5] In four of the five countries and in the total sample, these proportions are significantly higher than those supporting party politics. The single exception is Haiti, but in this case the difference between the two figures is not statistically significant.[6]

The greater sympathy for community organizations among the respondents is still more evident in the last rows of Table 2. They present the distribution of responses to a forced-choice item about how hypothetical inhabitants of a popular neighborhood spend their free time. With the exception of Guatemala, majorities in all countries endorsed the option of joining a community organization to "improve the neighborhood." In the full sample, two-thirds supported this alternative, while less than 10 percent opted for joining a party to "resolve the problems of this city." The Haitian and

Table 2.
Participation and Attitudes toward Party Politics and Community Grassroots Organizations in the Caribbean Basin, 1992

	Country					
Variable	**Costa Rica** %	**Dominican Republic** %	**Guatemala** %	**Haiti** %	**Jamaica** %	**Totals** %
1. Belongs to a Political Party						
	(40.0)[1]	21.3	4.0	4.0	98.1	47.0[2]
2. Belongs to a Community Organization[3]						
	12.5	11.4	4.5	12.0	2.3	7.3
3. Supports Participation in Party Politics						
	58.5	59.8	21.3	60.7	41.4	46.6
4. Supports Community Grassroots Organizations						
	74.5	87.1	65.8	55.0	86.0	76.6
5. Believes Community Organizations Can Accomplish:						
a. Nothing[4]	48.5	46.9	71.8	76.0	39.5	52.8
b. Something	28.3	36.2	21.0	21.3	44.1	32.9
c. A Great Deal	23.2	16.9	7.2	2.7	16.4	14.3
6. Best Use of Free Time Is:						
a. To Join a Political Party						
	7.5	12.9	3.3	8.0	6.8	7.5
b. To Join a Community Organization						
	62.3	60.3	45.8	54.7	83.8	65.5
c. To Remain at Home						
	30.2	26.8	50.9	37.3	9.4	28.0
N	400	403	400	300	792	2,295

1 = Estimate based on other published sources. See text.
2 = Weighted average, excluding Costa Rica.
3 = Missing cases classified as non-participants.
4 = Includes "don't know" responses.
N = Total number of respondents in each country.

Guatemalan sample had the highest proportion of respondents opting for the do-nothing option ("Remain at home"). The apathy toward popular partici-pation in these countries is again evident in the distribution of responses to another item inquiring how much community organizations can accomplish for their members. About 70 percent of Guatemalans and Haitians did not know or believed that community organizations could accomplish nothing; the corresponding figure among respondents in the three democratic coun-tries was less than 50 percent.[7]

These preliminary results show, first, a remarkable gap between theoretical expectations about the extent of popular involvement with the "new social actors" and actual participation in this type of organization. Second, they indicate an equally notable gap between verbal endorsements of these grassroots movements and involvement in them. Third, they demonstrate major disparities across countries in a pattern supportive of past theorizing on the effects of national political systems on popular mobilization (Leeds 1969, Portes and Walton 1976). However, this last conclusion must be tested against the real possibility that differences among national samples are a spurious result due to their different age, sex, educational, and occupational profiles. The following section examines this alternative.

Determinants of Participation

Despite the observed gap between attitudes and behavior, the two are not uncorrelated. Table 3 presents coefficients of association between party and community group participation and indices of attitudes toward the two forms of activism in the entire sample and in each individual country.[8] Results show positive and significant associations between each attitudinal index and the respective behavior and, with the partial exception of Haiti, higher correlations of attitudes and behavior within each type of political participa-tion than between them.[9] These results may be interpreted as supportive of the internal consistency and validity of the data rather than as indicative of causal direction. In a cross-sectional survey such as this, it is not possible to infer that statements of opinion "cause" behavior rather than vice versa. Instead, the following analysis treats political attitudes and reported partici-pation as separate dependent variables and cross-tabulates them against the individual-level predictors available for the sample.

Table 4 reveals wide variations by individual characteristics, especially in the attitudinal dimensions. Endorsement of community organizations is stronger among the better-educated and better-paid. It is also higher among workers (both formal and informal)[10] than among the unemployed and self-employed and higher among individuals who identify themselves as members of the working class. Interestingly, participation in political parties is also supported by the more educated and affluent although, in this instance, there are no statistically significant differences by type of occupation or class identification. Instead, ascriptive characteristics come into play with men being significantly more likely to endorse political party activism than women and the young more than the old.

Table 3.
Zero-order Correlations of Attitudes and
Participation in Political Parties and
Grassroots Community Organizations, 1992

		Attitudes toward:	
Country	Membership in:	Political Parties[1]	Community Organizations[2]
Costa Rica	Political Party	—	—[3]
	Community Organization	0.026	0.272*
Guatemala	Political Party	0.375**	0.049
	Community Organization	0.093	0.216*
Dominican Republic	Political Party	0.303**	0.029
	Community Organization	0.079	0.203*
Haiti	Political Party	0.276**	-0.019
	Community Organization	0.226**	0.187*
Total	Political Party	0.332**	0.107**
	Community Organization	0.127**	0.225**

1 = Summated index of positive responses to items 3 and 6a in Table 2.
2 = Summated index of positive responses to items, 4, 5, and 6b in Table 2. Item 5 was dichotomized as "nothing" versus "something/a great deal."
3 = Question about party membership omitted in the San José survey.
* = p < .01
** = p < .001

The data also reveal much less variation in actual participation in community groups that turns out to be quasi-constant across the entire sample. Neither gender nor age, occupation, income, or class identification lead to differential rates of community grassroots participation. There is only a slight positive relationship with education, but it is statistically nonsignificant. Political party membership is strongly affected, on the other hand, by several individual characteristics. Better educated people are much more likely to take part in this type of activity; this statistical association is the strongest found in the table. Workers (formal and informal) and individuals who identify themselves as workers are significantly more likely to engage in party politics than the self-employed, the unemployed, and those who define themselves as part of the middle class. There is also a marginally significant tendency for younger respondents to be more active in party politics.

These bivariate results are not surprising from the standpoint of classical theories of political participation. Education has been found repeatedly to be a significant determinant of political activism (Almond and Verba 1963, Banfield and Wilson 1970). So has occupation, insofar as wage workers who repeatedly interact with each other are more likely to develop class conscious-

Table 4.
Breakdowns of Community Grassroots and Political
Participation by Individual Characteristics, 1992

Predictor Variables	Community Organizations		Political Parties		Total[1]
	Attitudes Toward:[2] (Mean)	Partici- pation In: %	Attitudes Toward:[3] (Mean)	Partici- pation In: %	
Gender:					
Men	1.78	0.08	0.58	0.47	1,278
Women	1.51	0.06	0.49	0.47	1,009
	n.s.[4]	n.s.	$p < 0.01$[5]	n.s.	
			Eta = 0.08[6]		
Age:	1.76	0.09	0.58	0.51	1,062
Less than 40	1.78	0.06	0.53	0.42	879
41-60	1.65	0.06	0.45	0.47	345
60 or More	n.s.	n.s.	$p < 0.01$	$p < 0.01$	
			Eta = 0.07	Eta = 0.07	
Migration Status:	1.73	0.07	0.53	0.47	1,467
Migrant	1.76	0.07	0.56	0.48	819
City-Born	n.s.	n.s.	n.s.	n.s.	
Marital Status:	1.80	0.08	0.55	0.46	
Married[7]	1.67	0.07	0.53	0.48	
Non-Married	$p < 0.01$	n.s.	n.s.	n.s.	
	Eta = 0.07				
Education:					
Illiterate	1.47	0.05	0.43	0.10	175
Less than Primary School	1.67	0.08	0.48	0.22	765
Less than Secondary School	1.81	0.06	0.56	0.64	829
Secondary School Graduate or More	1.88	0.10	0.64	0.58	504
	$p < 0.001$[8]	n.s.	$p < 0.001$	$p < 0.001$	
	Eta = 0.13		Eta = 0.12	Eta = 0.41	

Continued on next page

Table 4 — Continued

	Community Organizations		Political Parties		
Predictor Variables	Attitudes Toward:[2] (Mean)	Partici- pation In: %	Attitudes Toward:[3] (Mean)	Partici- pation In: %	Total[1]
Occupation:	1.68	0.09	0.50	0.44	729
Jobless	1.89	0.06	0.53	0.56	357
Informal Worker	1.85	0.07	0.55	0.52	513
Formal Worker	1.65	0.07	0.56	0.42	507
Self-employed	1.74	0.08	0.65	0.42	171
Employer	$p < 0.001$	n.s.	n.s.	$p < 0.001$	
	Eta = 0.10			Eta = 0.11	
Income:[9]	1.66	0.08	0.46	0.40	639
Low	1.76	0.07	0.54	0.44	671
Medium	1.81	0.09	0.62	0.44	631
High	$p < 0.02$	n.s.	$p < 0.001$	n.s.	
	Eta = 0.07		Eta = 0.10		
Class Self- Identification:	1.71	0.06	0.51	0.46	943
Poor	1.87	0.07	0.57	0.55	965
Working Class	1.57	0.11	0.57	0.29	316
Middle Class	$p < 0.001$	n.s.	n.s.	$p < 0.001$	
	Eta = 0.12			Eta = 0.17	
Totals	**1.75**		**0.54**		**2,287**

1 = Totals vary because of missing values in independent and dependent variables.
2 = Summated index of positive responses toward community organizations. Range is 0 to 3.
3 = Summated index of positive responses toward community organizations. Range is 0 to 2.
4 = Statistically non-significant relationship.
5 = The statistical probability of this relationship occurring by chance is less than 1 in 100.
6 = Coefficient of non-linear strength of association. Higher values indicate a stronger relationship.
7 = Includes couples living together.
8 = The statistical probability of this relationship occurring by chance is less than 1 in 100.
9 = Income categorized as the lower, medium, and upper third of the respective income distribution in each country.

ness and participate on that basis than others, such as the self-employed and unemployed, who are cut off from the wage bond (Lipset 1963, Nielsen 1986, Wright 1985).

This pattern of empirical associations is much less supportive of the literature on the "new social actors" in Latin America since it reveals no sharp "disjuncture" in the individual correlates of this type of participation as contrasted with more traditional party activism. In both cases, significant effects tend to be associated with the same individual predictors — mainly education, occupation, and class identification — and the direction of results is generally the same. It remains to be seen, however, whether these individual differences can account for the observed variation across countries in the four dependent variables or whether, on the contrary, the contrast among national political systems overwhelms the effect of these individual characteristics. If the latter, this would be persuasive evidence against theories of popular mobilization that confine their focus to individual-level determinants.

The relevant data are presented in Table 5. It consists of a series of logistic regressions of the four dependent variables on all predictors including both individual characteristics and nationality, the latter variable serving as an indicator of differences in political systems. Regression coefficients indicate the net increase (or decrease) in the logarithm of the odds of endorsing or participating in either community or party politics associated with a unit increase in each predictor, controlling for others. To provide a clearer sense of the meaning of these results, the columns labelled Δp present the net increase (decrease) in the probability of endorsement or participation for each significant effect. Significant predictors are defined as those exceeding at least twice their standard errors.

The independent variables in these equations are somewhat different from those presented in Table 4. Education and income are entered as continuous variables with education measured in years completed and income as the logarithm of monthly income in 1992 dollar equivalents. Occupation also is entered as a continuous variable measured in Donald Treiman's international occupational prestige scores (Treiman 1977). Type of occupation also is included as a categorical variable. Coefficients associated with this and all other categorical variables have a somewhat different interpretation than the others. They represent effects relative either to the total effect of the variable or to its omitted category. In the case of occupational type, the omitted category is "employers"; for class identification, it is "middle class"; and for country, it is Guatemala.[11] In the first two cases, individual effects are estimated relative to the total variable effect; for country, effects are relative to those for Guatemala.[12]

Table 5 reveals a clear pattern of results in which inter-country differences are vastly more powerful as predictors of attitudes and behaviors than individual-level variables. Once national differences are introduced into the equation, no other predictor retains a significant effect in either grassroots organization or party membership. Attitudes are influenced by some individual characteristics, but there is no compelling pattern of effects: Married

Table 5.
Logistic Regressions of Community and
Political Participation by Selected Predictors, 1992

	Community Organizations					
Predictor[1]	Attitude Toward:			Participation In:		
	B[2]	S.E.[3]	ΔP[4]	B	S.E.	ΔP
Sex (Women)	0.148	0.121	—	-0.256	0.211	—
Age	-0.005	0.005	—	-0.008	0.008	—
Migrant	0.049	0.114	—	0.184	0.196	—
Married	0.400**	0.122	0.097	0.160	0.215	—
Years of Education	-0.017	0.015	—	0.047	0.025	—
Occupational Status	0.010	0.006	—	0.010	0.009	—
Type of Occupation:[1]						
Jobless	0.022	0.236	—	0.581	0.402	—
Informal Worker	0.252	0.237	—	0.308	0.405	—
Formal Worker	0.044	0.217	—	0.051	0.375	—
Self-Employed	-0.236	0.217	—	0.176	0.377	—
Income	0.169	0.107	—	-0.066	0.177	—
Class Identification:[5]						
Poor	0.162	0.164	—	0.495	0.271	—
Working Class	0.455**	0.161	0.109	-0.291	0.255	—
Country:[5]						
Jamaica	1.892**	0.194	0.351	-0.923*	0.439	-0.041
Costa Rica	0.530**	0.160	0.126	1.297**	0.318	0.147
Dominican Republic	0.998**	0.164	0.223	1.049**	0.320	0.108
Haiti	-0.150	0.197	—	0.886*	0.373	0.085
Model Chi-Square	233.906**			83.146**		
Degrees of Freedom	17			17		

Continued next page

Table 5 — Continued

	Political Parties					
	Attitude Toward:			**Participation In:**		
Predictor[6]	**B[7]**	**S.E.[8]**	**ΔP[9]**	**B**	**S.E.**	**ΔP**
Sex (Women)	-0.228*	0.104	-0.056	-0.256	0.234	—
Age	-0.004	0.004	—	-0.008	0.010	—
Migrant	-0.040	0.109	—	-0.487	0.258	—
Married	-0.122	0.114	—	-0.248	0.254	—
Years of Education	0.066**	0.015	0.016	0.030	0.029	—
Occupational Status	0.008	0.005	—	-0.009	0.011	—
Type of Occupation:[5]						
Jobless	-0.115	0.228	—	0.51	0.504	
Informal Worker	-0.357	0.223	—	-0.209	0.510	
Formal Worker	-0.325	0.209	—	0.305	0.461	
Self-Employed	-0.109	0.212	—	0.249	0.461	—
Income	0.301**	0.099	0.0007	0.076	0.205	—
Class Identification:[5]						
Poor	-0.233	0.167	—	-0.147	0.315	—
Working Class	-0.122	0.163	—	-0.381	0.316	—
Country:[5]						
Jamaica	0.941**	0.183	0.207	8.291**	0.616	0.666
Costa Rica	1.679**	0.175	0.317	1.983**	0.332	0.451
Dominican Republic	1.681**	0.175	0.317	0.456	0.451	
Haiti	1.346**	0.209	0.274			
Model Chi-Square	231.364**			1342.423**		
Degrees of Freedom	17			16		

* p < .05

** p < .01

1 = Variable coded in agreement with their labels. Words in parentheses indicate the higher-coded category.

2 = Beta weights for logistic regression coefficients.

3 = Standard errors of regression.

4 = Change in the probability of the dependent variable associated with a unit change in each predictor with the others controlled; significant effects only.

5 = See text for omitted category.

6 = Variable coded in agreement with their labels. Words in parentheses indicate the higher-coded category.

7 = Beta weights for logistic regression coefficients.

8 = Standard errors of regression.

9 = Change in the probability of the dependent variable associated with a unit change in each predictor with the others controlled; significant effects only.

individuals and those who identify themselves as members of the working class are significantly more likely to endorse community organizations; male, better-educated, and higher-income respondents are more likely to do so for political parties.

The combined effect of these three individual variables is quite strong. For example, a man with a high school (12-year) education and a monthly income of US$400 is 47 percent more likely to favor party membership than a woman with a grammar school education (six years) and a monthly income of US$150.[13] Nevertheless, the strongest effects in these equations are those associated with nationality, and they follow an unmistakable pattern. Relative to Guatemalans, all other members of the sample possess significantly higher levels of community grassroots participation, with the exception of Jamaicans, and all are significantly more likely to support such organizations, with the exception of Haitians.

Haitians share with Guatemalans a level of party membership significantly inferior to the other two national groups for which data are available, but Guatemalans are in a class apart in their negative attitudes toward the party system. Compared to them, Dominicans and Costa Ricans are 32 percent more likely to endorse party membership, Haitians 27 percent more likely, and Jamaicans 21 percent. Jamaicans are at the low end of attitudinal differences, but their probability of actual party membership exceeds that of Guatemalans by an extraordinary 67 percent.

These results clearly indicate that inter-country differences observed in the earlier bivariate tabulations are not explainable by differences in the sociodemographic profiles of the national samples. The opposite is the case, as most individual-level characteristics cease to have a significant association with political attitudes and behavior once nationality is taken into account. Hence, the obvious conclusion is that systemic factors associated with the polity play the decisive role in influencing patterns of popular participation. Within-country differences in political activism are still explainable through individual-level variables, but the "core" level of beliefs and behaviors of popular sectors is set largely by the characters of their historical interaction with the national political system.

A final word must be said about the direction in which the political system affects political attitudes and participation. Table 2 indicated that Dominicans, Costa Ricans, and Jamaicans shared a similar pattern of higher participation in political parties than in community organizations, but higher support for participation in community organizations than in political parties. This can be related to the fact that in democratic systems people have access to public and private goods through the party system (and hence they take part in it), but they do not value participation *per se*. The most notorious example is the Jamaican case, where the survey found an extremely high percent of membership in political parties (98 percent) and an extremely low endorsement of this form of political participation (4.4 percent). This may be explained by the fundamental importance of clientelist relations in the Jamaican political system. Guatemala, an example of a nondemocratic political system, shows a very low degree of participation and support for political parties. This can be explained by the fact that, in an authoritarian political system, people do not find incentives to either participate in or endorse political parties, leaving the field to the few politically committed.

Conclusion

In 1985, Luis Razeto, one of the most prominent students of Chilean popular grassroots organizations, had this to say about their future:

> For a long time, these groups have served efficaciously to maintain and develop popular organizations under difficult living conditions. Today, it is necessary that these groups do more than this. We know that these organizations were not created to protest or to present demands to the state, but many have known how to participate in protest rallies, in social demand-making, and in popular reivindications. Now that the *pueblo* begins to express itself anew, these organizations...also take part in the struggle of all for a new society. (Razeto 1985, 18-19)

In a more cautious tone, John Friedmann and Mauricio Salguero also concluded their analysis of the Latin American "*barrio* economy" thus:

> If civil society is to be mobilized for political ends, the factory cannot remain the primary locus. As the home terrain for the self-production of life, the *barrio* economy is the more inclusive alternative. It brings in the long-term unemployed, the young first-time job seekers, the workers active in the informal sector, older folks, and even small children, in short *the entire working class sector of civil society*....To be sure, the possibility of a counter-hegemonic mobilization in the popular *barrios* of Latin American cities is only a latent possibility at this time, though there is growing evidence for it from a wide spread of cities, from São Paulo to Santiago to Lima to Medellin. (Friedmann and Salguero 1988, 38; emphasis in original)

Whatever this "growing evidence" was in the mid-1980s, it was scarcely apparent in the capital cities of the Caribbean Basin in the early 1990s. Compared with the eloquent rhetoric about the counter-hegemonic and innovative potential of grassroots organizations, survey figures on the actual extent of popular participation in these organizations look rather dismal. To be sure, there is widespread sympathy for their goals, but when the moment comes to translate sentiments into action, it is the traditional political parties rather than the "new" movements that have the upper hand.

Still more important is the finding that individual-level influences on both sympathy for and participation in popular organizations do not form a distinct causal sequence. Instead, the same general set of characteristics that incite support for political party membership do so for grassroots organizations, suggesting the existence of a more general participatory syndrome. The more educated rather than the illiterate, the better off rather than the destitute, those who see themselves as members of the working class rather than the poor lean more strongly toward both forms of participation. This pattern of relationships is, of course, at variance with the expectations of much of the earlier grassroots movement literature.

The key finding of the analysis is, however, that when country differences in political systems are introduced, they do away with most of the observed individual influences on participation. This pattern of results indicates that what ultimately matters is the size, durability, and character of the political "space" opened by the dominant system for popular participation. Low-income groups are quick to seize such spaces when they emerge, but they lapse into indifference and apathy when these opportunities close due to systematic repression. In this sense, the best characterization of political action by low-income urban groups is rational adaptation to the existing structures of power rather than radical confrontation with them or the creation of an alternative civic order.

Twenty-three years ago, a study of politics in the *favelas* of Rio de Janeiro concluded on the following note:

> Our evidence shows beyond the shadow of a doubt that *squatment* populations are shrewdly aware of [political] changes and make appropriate responses to them, shifting their form of behavior as is convenient, attempting to make the best use of the changing structure in their bad situation. Thus, there has always been a keen interplay between residents and politicians or candidates looking for votes in return for which gifts are given. (Leeds 1969, 79)

The findings of this comparative study agree in essence with that conclusion. They extend it by showing the key disjunction between endorsement of grassroots organizations, on the one hand, and membership in traditional parties, on the other, in the three democratic countries where both forms of participation are possible. Sympathy for grassroots organizations there is aplenty, but rational adaptation to reality dictates that actual investments of time and effort should go mostly toward those organizations capable of delivering individual favors and improvements in precarious living conditions.

A final issue to consider is the extent to which these findings apply to other Latin American countries beyond the Caribbean Basin. The diversity of political regimes of the countries included in the study presents the possibility that these results can be extended to other countries of the area. Moreover, the results coincide with a number of studies that show the dependency of the new social movements on the political parties and the political system (Cardoso 1983, Tironi 1986). As Elizabeth Jelin points out in this volume, with the return to democracy, the political parties reoccupied spaces formerly occupied by social movements. Hence, although a final answer to this can be provided only by additional comparative research, there is every reason to think that these results should not be confined to the Caribbean Basin.

Notes

1. The research reported herein was conducted with the support of a grant from the Mellon Foundation. The project was a collaborative effort between institutions and research teams in each of the countries studied. The project directors and institutions involved were as follows: Mario Lungo, Central American University Confederation (CSUCA), Costa Rica; Wilfredo Lozano, Latin American Faculty of Social Science (FLASCO), Dominican Republic; Juan Pablo Pérez-Sáinz, FLASCO, Guatemala; Sabine Manigat, National University of the Republic, Haiti; Derek Gordon and Patricia Anderson, University of the West Indies, Jamaica. None of them bears responsibility for the analysis presented in this chapter.

2. The CBI was created during the Ronald Reagan administration to stimulate the economies of the countries of the Caribbean Basin by granting them preferential access to the U.S. market for a variety of industrial products. During the late 1980s and early 1990s, it triggered a rapid growth in export processing zones (EPZs) and export plants to take advantage of the new concessionary facilities and of the very low labor costs throughout the region (see Schoepfle and Pérez-López 1989).

3. The original version of the questionnaire in Spanish was pretested by the research teams in all sites, including Jamaica (English) and Haiti (French Creole), to guarantee that the wording of questions conveyed comparable meanings to all respondents.

4. The question on party membership was omitted in the San José survey because its timing coincided with a hotly contested election and was judged too "sensitive" by the local research team. The figure in Table 2 is an estimate drawn from results of primary elections in the two main parties — Partido Liberación Nacional (PLN) and Partido Unidad Social Cristiana (PUSC) — that took place in the first half of June 1993. The percentage of voters in popular areas was estimated by the sum of votes for all candidates divided by the number of registered voters in these areas (calculations based on results of the primary elections obtained in San José by the authors).

5. The English version of all items used in these surveys is presented in the Appendix.

6. The high endorsement of political parties in Haiti may be the result of the timing of the survey, which took place mainly during the Aristide presidency. Aristide was elected with heavy popular support, and his triumph stimulated hopes that involvement by common people in the political system would help transform the country (Trouillot 1990). Such hopes may be reflected in the respondents' answers to this item.

7. A test of significance of the difference between responses in Guatemala and Haiti versus the other countries combined yields a chi square of 246 with 3 degrees of freedom, significant at the .001 level.

8. Jamaica is excluded from this analysis because party membership is a near-constant that biases the pooled-sample results.

9. A series of cluster and factor analyses were conducted of attitudinal items 3, 4, 5, and 6 in Table 2. Item 6 was broken down into dummy variables representing endorsement of participation in political parties and community organizations, respectively. The analysis reveals a clear dual structure with "poltical party" items clustering together and loading on a single factor and "community group" items loading on a second factor. These results are available from the authors upon request.

10. Formal employment was defined in the survey as that covered by existing labor and social security regulations; informal employment is that not covered by all or most of these provisions.

11. Estimation of categorical-variable effects requires the exclusion of one category. Otherwise, there is singularity in the moments matrix preventing accurate maximum likelihood estimates.

12. This mode of presentation of nationality effects does not alter the substantive conclusions. They would be the same if the alternative total-variable contrast were used.

13. The probabilities were calculated for the Guatemalan sample as the omitted national category. The actual probabilities of favoring party membership were 45.8 percent for the hypothetical man and 31.1 percent for the woman.

References

Almond, Gabriel, and Sidney Verba. 1963. *The Civic Culture: Political Attitudes and Democracy in Five Nations.* Princeton, N.J.: Princeton University Press.

Banfield, Edward, and James Q. Wilson. 1970. *The Unheavenly City: The Nature and Future of our Urban Crisis.* Boston: Little, Brown.

Beyer, Glen H. 1967. *The Urban Explosion in Latin America.* Ithaca, N.Y.: Cornell University Press.

Campero, Guillermo. 1987. *Entre la sobrevivencia y la acción política.* Santiago de Chile: ILET.

Cardoso, Ruth C.L. 1983. "Movimentos sociais no Brasil pós-64. Balanço crítico." In *Sociedade e política no Brasil pós-64*, eds. B. Sorj and M.H. Tavares de Almeida. São Paulo: Brasiliense.

Cardoso, Ruth C.L. 1992. "Popular Movements in the Context of the Consolidation of Democracy in Brazil." In *The Making of Social Movements in Latin America*, eds. A. Escobar and S.E. Alvarez. Boulder, Colo.: Westview Press.

Castells, Manuel. 1983. *The City and the Grassroots.* London: Edward Arnold.

CEPAL (Comisión Económica de América Latina y el Caribe). 1990. *Transformación productiva con equidad.* Santiago de Chile: CEPAL.

Dore-Cabral, Carlos. 1985. "La distribución espacial de los movimientos sociales de abril del 84." *Impacto socialista* 1(April-May):16-26.

Eckstein, Susan. 1977. *The Poverty of Revolution, the State and the Urban Poor in Mexico.* Princeton, N.J.: Princeton University Press.

Eckstein, Susan. ed. 1989. "Power and Popular Protest in Latin America." In *Power and Popular Protest: Latin American Social Movements.* Berkeley: University of California Press.

Fals Borda, Orlando. 1992. "Social Movements and Political Power in Latin America." In *The Making of Social Movements in Latin America*, eds. A. Escobar and S.E. Alvarez. Boulder, Colo.: Westview Press.

Friedmann, John. 1989. "The Latin American Barrio Movement as a Social Movement: Contribution to a Debate." *International Journal of Urban and Regional Research* 13:501-510.

Friedmann, John, and Mauricio Salguero. 1988. "The Barrio Economy and Collective Self-Empowerment in Latin America." In *Power, Community and the City*, ed. P.D. Smith. New Brunswick, N.J.: Transaction Books.

Gordon, Derek, and Cheryl Dixon. 1991. "La urbanización en Kingston, Jamaica." In *Urbanización en el Caribe*, eds. A. Portes and M. Lungo. San José: FLACSO.

Hardy, Clarisa. 1987. *Organizarse para vivir. Pobreza urbana y organización popular.* Santiago de Chile: Programa de Economía del Trabajo.

Hechter, Michael. 1987. *Principles of Group Solidarity.* Berkeley: University of California Press.

Iglesias, Enrique. 1985. "The Latin American Economy during 1984: A Preliminary Overview." *CEPAL Review* 35(April):7-44.

Jelin, Elizabeth. 1985. *Los nuevos movimientos sociales*. 2 vols. Buenos Aires: Centro Editor de América Latina.

Jonas, Susanne. 1991. *The Battle for Guatemala: Rebels, Death Squads, and U.S. Power*. Boulder, Colo.: Westview Press.

Lagos, Ricardo, and Victor Tokman. 1983. "Monetarismo global, empleo y estratificación social." *El Trimestre Económico* 50(July-September):1437-1474.

Leeds, Anthony. 1969. "The Significant Variables Determining the Character of Squatter Settlements." *América Latina* 12 (July-September):44-86.

Lehman, David. 1990. *Democracy and Development in Latin America*. Philadelphia: Temple University Press.

Lipset, Seymour Martin. 1963. *Political Man*. Garden City, N.Y.: Doubleday.

Lozano, Wilfredo, and Isis Duarte. 1991. "Proceso de urbanización, modelos de desarrollo y clases sociales en República Dominicana, 1960-1990." In *Urbanización en el Caribe*, eds. A. Portes and M. Lungo. San José: FLACSO.

Lungo Uclés, Mario, Marian Pérez, and Nancy Piedra. 1991. "La urbanización en Costa Rica en los '80." In *Urbanización en Centroamérica*, eds. A. Portes and M. Lungo. San José: FLACSO.

Mangin, William. 1967. "Latin American Squatter Settlements: A Problem and a Solution." *Latin American Research Review* 2 (Summer):65-98.

Manigat, Sabine. 1992. "L'urbanisation de Port-au-Prince dans les annees 1980: economie et conditions de vie des Port-au-Princiens." Paper presented at the conference on Caribbean Urbanization in the Years of the Crisis, sponsored by the Latin American Faculty of Social Sciences (FLACSO) and The Johns Hopkins University. Santo Domingo, July 29-August 2.

Matos Mar, José. 1985. *Desborde popular y crisis del estado*. Lima: Instituto de Estudios Peruanos.

Melucci, Alberto. 1991. "La Acción Colectiva Como Construcción Social." *Estudios Sociológicos* 26 (May-August): 357-364.

Nielsen, François. 1986. "Structural Conduciveness and Ethnic Mobilization: The Flemish Movement in Belgium." In *Competitive Ethnic Relations*, eds. S. Olzak and J. Nagel. Orlando, Fla.: Academic Press.

Pérez-Sáinz, Juan Pablo. 1991. "Ciudad de Guatemala en la década de los ochenta: Crisis y urbanización." In *Urbanización en Centroamérica*, eds. A. Portes and M. Lungo. San José: FLACSO.

Pinkow, Linda. 1993. "Producing Development: The Structure and Dynamics of the Broadcast Media in Jamaica." Ph.D. dissertation. Baltimore: The Johns Hopkins University.

Portes, Alejandro, and Michael Johns. 1989. "Class Structure and Spatial Polarization: An Assessment of Recent Urban Trends in Latin America." In *Lost Promises: Debt, Austerity, and Development in Latin America*, ed. W.L. Canak. Boulder, Colo.: Westview Press.

Portes, Alejandro, and John Walton. 1976. *Urban Latin America, the Political Condition from Above and Below*. Austin: University of Texas Press.

PREALC (UN Program on Employment in Latin America). 1990. *Empleo y equidad: el desafío de los 90*. Santiago de Chile: PREALC.

Przeworski, Adam. 1985. *Capitalism and Social Democracy.* Cambridge: Cambridge University Press.

Razeto, Luis. 1985. *Las organizaciones populares. Más allá de la subsistencia.* Santiago de Chile: Academia de Humanismo Cristiano.

Schoepfle, Gregory K., and Jorge F. Pérez-López. 1989. "Export Assembly Operations in Mexico and the Caribbean." *Journal of Interamerican Studies and World Affairs* 31(Winter),4:131-161.

Schkolnik, Mariana. 1986. *Sobrevivir en la población José M. Caro y en lo Hermida.* Santiago de Chile: Programa de Economía del Trabajo.

Slater, David, ed. 1985. "Social Movements and a Recasting of the Political." In *New Social Movements and the State in Latin America.* Amsterdam: CEDLA.

Tironi, Eugenio. 1986. "El fantasma de los pobladores." *Estudios Sociológicos* 4(September-December):391-397.

Treiman, Donald J. 1977. *Occupational Prestige in Comparative Perspective.* New York: Academic Press.

Trouillot, Michel-Rolph. 1990. *Haiti, State Against Nation.* New York: Monthly Review Press.

Vargas, Jorge. 1992. "Los movimientos urbanos en Costa Rica durante los ochenta." In *El nuevo rostro de Costa Rica,* ed. J. M. Villasuso. Heredia: Centro de Estudios Democráticos de América Latina.

Ward, P. 1964. "Uses of Prosperity." *Saturday Review.* August 29: 191-192.

Wright, Erik O. 1985. *Classes.* London: Verso.

Appendix

English Version of Items Measuring Attitudes and Participation in Community Grassroots Organizations and Political Parties

1. Belongs to a Political Party: Do you belong to any political party today?
   1. Yes ＿＿ Which? ＿＿＿＿＿＿＿＿＿＿＿＿＿＿＿＿＿＿＿＿＿＿＿＿＿＿＿＿
   2. No ＿＿

2. Belongs to a Community Organization: To what community organizations do you belong? (This question is part of a battery of questions about community organizations.)
   1. None＿＿＿
   2. One or More ＿＿ Number: ＿＿＿＿＿＿＿＿＿＿＿＿＿＿＿＿＿＿＿＿＿＿
      Names: ＿＿＿＿＿＿＿＿＿＿＿＿＿＿＿＿＿＿＿＿＿＿＿＿＿＿＿＿＿＿
      ＿＿＿＿＿＿＿＿＿＿＿＿＿＿＿＿＿＿＿＿＿＿＿＿＿＿＿＿＿＿＿＿＿
      ＿＿＿＿＿＿＿＿＿＿＿＿＿＿＿＿＿＿＿＿＿＿＿＿＿＿＿＿＿＿＿＿＿

3. Supports Participation in Party Politics: Please, tell me with whom do you agree:

   James said: It is better to stay out of politics. After all, common people have very little say in how the country is run.

   George said: It is important to take part in politics. If common people get together, they can have a say in how the country is run.

   Who is right?
   1. James ＿＿
   2. George＿＿
   3. None ＿＿Why? ＿＿＿＿＿＿＿＿＿＿＿＿＿＿＿＿＿＿＿＿＿＿＿
   4. Don't know ＿＿

4. Supports Community Grassroots Organizations: Please, tell me with whom do you agree:

Helen said: The city government should give more participation to neighborhood organizations because those are the true voices of the people.

Laura said: The city government should not give more participation to neighborhood organizations because they represent only the interest of small groups.

Who is right?

1. Helen ____
2. Laura   ____
3. None   ____   Why?_____
4. Don't know ____

5. Effectiveness of Community Organizations: How much would you say that community organizations can help improve the neighborhood? (Interviewer: If the respondent says some can help and others can't, try to obtain a general answer regarding these organizations.)

1. A great deal ____
2. Some   ____
3. A little   ____
4. Not at all   ____

6. Best Use of Free Time: I am going to read you a story and would like you to tell me with whom do you agree. John, Paul, and George all live in the same neighborhood. Each uses his free time differently. John joined a political party. He says that only by participating in politics is it possible to solve the problems of the city. Paul joined a neighborhood committee that works to improve the conditions where he lives. George did not join any organization and spent his free time at home or with his friends. Who is making better use of his time?

1. John   ____
2. Paul   ____
3. George ____
4. None of them ____ Why?_____
5. Don't know____
6. No answer ____

Part IV.

Social Change and the World Economy

Chapter 10

The Deepening Differentiation of States, Enterprises, and Households in Latin America[1]

Roberto Patricio Korzeniewicz

Introduction

Speculations about current social and political transformations in Latin America have centered around three related debates. The first debate is over current economic strategies. Are these policies likely to result in sustained economic growth? How will they affect social inequalities? The second debate is over the social response to these transformations. Have new social movements become the new axis of political action? Are these new social movements essential to the consolidation or deepening of democracy in the region? Finally, participants and observers debate the extent and likely future of democracy in the region. Has democracy in Latin America acquired a more restricted character than elsewhere? Will substantive democracy give way to authoritarianism in the near future? This chapter seeks to identify some fruitful ways of addressing these questions.

The chapter is divided into three sections. The first section suggests that while in some countries (e.g., Chile), economic restructuring and growth are claimed to have led to an improvement in several measures of social welfare (in regard to poverty, unemployment, and income distribution), the social impact of processes of adjustment and restructuring has shown great spatial and temporal heterogeneity, making it difficult to offer precise predictions regarding the social consequences of these change processes. The second section seeks to evaluate the character of restructuring under the new paradigms of development that have come to prevail in the region. This section emphasizes that in recent times, innovation has displaced industrialization as the lodestar of development and modernization, entailing a transcendental shift in the paradigms guiding market strategies and state policies in Latin America and promoting a deepening differentiation between enterprises, households, and states. The last section of the chapter explores some linkages between this deepening differentiation and the new social movements that have characterized the region in recent years. Special consideration is given to changes in patterns of female labor force participation and the role of women in the new social movements. This section argues that beyond recognizing the existing heterogeneity in the constitution of social identities, it is important to distinguish between the sites (states, enterprises, households) and the processes (accumulation, rule, resistance) in which current social transformations are embedded.

The Social Impact of Adjustment and Restructuring

Many studies have sought to assess the impact of economic restructuring on the labor force and households, often emphasizing that enterprises appear to have enhanced their bargaining power vis-à-vis the households that supply their labor. For example, Carlos Acuña and William C. Smith (1994, 18) indicate that "since the end of the 1970s, a sharp decline in per capita income in most countries has exacerbated poverty and worsened already egregious patterns of inequality and concentration of income and wealth." Analyzing the case of Mexico, Sergio Zermeño (1993, 274) concludes that a new modernization, "in the midst of the disorganization, pauperization and growing anomie that today characterizes seven of every ten Mexicans, is implying the dismantling of modern actors in favor of a reduced strong core of transnational enterprises associated with the leadership of state political power." Such a critical perspective on the social impact of restructuring is not limited to the academic sphere. Policymakers in international agencies themselves acknowledge that through their social impact, reforms are producing "adjustment fatigue," so they now emphasize that "the political challenge in the 1990s consists therefore of generating broad-based social support for the reform process by spreading the benefits of renewed growth more equally over all groups of the population" (Inter-American Development Bank 1992, 1; see also Ames 1987).[2]

A precise comparative evaluation of the performance of social indicators during recent times is hampered by the limited availability of data. For example, there are difficulties in obtaining comparable series of data on unemployment or real wages. Besides procedural aspects in the compilation of this information that might underestimate unemployment (for example, the focus on individuals actively seeking employment), the available data are generally restricted to selected urban areas; of course, these biases are particularly problematic for countries characterized by large rural populations. Keeping these biases and general problems in mind, however, available data on various social indicators (unemployment, wages, poverty, income distribution) can be used to arrive at a preliminary assessment of recent regional trends. Reviewing these data, the following pages suggest that the social impact of adjustment policies and economic restructuring has been rather heterogeneous both through time and in different countries and areas within the region.

Economic Growth

The heterogeneity in question begins to become evident in contrasting recent patterns of economic growth in Latin America (see Table 1 below). The region as a whole, since the early 1980s, has been characterized by a considerable growth of exports and new flows of capital from both foreign and local investors (ECLAC 1993). Some countries (Brazil, Nicaragua and, to some extent, Venezuela) have been characterized not only by a relative lack of economic growth but also by high rates of inflation that further undermine the viability of state and entrepreneurial strategies. Other countries (Bolivia and Mexico) have introduced strong adjustment programs without experiencing much growth. A few (Argentina, El Salvador, Colombia, Uruguay, and, to a lesser extent, Honduras and Guatemala) have been able to achieve both remarkably high rates of economic growth and a reduction of inflation.

The search for a new model of development, conducive to both economic growth and enhanced social welfare, calls attention to the case of Chile. The data presented in Table 1 indicate some of the trends that have generated this interest. Over the last 10 years, Chile has experienced uninterrupted economic growth at an average annual rate of over 6 percent (ECLAC 1993, 4). To be sure, this economic growth followed a prolonged period (1973-1982) characterized by the implementation of adjustment policies that had painful social consequences and were sustained through repressive political arrangements under military rule. Furthermore, it is unlikely that these adjustment policies, in and of themselves, could produce a viable strategy of growth. Yet adjustment was followed by a process of economic restructuring that provided a basis for the significant growth experienced over the last decade. Hence, since 1982-1983, economic restructuring has been characterized generally "by a fall in the rate of unemployment, a reduction in informality and tertiary employment, and an increase in waged work among the labor force" (Díaz 1993, 1). However, the Chilean "road" has been difficult to replicate elsewhere in Latin America.

Unemployment

Although average rates of urban unemployment for Latin America as a whole have shown no drastic changes over the past five years (ECLAC 1993, 4), there have been considerable differences within the region (see Table 2 below). Again, Chile appears as a relatively successful model. In the early 1980s, urban unemployment rates hovered around 20 percent. Subsequently, high rates of economic growth over the late 1980s and early 1990s were accompanied by a substantial reduction in rates of urban unemployment, to less than 5 percent by 1993. In addition, the workforce as a whole has begun to grow more rapidly in Chile as women and youth are incorporated into the labor market (ECLAC 1993, 4).

Yet the Chilean model has been difficult to replicate. Argentina has shown among the fastest rates of economic growth in recent years, but urban unemployment has been reaching the highest levels since the 1930s rather than declining, and the only sources of employment that have shown some growth

Table 1.
Growth of Gross Domestic Product Per Capita in Selected Latin American Countries, 1981-1995
1980 Prices

	Average Annual Rate of Variation 1981-1990	Annual Rate of Variation						Average Annual Rate of Variation 1991-1995(a)
		1990	1991	1992	1993	1994	1995 (a)	
Argentina	-2.1	-1.4	7.5	7.3	4.8	6.1	3.6	5.9
Bolivia	-1.7	2.4	2.7	-1.2	1.6	1.7	1.2	1.2
Brazil	-0.5	-6.1	-1.4	-2.6	2.4	4.0	2.4	1.0
Chile	1.2	1.6	5.0	8.8	4.2	2.4	6.4	5.4
Colombia	1.8	2.2	0.1	2.0	3.0	3.9	3.6	2.5
Costa Rica	-0.6	0.7	-0.4	4.6	3.5	1.9	0.2	2.0
Dominican Republic	0.2	-7.2	-1.5	4.7	0.4	2.4	2.9	1.8
Ecuador	-0.7	-0.3	2.5	1.1	0.0	2.0	0.4	1.2
El Salvador	-1.9	2.4	0.3	4.9	4.0	2.0	4.0	3.0
Guatemala	-1.8	0.0	0.6	1.9	0.8	0.9	1.6	1.2
Honduras	-0.8	-3.4	-0.7	3.0	3.6	-4.8	0.7	0.4
Mexico	-0.6	2.5	1.7	0.9	-1.2	1.7	-8.6	-1.1
Nicaragua	-3.4	-3.0	-3.6	-3.4	-4.3	-0.7	0.4	-2.3
Panama	-0.2	4.3	6.6	4.1	2.2	0.0	1.0	2.8
Paraguay	-0.1	0.1	-0.5	-1.1	1.1	0.2	1.3	0.2
Peru	-2.9	-7.4	0.7	-2.9	4.0	10.9	5.7	3.7
Uruguay	-0.1	0.3	2.6	7.2	1.9	4.5	-2.1	2.8
Venezuela	-1.9	4.2	7.1	3.4	-2.4	-5.1	-0.1	0.6
Latin America and the Caribbean (b)	**-0.8**	**-1.6**	**1.4**	**0.9**	**1.1**	**2.7**	**-1.1**	**1.0**

(a) = Estimated.   (b) = Does Not Include Cuba.   Source: ECLAC (1995, 48), on the basis of official figures.

Table 2

Unemployment in Selected Latin American Countries, 1980-1995

	1980	1981	1982	1983	1984	1985	1986	1987	1988	1989	1990	1991	1992	1993	1994	1995
Argentina	2.6	4.7	5.3	4.6	4.6	6.1	5.6	5.9	6.3	7.6	7.5	6.5	7.0	9.5	11.5	18.6
Bolivia	7.1	5.9	8.2	8.5	6.9	5.8	7.0	7.2	11.6	10.2	9.5	10.2	5.8	5.4	5.8	n/a
Brazil	6.3	7.9	6.3	6.7	7.1	5.3	3.6	3.7	3.8	3.3	4.3	5.0	5.8	5.6	5.1	4.7
Chile	11.8	11.1	22.1	22.2	19.3	17.0	13.1	11.9	10.2	7.2	6.5	7.3	5.0	4.7	6.3	5.6
Colombia	9.7	8.2	9.3	11.8	13.5	14.1	13.8	11.8	11.2	9.9	10.3	10.0	10.0	8.5	8.9	8.6
Costa Rica	6.0	9.1	9.9	8.6	6.6	6.7	6.7	5.9	6.3	3.7	5.4	6.0	4.3	4.0	4.3	n/a
Ecuador	5.7	6.0	6.3	6.7	10.6	10.4	10.7	7.2	7.4	7.9	6.1	8.5	8.9	8.9	7.8	8.4
El Salvador	n/a	n/a	n/a	n/a	n/a	n/a	n/a	n/a	9.4	8.4	10.0	7.5	7.9	8.1	7.2	7.5
Guatemala	2.2	1.5	6.0	10.0	9.1	12.0	14.0	11.4	8.8	6.2	6.4	6.7	5.7	5.5	5.2	4.3
Honduras	8.8	9.0	9.2	9.5	10.7	11.7	12.1	11.4	8.7	7.9	7.8	7.4	6.0	7.1	6.3	4.5
Mexico	4.5	4.2	4.2	6.6	5.7	4.4	4.3	3.9	3.5	2.9	2.9	2.7	2.8	3.4	3.7	6.4
Panama	9.7	11.8	10.1	11.7	12.4	15.7	12.7	11.8	16.3	16.3	16.8	16.0	14.7	13.2	13.7	14.3
Paraguay	4.1	2.2	5.6	8.4	7.4	5.1	6.1	5.5	4.7	6.1	6.6	5.1	5.3	5.1	4.4	4.8
Peru	7.1	6.8	6.6	9.0	8.9	10.1	5.4	4.8	7.9	7.9	8.3	5.9	9.6	9.9	8.8	8.2
Uruguay	7.4	6.7	11.9	15.5	14.0	13.1	10.7	9.3	9.1	8.6	9.3	8.9	9.0	8.4	9.1	10.7
Venezuela	6.6	6.8	7.8	10.5	14.3	14.3	12.1	9.9	7.9	9.7	11.0	10.1	8.1	6.8	8.7	10.3

Source: ECLAC (1987, 1988, 1993, 1995), on the basis of official data, with considerable variation in geographical and temporal coverage.

are in non-wage jobs and the service sector (ECLAC 1993, 4). The recovery of urban employment also has been slow in Brazil, Ecuador, Mexico, Panama, Paraguay, Peru, and Uruguay (ECLAC 1993, 5). In 1993, substantial declines in urban unemployment (of over one percentage point) only took place in Colombia and Panama, and there was a substantial increase in Argentina, where the unemployment rate reached 9.5 percent (ECLAC 1993, 4).

These data on unemployment suggest that the relationship between economic growth and employment is not immediate and that the impact of economic restructuring might differ from the consequences of adjustment policies. Economic growth might involve sectoral readjustments (such as a growth of services but a decline of employment in manufacturing or agriculture) that result in growing unemployment rates, as in the case of Argentina. Once a threshold of sectoral readjustments is reached, however, economic restructuring again might promote a reduction in unemployment and a shift toward tight labor markets (as in the case of Chile). The data, therefore, suggest considerable differences throughout Latin America but are insufficient to assess whether these differences entail a necessary or even probable sequence (from adjustment and rising unemployment to restructuring and declining unemployment).

The data are also insufficient to assess precisely the evolution of informal activities under adjustment and economic restructuring. Several authors have argued that processes of adjustment and economic restructuring have been accompanied by a more rapid growth of informal economic activities (Bonilla 1990, Portes 1985). However, other authors have indicated that, at least in some instances, economic restructuring not only has increased employment in the formal sector of the economy but also has reduced the relative importance of the informal sector. For example, Alvaro Díaz (1993, 11) suggests that in recent times, the Chilean case has been characterized by a decline of self-employment and unpaid family labor, as well as the growth of a "new type of informality" based on "small capitalist production" rather than "the expansion of small mercantile production, as in the past."

Wages

These data again show considerable heterogeneity throughout Latin America in regard to the evolution of wages (see Table 3 below). According to most indexes, and accompanying the drop in unemployment, real wages in Chile have increased steadily since 1987.[3] Colombia (and to a much lesser extent, Bolivia) shows a somewhat similar pattern to Chile.

Yet other than these two countries, the pattern has been one of falling real wages (Férez and León 1990, Infante and Klein 1991). The data suggest that on average, the crisis of the 1980s has a clearly detrimental impact on the labor force. In some countries, there has been a dramatic (Ecuador, Nicaragua, Peru, and Venezuela) or continuing (Argentina and Guatemala) decline in average real wages through the late 1980s and early 1990s. In others, there has been a slight improvement in wages over the early 1990s, but wages appear to remain below their level in the early 1980s (Mexico, Uruguay, and perhaps

Table 3.
Real Wages in Selected Latin American Countries, 1980-1993 (1980=100)

	1980	1981	1982	1983	1984	1985	1986	1987	1988	1989	1990	1991	1992	1993
Argentina	100.0	89.3	79.9	93.8	115.0	96.3	95.6	90.4	85.5	80.6	77.9	69.4	65.8	64.7
Bolivia	100.0	93.6	86.2	88.6	87.2	69.7	53.6	56.5	67.5	69.2	73.6	78.7	84.2	n/a
Brazil	100.0	85.7	86.6	78.2	71.7	74.2	74.0	56.6	55.7	72.8	41.7	47.9	50.5	49.8
Chile	100.0	108.9	108.8	96.8	97.1	92.7	94.6	94.4	100.5	102.5	104.3	109.4	114.3	120.2
Colombia	100.0	102.0	105.7	111.7	118.6	116.2	120.8	120.3	119.7	122.0	122.5	120.3	123.0	130.6
Costa Rica	100.0	90.9	72.8	80.7	86.6	94.5	100.1	99.2	97.8	101.8	104.3	101.8	102.6	111.5
Dominican Republic	100.0	92.6	86.1	80.5	81.7	80.1	85.7	83.7	87.1	77.5	73.9	78.4	90.1	94.6
Ecuador	100.0	86.2	77.8	70.4	70.9	69.1	71.2	65.9	55.4	44.6	40.1	34.0	37.4	39.6
El Salvador	100.0	92.2	82.3	92.6	89.8	77.5	70.4	77.5	69.9	66.6	62.9	58.3	57.6	54.6
Guatemala	100.0	117.7	124.8	115.7	105.2	90.8	74.2	79.2	83.3	88.7	75.6	70.8	82.4	91.3
Honduras	100.0	115.2	104.7	95.8	91.6	88.6	84.9	82.9	79.3	72.1	84.2	84.3	95.5	97.3
Mexico	100.0	101.6	102.3	79.0	73.4	71.4	67.2	65.9	65.0	70.9	73.0	77.7	84.5	91.4
Nicaragua	100.0	101.5	88.6	77.4	73.4	56.3	22.5	15.1	8.7	11.7	19.3	18.5	20.6	19.1
Panama	100.0	98.0	98.8	101.5	104.2	109.4	109.1	114.7	115.1	115.1	116.1	116.5	118.0	122.8
Paraguay	100.0	105.3	102.4	95.1	86.7	87.3	88.7	92.7	105.0	103.7	102.3	105.3	101.8	101.4
Peru	100.0	101.7	109.7	94.0	86.5	79.3	100.3	106.5	81.3	43.3	37.1	41.4	40.9	42.6
Uruguay	100.0	107.5	107.2	85.0	77.3	88.2	94.1	98.5	100.0	99.6	92.3	95.8	97.9	102.6
Venezuela	100.0	94.3	93.9	89.4	76.4	71.4	68.3	58.0	52.9	44.5	41.0	37.7	39.1	36.4

Source: On the basis of data in Inter-American Development Bank 1990, 1992, and 1994.

Honduras). Finally, for some countries (Costa Rica and Brazil), the data are inconclusive, although a comparison of available indexes suggests that while average real wages have fallen, limited sectors of the labor force have been privileged by steady or higher earnings (see Tables 3 and 4). For Latin America as a whole, for example, the Inter-American Development Bank (1992, 19) has observed that the late 1980s and early 1990s appeared to be characterized by "a widening wage differential between white-collar and blue-collar workers, which has exacerbated the feeling that the recovery has hardly improved the welfare of those at the lower end of the wage scale." It is more difficult to assess the evolution of indirect wage benefits, such as social security and family benefits.

Poverty

Available data and studies indicate that the incidence of poverty grew throughout the region in the 1980s (CEPAL 1992, Felix 1983, Férez and León 1990). For example, between 1980 and 1985, the incidence of poverty among households in Latin America increased from 33 percent to 39 percent (Bonilla 1990, 215) (see Table 5 below). In Argentina and Chile, according to CEPAL (1992, 6), there was a doubling of the population lacking sufficient income to meet basic needs.

Furthermore, the available evidence suggests a rapid increase in the incidence of poverty during recessionary periods but a slow reduction of poverty during periods of economic growth (CEPAL 1992, 5). In many countries in the region, poverty has remained at considerably high levels throughout the 1990s. Even in Chile, where there was a noticeable reduction of poverty in the late 1980s and early 1990s, the rate of decline of poverty in recent years has been less pronounced than in the earlier years of the current cycle of economic growth (ECLAC 1995).

The data also suggest differences between urban and rural areas. In several countries (Argentina, Brazil, Costa Rica, Guatemala, Mexico, and Peru), indicators of poverty have risen in urban areas while declining in rural areas (see Table 6). Historically, the extent of poverty in different nations was a direct consequence of the relative predominance of a rural population, and the magnitude of poverty in rural areas tended to decline primarily as a consequence of the migration of the poor to urban areas (Infante and Klein 1991). However, to the extent that the impact of the crisis of the 1980s varied according to the extent to which household units could use their own production to counter detrimental exposure to markets, these households tended to fare better in rural rather than in urban areas (CEPAL 1992, 6). Furthermore, poverty initially grew more rapidly and subsequently declined more slowly in urban areas. For these reasons, although the relative incidence of poverty might still be higher in rural areas, most of the poor in Latin America today reside in urban areas.

Moreover, there are some indications that the relationship between poverty and informality might be undergoing changes as a consequence of economic restructuring. In Chile, for example, Díaz (1993, 23) comments that

Table 4.
Average Real Wages in Selected Latin American Countries, 1980-1995
1980=100

	1980	1981	1982	1983	1984	1985	1986	1987	1988	1989	1990	1991	1992	1993	1994	1995
Argentina	100.0	89.4	80.1	100.5	127.1	107.8	109.5	103.0	97.3	78.7	82.4	83.5	84.7	83.2	84.0	83.1
Brazil																
Rio de Janeiro	100.0	108.5	121.6	112.7	105.1	111.8	121.5	105.4	103.2	105.2	94.0	74.6	74.8	80.6	81.9	82.6
São Paulo	100.0	104.7	107.2	94.0	97.9	120.4	150.7	143.2	152.1	157.3	140.8	124.3	120.1	133.2	137.9	138.2
Chile	100.0	108.9	108.6	97.1	97.2	93.5	95.1	94.7	101.0	103.0	104.9	110.0	115.0	119.1	124.7	129.4
Colombia	100.0	101.3	104.7	110.1	118.1	114.6	120.1	119.2	117.7	119.2	117.7	114.6	116.0	121.4	122.5	122.7
Costa Rica	100.0	88.3	70.8	78.5	84.7	92.2	97.8	89.2	85.2	85.7	87.1	83.1	86.5	95.3	98.9	96.9
Guatemala	100.0	117.6	124.7	126.2	114.8	99.2	81.0	86.5	89.5	91.2	n/a	n/a	n/a	n/a	n/a	n/a
Mexico	100.0	103.6	104.4	80.7	75.4	75.9	71.5	71.3	71.7	75.1	77.8	82.9	89.0	96.9	100.5	87.2
Nicaragua	100.0	101.1	95.8	97.4	90.9	75.5	55.9	62.4	17.4	17.7	n/a	n/a	n/a	n/a	n/a	n/a
Panama	100.0	98.7	94.1	98.2	105.8	107.0	110.0	n/a	n/a	n/a	n/a	n/a	n/a	n/a	n/a	n/a
Paraguay	100.0	105.3	102.4	95.2	91.8	89.8	85.9	96.5	103.9	105.9	n/a	n/a	n/a	n/a	n/a	n/a
Peru	100.0	101.8	110.2	93.4	87.2	77.6	97.5	101.3	76.1	41.8	36.5	42.0	40.5	40.2	46.4	44.7
Uruguay	100.0	107.5	107.1	84.9	77.1	67.3	71.9	75.2	76.3	76.0	70.4	73.1	74.7	78.3	79.0	76.8

Source: ECLAC (1987, 1988, 1993, 1995), on the basis of official data, with considerable variation in breadth of coverage.

Table 5.
Poor and Indigent Households in Selected Latin American Countries, 1970-1994

as percentage of all households

	Households Under the Poverty Line																	
	Urban						Rural						National					
	1970	1980	1986	1990	1992	1994	1970	1980	1986	1990	1992	1994	1970	1980	1986	1990	1992	1994
Argentina	5	7	12				19	16	17				8	9	13			
Metropolitan		5	9	16	10													
Bolivia				50(b)	46													
Brazil	35	30	34(a)	39			73	62	60	56			49	39	40(a)	43		
Chile	12		38(a)	33	28	24	25		45	34	28	26	17		39(a)	33	28	24
Colombia	38	36	36	35	38		54	45	42				45	39	38			
Costa Rica	15	16(c)	21(d)	22	25		30	28(c)	28(d)	25	25		24	22(c)	25(d)	24	25	
Guatemala		41	54					79	75	72				65	68			
Honduras	40		53	65	66		75		81	84	79		65		71	75	73	
Mexico	20		28(e)	34(b)	30		49		45(e)	49(b)	46		34	32(f)	34(e)	39(b)	36	
Panama		31(h)	30	34(b)	34(g)	36		45(h)	43	48(b)	43(g)			36(h)		38(b)	36(g)	
Paraguay (i)			46	37														
Peru	28	35(h)	45				68	65(h)	64				50	46(h)	52			
Uruguay	10	9(c)	14	12	8			21(c)	23					11(c)	15			
Venezuela	20	18(c)	25	33	32		36	35(c)	34	38	36		25	22(c)	27	34	33	
Latin America	26	25	30	34			62	54	53	53			40	35	37	39		

Continued on next page

Table 5—Continued

Households Under the Indigence Line

	Urban						Rural						National					
	1970	1980	1986	1990	1992	1994	1970	1980	1986	1990	1992	1994	1970	1980	1986	1990	1992	1994
Argentina	1	2	3				1	4	6					1	2	4		
Metropolitan		1	9	16	10													
Bolivia				50(b)	46													
Brazil	15	10	13(a)	22			42	35	34(a)				25	17	18(a)			
Chile	3		14(a)	10	7	6	11		17(a)	12	8	8	6		14(a)	11	7	7
Colombia	14	13	15	12	15		23	22	22				18	16	17			
Costa Rica	5	5(c)	6(d)	7	8		7	8(c)	10(d)	12	12		6	6(c)	8(d)	10	10	
Guatemala		13	28					44	53	45				33	43			
Honduras	15		28	38	38		57		64	66	59		45		51	54	50	
Mexico	6		7(e)	9(b)	7		18		20(e)	23(b)	20		12	10	11(e)	14(b)	12	
Panama		14(h)	13	15(b)	14(g)			27(h)	22	25(b)	21(g)			19(h)	16	18(b)	16(g)	
Paraguay			16	10	13													
Peru	8	12(h)	16				39	37(h)	39				25	21(h)	25			
Uruguay	4	2(c)	3	2	1			7(c)	8					3(c)	3			
Venezuela	6	5(c)	8	11	10		19	15(c)	14	17	10		10	7(c)	9	12	11	
Latin America	10	9	11	13			34	28	30	30			19	15	17	18		

(a) 1987; (b) 1989; (c) 1981; (d) 1988; (e) 1984; (f) 1977; (g) 1991; (h) 1979; (i) metropolitan area.
Source: CEPAL (1992, 17) and ECLAC (1995).

"informality and poverty are not the same thing," and "many of those who are formally employed are poor." In part, the changes involved are related to the adjustment of some households/household members to market opportunities and constraints in rural areas and the migration of other households/ household members to urban areas. In the process, poor households themselves also undergo greater differentiation.

Income Distribution

Of all the areas reviewed in this section, the quality and availability of data on income inequalities are probably the poorest. As suggested by Table 6 below, data are only available for a few nations, and they seldom allow for comparisons over time. In Brazil between 1983 and 1989, the income share of the top 20 percent of households rose from 62.6 percent to 67.5 percent, while the share of income of the lowest quintile declined from 2.4 percent to 2.1 percent (World Bank 1993b, Table 30). In Venezuela and Costa Rica, on the other hand, available data suggest a slight redistribution of income toward the lower household quintiles (World Bank 1993b, Table 30). In Chile, the share of the lowest quintile increased from 3.1 percent to 3.2 percent between 1978 and 1988, while the share of the highest quintile rose from 58.2 percent to 64.2 percent during the same period (Programa de Economía del Trabajo 1992, 72). A more limited study of income distribution in Santiago showed the share of the lowest income fluctuating from 3.7 percent in 1969, to 3.8 percent in 1979, to 3.4 percent in 1988, and 3.7 percent in 1991; during the same years, the share of the highest quintile moved from 56.4 percent, to 57.2 percent, to 58.6 percent, and to 57.9 percent (Programa de Economía del Trabajo 1992, 73). This suggests that the concentration of income was not as pronounced in urban as in rural areas.

Table 6 below shows the ratios of the income shares of the richest 20 percent and the poorest 20 percent of the population of selected Latin American countries. These ratios provide a rough indication of trends in income inequality during the period under consideration. No single pattern can be identified from these data. In Brazil the ratio has increased, suggesting greater income inequality, but the observations are limited to a few years. In Chile, the national data show a slight increase between 1978 and 1988; data from Santiago, on the other hand, suggest a decrease in subsequent years.

The interpretation of these data, furthermore, is problematic. As suggested by Acuña and Smith (1994, 24), "How should one analyze statements affirming the 'regressive redistribution of income,' when in some cases this signified a decline in the relative income of the popular sectors combined with an increase in their absolute income levels (as in Brazil), while in others it meant both relative and absolute declines in the incomes of workers and the popular sectors (as in Argentina)?"

What conclusions can be reached from this brief review of social indicators? Clearly, there is significant variation across Latin America in the social impact of adjustment policies (that have generally sought to reduce a fiscal crisis primarily, but not exclusively, through a reduction in the size of

Table 6.
Proportion of the Income of the Highest to the Lowest Population Quintile, Selected Latin American Countries, 1965-1994

	Circa						
	1965	**1970**	**1975**	**1980**	**1985**	**1990**	**1994**
Argentina							
Bolivia			14.8			8.6	
Brazil			20.7		26.1	32.1	
Chile	12.8			18.8		20.1	17.4
Santiago		15.2		15.1	17.2	15.6	
Colombia	34.0		14.8		13.3	15.5	
Costa Rica			18.3		16.5	12.7	
Dominican Republic			9.0			13.3	
Ecuador			36.0				9.7
El Salvador			10.6				
Guatemala		12.0				30.0	
Honduras							15.1
Mexico	20.3		20.3			13.5	
Nicaragua			21.7				13.1
Panama			31.0			29.9	
Peru			30.5		11.8		10.3
Uruguay	7.2		7.8				
Venezuela	19.7		18.0		10.8	16.2	

Source: World Bank (1980-1996).

the state) and economic restructuring (or the constitution of new institutional arrangements between states, enterprises, and households). More importantly, the limited data available suggest that adjustment and restructuring might differ in their consequences. Frequently, there is considerable temporal overlap between those policies aiming at adjustment and those seeking to promote economic restructuring. Yet while the introduction of adjustment policies in the 1980s was generally linked, in the midst of a profound economic crisis, to growing social inequalities, the more recent impact of economic restructuring in the 1990s, particularly in contexts of rapid economic growth, has been less clear.[4]

For example, existing data support the hypothesis that differences in the relative intensity of poverty and social inequalities among and within the Latin American countries reviewed in this section might be a consequence of processes entailing the exclusion of some sectors of the population from markets (this use of the term "exclusion" differs from that employed by Baño 1993). While adjustment was more likely to intensify exclusion, restructuring has been more likely to both extend the role of markets in regulating the activities of households (through a decline of petty commercial activities and subsistence production) and promote new patterns of organization within household units (through changes in gender roles). Households and household members have been active participants in these transformations, tending to choose exploitation as a preferable option to exclusion. The third section of this chapter will return to this issue so as to assess the relative weight of processes of exclusion in processes of economic restructuring.

The next section of the chapter analyzes the orientation of the new model of development prevalent in the region, so as to evaluate the likely characteristics of economic growth in the near future. In their contributions to this volume, Alvaro Díaz and Sergio Zermeño propose alternative interpretations of processes of adjustment and economic restructuring. While Zermeño emphasizes that these processes have resulted in deep social disorganization, Díaz indicates that the recent trajectory of Chile serves to highlight the differences between adjustment and restructuring. Yet is the Chilean path likely to continue without major changes? Is the Chilean path likely to be replicated elsewhere in Latin America? Studies of similar change processes in other regions (see Maravall 1993 on Southern Europe) have suggested that there is no single outcome to restructuring or even adjustment policies. These are some of the main issues addressed in the following section.

Toward New Paradigms of Development: Innovation and Differentiation

Over the last decade, there has been a fundamental change in the paradigm that guides the prevalent models of development in the region. As opposed to previous exposures to economic stagnation or political instability, the crisis of the 1980s was represented by observers as a wholesale challenge to the strategy of development that had prevailed for most of the postwar period in the region. Innovation has displaced industrialization as the key component of development strategies, inherently justifying and promoting a deepening differentiation between states, enterprises, and households.

The main premises guiding postwar models of development had been drawn by policymakers and political leaders in Latin America from the interwar experiences of the 1920s and 1930s. One of these key premises was that wealth could be pursued most effectively through industrialization rather than through reliance on comparative advantages and market mechanisms (see Prebisch 1950 and 1959, Singer 1950, Myrdal 1957, and also Rostow 1960). Additionally, and related to this point, industrialization was expected to provide a more effective mechanism for generating employment opportunities (Hirschman 1965). Domestic industrialization would counter the deterioration of the terms of trade in the world market, and its extensive vertical and horizontal linkages would promote greater production, wealth, and employment than specialization in raw materials.

Another key premise was that autonomous industrialization had to be induced and promoted through state regulation, for it was unlikely to result from open exposure to world markets (Hirschman 1965, Gerschenkron 1962). State regulation also was deemed necessary to ensure social cohesion either through income redistribution (as in the different versions of the social-democratic model) or through repression (as in the different versions of authoritarian regimes).

Even when industrial development policies faced bottlenecks or periodic crises within specific Latin American nations in the 1950s and 1960s, the overall importance of state regulation — or Luiz Carlos Bresser Pereira's (1993, 53) "economic populism" or Marcelo Cavarozzi's (1994, 127) "state-centric matrix" — was not significantly challenged, by either civilian or military regimes. At least in part, this was because state regulation appeared to be legitimated by the perceived success of the socialist experience in promoting industrialization in the Soviet Union and Eastern Europe, areas that appeared to enhance their relative position in the interstate system.[5] In this sense, political discourses and the representation of social forces addressed not only specific national circumstances but also the perceived existence of alternative models of development at a global level (such as socialism).

These premises came to be challenged fundamentally in the 1980s. Criticisms had been directed against protectionism and state regulation throughout the postwar period, and there were some noticeable efforts to guide state policies according to these critiques during the 1970s — for example, by shifting resources from manufacturing to agricultural growth (Oman and Wignaraja 1991). Only in the 1980s, however, did these challenges begin to coalesce into a widely accepted, alternative paradigm of development (Bresser Pereira 1993, Williamson 1990). This shift was due in part to the comparative performance of regional models of development during the 1980s, when the East Asian experience appeared to suggest the supremacy of export-led or outward-oriented industrialization as a strategy of growth. Eventually, support for this strategy entailed a shift away from industrialization toward the adoption of market mechanisms and innovative practices as a basis for development.

Figure 1 below traces the average gross national product per capita (GNPPC) in Latin America, as compared to high-income nations in the world economy, to suggest possible explanations for the relative popularity of alternative models of development. Despite advances in industrialization, there were no substantial advances in the relative status of Latin America vis-à-vis high-income nations. Yet until the 1980s, most Latin American nations grew enough at least to maintain their relative position vis-à-vis high-income nations.

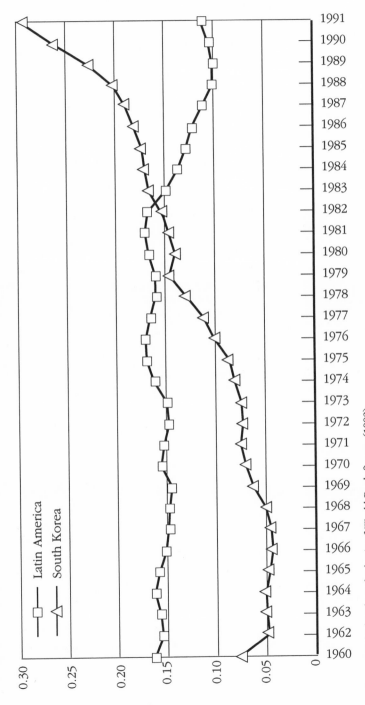

Figure 1.
Proportion of the GNPPC of Latin America and South Korea to Core Nations (= 1.00), 1960-1991

Source: Calculated on the basis of World Bank figures (1992).

After the early 1980s, on the other hand, the average GNPPC of most Latin American nations, as compared to high-income nations, underwent a precipitous decline. Not only were most Latin American nations characterized by stagnant economic growth, but this was perceived as a generalized crisis of market regulation. For by the 1980s, as illustrated by Figure 1, the apparent failure of state-regulated economies was all the more evident when compared to the dramatic success of East Asian development (as indicated in the figure by the trajectory of GNPPC in South Korea). These success stories seemed to indicate that the Japanese model of the 1960s could be replicated elsewhere in the world economy.

In comparison to Latin America, the East Asian nations indeed appeared as success stories. In the midst of the Latin American crisis, between 1980 and 1991, the average annual growth rate of GNPPC was 8.7 percent in South Korea, 5.6 percent in Hong Kong, and 5.3 percent in Singapore (World Bank 1993b, Table 1). During the same period, economic growth was stagnant in most of Latin America, for an average annual growth rate of GNP per capita of -0.3 percent for Latin America as a whole (including, for example, -1.5 percent in Argentina, -2.0 percent in Bolivia, -0.5 percent in Mexico, -4.4 percent in Nicaragua, -1.3 percent in Venezuela, and -0.4 percent in Uruguay) (World Bank 1993b, Table 1). Average annual rates of growth were meager even among the few Latin American countries that did experience growth in their GNP per capita during this period, such as Brazil (0.5 percent), Chile (1.6 percent), Colombia (1.2 percent), Costa Rica (0.7 percent), and Peru (2.4 percent) (World Bank 1993b, Table 1).

Policymakers and scholars invested considerable effort during the 1980s debating the character of this regional divergence between Latin America and East Asia. The literature generally agreed in characterizing the East Asian countries as pursuing an export-led model of development.[6] However, on one side of the spectrum of interpretations, these differences were used to endorse an outward-oriented, market-based strategy of economic growth (Balassa 1981, World Bank 1987). On the other side of the spectrum, economic growth in East Asian was characterized as a product of authoritarianism and low labor costs (see, for example, Fröbel, Heinrichs, and Kreyo 1979). These contending interpretations generally were represented as leading to alternative and largely irreconcilable strategies of development.[7] As such, these interpretations had an immediate and profound impact on the design and implementation of development and stabilization policies among national governments and international agencies.[8]

The apparent importance of exports and international markets in explaining successful economic strategies led to a substantial reevaluation of the basic characteristics of industrialization in Latin America, particularly in regard to state regulation of markets and production. Observers challenged the direct involvement of states in promoting industrialization, as well as the use of state regulation to limit the exposure of enterprises to competition, to maintain that greater efficiency could be gained by exposing enterprises to competitive pressures. In some cases, this critique of state regulation drew from the arguments of public-choice theory to emphasize that rent-seeking activities on the part of states tend to rigidify markets and divert resources from wealth-producing activities (Krueger 1974, Olson 1982). In other cases, the crisis of state regulation and import-substitution industrialization was recognized but attributed to a fiscal crisis that had been precipitated by military rule or the debt crisis (Bresser Pereira 1993; Fanelli, Frenkel, and Rozenwurcel 1994). Both criticisms formulated a major challenge to the premises guiding state regulation since the interwar period. Yet another fundamental challenge would arise around a critique of industrialization itself.

Initially, most analyses of the East Asian and Latin American models continued to emphasize the crucial importance of industrialization. Gary Gereffi (1989, 511), for example, suggested that "manufacturing has been the cornerstone of development for the Latin American and East Asian NICs [newly industrializing countries]." Such a line of interpretation continued to portray primary or labor-intensive productive activities and trade as characteristic of peripheral nations and manufacturing/capital-intensive activities and diversified trade as predominating among core nations (Chase-Dunn 1975, 1990a, and 1990b; Bollen 1983; Taylor 1985; Gonick and Rosh 1988). Given this continuing emphasis on industrialization, the divergence between East Asia and Latin America was explained primarily in terms of the manner in which industrialization or manufacturing had been promoted (for example, see Whitehead 1989 and some of the essays in Appelbaum and Henderson 1992). For some (see Gereffi 1989), the differences between East Asia and Latin America involved distinct paths of industrialization, some of which (such as import-substitution industrialization oriented toward domestic markets) could generate constraints that made it difficult to promote manufactured exports. This line of interpretation generally reintroduced the timing of industrialization as an important variable and continued to highlight the importance of the state as an actor shaping the developmental process.[9]

Developing into a more substantial critique of prevailing strategies of development, several studies have indicated that the relationship between industrialization and control over wealth has weakened over time. In this line of interpretation, world economic status is portrayed not as derived from the ability to shift production from raw materials to complex manufacturing but as contingent upon the ability of states and enterprises to engage in innovation (Wallerstein 1983, Cumings 1984, Arrighi and Drangel 1986, Arrighi 1991). There is nothing inherent about the character of certain production processes or commodities (for example, iron versus apples) that determines their yield of relative wealth. Instead, production processes and commodities "have had 'production cycles,' starting off as core products and eventually becoming peripheral products" (Wallerstein 1983, 36). This interpretation is linked to Joseph Schumpeter (1934 and 1942), for whom innovative processes were at the root of the "creative destruction" that characterizes capitalism as a system. More recently, this focus on innovation rather than industrialization as the basis for comparative advantages in the world economy has been at the fore of influential studies on economic organization (Vernon 1979, Porter 1985 and 1990).

This focus on innovation allows one to abandon the concept of dependent development while retaining an emphasis on the relational character of world economic processes. Even Gereffi (1989) has retained the concept of dependent development, arguing that the nature of this dependency varies among regions (for example, Asia and Latin America). In this use, "dependency" means "external linkages," and "the developmental consequences of...different types of dependency turn, in large degree, on the ability of the state to convert these external linkages to national advantage" (Gereffi 1989, 510). Rather than move toward this soft use of the notion of dependency, one can dispense with the concept of dependent development altogether and focus instead on the spatial dimensions of the processes of competition and exploitation shaping commodity chains (Wallerstein 1983; along these lines, see, for example, the essays edited by Gereffi and Korzeniewicz 1994).

Furthermore, this emphasis on the crucial role of innovation recasts current comparisons of development strategies away from a simple emphasis on the constraints of inward-oriented state-centered policies and the advantages of outward-oriented market-centered policies. Of course, state regulation often has been associated with resistance to innovations. Along these lines, Albert Hirschman (1965, 59) noted that innovations are accompanied by creative destruction, leading planned economies to resist these innovations, for "destruction here means self-destruction rather than destruction of somebody else." Hence, there certainly has been a close relationship between state restructuring and efforts to promote innovative practices. However, the most important lesson to be drawn from a comparison of East Asian success and Latin American constraints during the 1980s is the relational character of these outcomes.

In this sense, rigidities and institutional constraints operating in some areas of the world economy generated competitive opportunities that could be exploited by enterprises and state agencies in countries where institutional innovations could be adopted relatively free from these rigidities and constraints. To draw on Hirschman (1970, 4), "the very process of decline activates certain counterforces." These innovations sometimes involved new organizational linkages to production or market niches within commodity chains (Gereffi 1989, Gereffi and Korzeniewicz 1994). However, innovative practices were not limited to enterprises and markets. They often involved the organization of state regulation around new strategic objectives (Cumings 1984, Wade 1990). In this sense, successful growth policies in the 1980s and 1990s, as generated by both businesses and states, have been characterized not by specific forms of organizing production and trade but by the organizational ability to mold and shift strategic goals according to rapidly changing opportunities and constraints. Here, to borrow from a previous analogy, the medium is the message.

This is an important point to make because scholars and policymakers have continued their efforts to construct a new lodestar for development out of successful growth experiences. Some have emphasized the importance of continuing integration with the world market and the adoption of outward-oriented strategies. For others, the path to development can be found in tighter controls over capital and resource flows and an effective developmental state. For yet others, development requires states and enterprises to promote greater economic integration or move into more complex areas of production. Yet if greater control over wealth has been an outcome of innovation rather than specific commodities or production processes, there is no single model or specific strategy to be derived from the successful experiences (as in East Asia, Spain, or Chile).[10] In fact, the very implementation of innovative practices initiates their diffusion, their eventual elimination as innovations, and the creation of new technological, organizational, and institutional rigidities.

Pursuing specific combinations of production processes, trade patterns, or institutional arrangements in search of greater control over wealth often has led enterprises and states to run very fast and yet stand still. In fact, this was the most important lesson to draw from the failure of postwar industrialization to deliver greater approximation to the standards of wealth enjoyed in high-income or core nations (Arrighi 1991). If innovation constitutes the principal mechanism through which world income inequalities have been reproduced, no specific or single strategy can be expected to provide a fully reliable lodestar of development.

This skepticism regarding the ability of the world economy to deliver a more even distribution of wealth among nations in the near future, however, should not distract from the profound changes accompanying innovation. The next section analyzes the character of these transformations in terms of a deepening differentiation between states, enterprises, and households.

The Deepening Differentiation Among States, Enterprises, and Households

While a process of differentiation among states, enterprises, and households has been a constant feature of modern history, the intensity of this differentiation has varied over time. In each of the three sites in question (states, enterprises, households), this process of differentiation implies the creation of new activities and forms of organization as well as the elimination or destruction of some previous activities and forms of organization. While it is difficult at times to assess the relative weight of inclusion and exclusion within this process of differentiation, one can expect that a heightened intensity in this process would lead to an accelerated transformation in the character and forms of expression of social actors. Such are the characteristics of change processes in Latin America in recent years.

Institutional arrangements through most of the postwar period shielded enterprises and households in Latin America from competition.[11] Import tariffs and the manipulation of exchange rates were often used by policymakers to enhance the competitive standing of domestic enterprises and to improve the bargaining power of state agencies in their efforts to regulate economic growth. Yet state regulation of import tariffs and exchange rates also has sustained a set of institutional arrangements that enhanced income redistribution by protecting labor from world market competition (Canitrot 1975 and 1981). It is in this sense that state regulation played a fundamental role not only in promoting industrialization but also in limiting the exposure of state agencies, enterprises, and households to market competition.[12]

Through economic restructuring, state agencies in Latin America are deeply involved in the process of introducing changes to transform markets.[13] The general features of these changes are clear, although the extent of their implementation has varied among countries. Policymakers have attacked state budget deficits primarily by cutting expenditures, by privatizing state-run enterprises, and, less often, by enhancing the ability of state agencies to collect revenues. They also have sought to enhance market regulation of interest and exchange rates and to lift restrictions on investments and markets in general.

It is not altogether clear that processes of adjustment and restructuring have indeed weakened state structures. Moisés Naim (1993, 133) has argued that "Latin America, which has spent the last 10 years demolishing the state, will spend the next 10 rebuilding it."[14] Bresser Pereira (1993, 20), on the other hand, notes that "even in Chile and Bolivia...the economic role of the state remains crucial" but joins Naim's call for strengthening the strategic role of the state in promoting growth. For yet others, states in Latin America are becoming both weaker and stronger — weaker in relation to direct involvement in production but stronger in terms of their independence from civil society and specific interests. Along this latter line of interpretation, Acuña and Smith (1994, 21) argue that "state strengthening is unavoidable during market strengthening."

The new strategies of growth adopted by states — privatizing state firms, removing trade barriers, and facilitating foreign investments — have created new opportunities and constraints for the expansion of enterprises in Latin America. To deal with these new conditions effectively, enterprises have found it necessary to alter their organizational strategies significantly. This has been true in all lines of production, regardless of whether the enterprises involved produce manufactures or raw materials, are large or small, or sell in domestic or export markets.

Not all enterprises have found it possible to survive under these new competitive conditions. The new competitive conditions have greatly affected those enterprises that developed earlier in the postwar period and were geared toward captive or mass markets. Such an orientation generally implied the adoption of production techniques and organizational structures that proved to be burdensome in adapting production processes and market strategies to the new competitive opportunities of the 1980s and 1990s (on this topic, see Morawetz 1981). For example, many enterprises in the region sought to deal with inflationary pressures in the 1970s and 1980s by adopting speculative strategies (for example, by transforming finance departments and executives into the centerpiece of the firm) that shifted resources away from effective administrative controls over costs, eventually undermining the ability of these firms to adapt to the new conditions of the 1990s.

There are many indications that competitive pressures also have resulted in greater differentiation between enterprises and households. Díaz (1993), for example, suggests that changes in the informal sector in Chile over the past 10 years have involved both a retreat from self-employment and the use of family labor to their replacement by small capitalist firms. Likewise, Elssy Bonilla (1990) has indicated that throughout Latin America, households supplying labor in rural areas have become increasingly differentiated from (large and medium) agricultural enterprises. Similarly, Infante and Klein (1991, 125) indicate that both the rural and the informal urban sectors have been undergoing considerable internal differentiation, resulting in "social strata of higher incomes and good possibilities of growth in the economic area." The precise magnitude of these changes is difficult to establish, and once again it is often difficult to assess the extent to which these transformations are an outcome of adjustment or economic restructuring.

To evaluate the social impact of these transformations, most studies focus on two alternative, but often complementary, dimensions. First, efforts often are made to study households as a site of social organization, bounded as income-pooling units and competing for wealth and power with enterprises and states. In this line of analysis, most studies have emphasized the relative loss of income and growing vulnerability of households since the early 1980s.

Second, efforts are made to identify a sphere of resistance to markets and states, involving actors such as new social movements and often located directly either in the household or in arenas (such as neighborhoods) in which households are particularly active. In this line of analysis, most studies tend to emphasize the growing importance of households, new social movements, and new identities in shaping the organization and distribution of political power. Both lines of analysis often intersect to emphasize that households have sought to counter their declining bargaining power in markets with a growing bargaining power in shaping alternative political identities.

For example, the literature on the social impact of adjustment policies among labor and poor households has been accompanied by a strong emphasis on the emergence of new social movements (Melucci 1980, Castells 1983, Lechner 1982). In part, these social movements have been explained as the outcome of worsening status inequalities that generated collective demands around new arenas of action (for example, households or neighborhoods).[15] These informal organizations gained importance during the military regimes of the 1970s and 1980s, for they were a less vulnerable target of repression than organized labor or other more traditional political institutions (Portes 1985, Jelin 1990b). Some observers initially expected these new social movements to transform the arena of politics. Later studies have evaluated more critically the extent to which these movements represented new social practices (see Escobar and Alvárez 1992).

These social movements do not appear to be inherently incompatible with economic restructuring. Studies of these social movements often assume that economic restructuring has tended to weaken the bargaining power of labor or poor households in existing markets, pushing affected groups to raise demands in a redefined political terrain. In other words, existing studies often have assumed that adjustment policies and economic restructuring tend to promote voice (rather than exit) as a social and political response.[16] However, the very existence of these social movements and their demands often presuppose, or revolve around enhancing, the option of exit and entry for individuals and groups. Migration from rural to urban areas, efforts by women to enter the wage labor force, and even the legalization of divorce, suggest that exit remains a viable and sometimes preferred option. These dynamics can be illustrated with the shifts in patterns of female labor force participation.

While observers tend to emphasize the multiplicity of sites around which these new social movements have risen, gender issues or women are the epicenter of the overwhelming majority of these phenomena (see Jelin 1984 and the essays in Jelin 1990a). In part, new gender roles have been explained as an outcome of demographic changes: "Women's biological reproductive role has lost its pre-eminence and in many societies it is declining," leading women to pursue new goals (Arizpe 1990, xv). Others have attributed these new roles to urbanization, emphasizing the loosening of traditional social controls over women (Krawczyk 1990). Clearly, the growth in female labor force participation has been most noteworthy among young women (Infante and Klein 1991).

These new roles also have been tied to deepening differentiation: "To the extent that nowadays the capitalist market and/or the state penetrate daily life, this is no longer the domain reserved mainly for women, but rather for the impersonal institutions that usurp their functions" (Arizpe 1990, xv). According to this perspective, new social movements, organized, for example, around women, emerge in response to this encroachment on the private sphere, for "it is the loss of [the power previously derived from this sphere] which increases the feeling among women that they are being more and more excluded and marginalized" (Arizpe 1990, xviii).

Thus, several studies have emphasized that female labor force participation has risen due to growing income inequalities, for "the low levels of working-class income make it essential for women to take on some form of income generating activity" (Arizpe 1990, xv; see also Jelin and Feijoó 1980, Blondet 1990, Gálvez and Todaro 1990). According to these arguments, there was a disproportionate impact of adjustment programs on women, who compensated for the "social disinvestment" that characterized adjustment policies through their "nonremunerated household work and by the way they assume responsibility for the economic and physical welfare of the family" (Bonilla 1990, 215). For these reasons, there were expectations that the crisis of the 1980s would be accompanied by a significant expansion of women's participation in the labor force (Bonilla 1990, 207).

Although available data suggest that women's labor force participation indeed has increased throughout the 1970s and 1980s in most Latin American countries (except Paraguay), the rate of increase in most countries was higher in the 1970s than in the 1980s (see Table 7). This was the pattern that characterized Argentina, Brazil, Chile, Costa Rica, El Salvador, Mexico, Peru, Uruguay, and Venezuela. In Colombia and Ecuador, women's share of the labor force during the 1980s remained the same or actually declined. The only nations in which women's share of the labor force increased more rapidly in the 1980s than in the 1970s were Bolivia, the Dominican Republic, Guatemala, Honduras, Nicaragua, and Panama (World Bank 1993c, various tables).[17] Of course, several of these countries (such as Bolivia and the Dominican Republic) have long been characterized by a high rate of participation of women in small commerce.

As suggested in Table 7, there also have been pronounced changes in patterns of female labor force participation. Agricultural employment has declined in relative importance for both men and women. Service activities have become increasingly important as a source of female employment, accounting for roughly two-thirds of the jobs held by women in the 1980s. While employment in service activities also has risen for men, the latter also have moved in considerably larger numbers into manufacturing jobs. As suggested in the literature, the service jobs held by women are less likely to be covered by labor laws and are characterized generally by greater job instability (Bonilla 1990, 221).

Of equal importance, there also has been a growing income contribution of women through their work in the informal sector, where greater flexibility in work schedules allows women to reconcile paid employment with family responsibilities (Bonilla 1990). Women's work also has intensified in rural areas (ECLAC 1988) and within domestic units themselves (Jelin and Feijoó 1980, Gálvez and Todaro 1990). Several authors have indicated that growing female participation in the paid labor force was not accompanied by a proportional increase in income and that poverty has been disproportionately higher among households headed by women (Bonilla 1990). These observations have been used to promote demands that others (states, enterprises, male family members) assume greater responsibility in alleviating women from the burden of reproductive activities.

While much of the pertaining literature emphasized the exploitative character of labor market conditions, more studies are needed on how women are experiencing paid employment.[18] In the study of fresh fruit workers carried out in Chile by Julia Medel R., Soledad Olivos M., and Verónica Riquelme G. (1989, 35), for example, a female homemaker (44 years old) indicated that wage labor "is also like a therapy. Because there one really forgets that she has a house, that she has children." Another female worker, a 26-year-old single mother, indicated to the same authors that "going to [work] I felt as 'yo mujer,' not 'yo madre,' but 'yo mujer'....That is to say, to get the pleasure of being with my friends, being with my *amiga*....When I board the bus (returning home), I am thinking how will I look again as *madre*" (Medel R., Olivos M., and Riquelme G. 1989, 37).[19] Gonzalo Falabella (1988, 7) has indicated that gender relations in fruit production are characterized by "a level of gender equality (women earn even more money and due to this have greater status than men) never seen in the countryside."

Table 7.
Female Labor Force Participation in Selected Latin American Countries, 1960-1990

	Women as Percent of the Total Labor Force							1960 Distribution of the Female Labor Force			1980 Distribution of the Female Labor Force			1980 Distribution of the Male Labor Force		
	1960	1970	1975	1980	1985	1990	2000ᵃ	% Agric.	% Manuf.	% Serv.	% Agric.	% Manuf.	% Serv.	% Agric.	% Manuf.	% Serv.
Argentina	21.0	24.9	26.0	26.9	27.5	28.1	29.1	4.9	26.7	68.4	3.1	18.3	78.7	16.7	39.6	43.8
Bolivia	20.4	21.4	22.0	22.5	24.2	25.8	25.6	26.2	27.3	46.6	27.5	16.5	56.1	52.0	20.6	27.5
Brazil	17.5	21.7	24.4	26.9	27.2	27.4	28.8	27.8	24.3	48.0	15.3	19.0	65.7	37.0	29.4	33.6
Chile	21.7	22.4	24.8	27.2	28.0	28.5	28.9	3.6	20.3	76.1	2.3	16.4	81.3	21.8	28.4	49.9
Colombia	19.4	21.3	21.9	22.5	22.2	21.9	22.3	11.3	22.3	66.4	5.0	21.0	74.0	42.7	24.2	33.1
Costa Rica	15.8	18.1	19.7	21.3	21.6	21.8	22.6	7.5	17.0	75.5	4.0	20.0	76.0	38.0	24.0	38.0
Dominican Republic	10.0	10.9	11.7	12.4	13.7	15.0	17.9	13.2	16.2	70.7	7.8	7.6	84.6	51.1	16.6	32.4
Ecuador	16.3	16.3	17.7	19.3	19.3	19.3	19.7	21.5	30.8	47.7	12.8	18.0	69.2	44.7	20.3	35.0
El Salvador	16.8	20.4	22.6	24.9	25.1	25.1	25.3	7.3	25.0	67.7	5.0	18.2	76.8	55.8	19.8	24.4
Guatemala	12.3	13.1	13.5	13.8	15.1	16.4	19.5	11.0	22.9	66.1	9.4	20.0	70.6	64.5	16.0	19.0
Honduras	12.3	14.2	14.9	15.7	17.3	18.8	22.7	5.3	18.6	76.1	7.3	30.2	62.5	70.4	13.6	16.1
Mexico	15.3	17.8	22.6	27.0	27.0	27.1	27.7	32.8	14.0	53.3	19.3	27.9	52.8	42.9	29.4	27.7
Nicaragua	17.9	19.7	20.6	21.6	23.4	25.2	29.1	14.2	19.7	66.1	8.0	15.0	77.0	57.2	16.0	26.8
Panama	20.9	25.2	25.8	26.1	26.7	27.2	28.7	9.1	10.8	80.2	8.0	10.5	81.6	40.2	20.9	39.0
Paraguay	21.4	21.3	21.0	20.8	20.8	20.7	20.8	21.5	31.0	47.6	12.5	24.5	63.1	58.0	19.5	22.5
Peru	20.9	20.3	22.3	24.3	24.2	24.1	24.4	33.7	19.1	47.3	24.4	13.5	62.2	45.1	19.8	35.2
Uruguay	24.1	26.3	27.9	29.6	30.4	31.1	32.5	4.1	26.3	69.7	2.9	23.1	74.1	21.2	31.7	47.2
Venezuela	18.3	20.7	23.3	25.8	26.7	27.6	28.8	4.6	19.7	75.8	2.6	18.4	79.1	20.7	31.9	47.5
Latin America	19.2	21.7	n/a	26.1	n/a	26.6	27.5	24.4	21.0	54.7	14.9	19.9	65.2	38.6	27.8	33.6

Source: Bonilla (1990, 222-225); World Bank (1993c, Various Tables).
a = projected.

These observations suggest that changes in female labor force participation may alter the internal organization of households and their relationship to enterprises and the state (for example, by intensifying anxiety and concern around new issues such as child care). Hence, while householding might in certain instances be used as a defense against market pressures, new patterns of market participation also might provide grounds for challenging existing patterns of authority and domination within households.

In much of the literature, social movements were seen not only as agents that would promote or at least accelerate the demise of authoritarianism but also as a key mechanism for deepening democracy, transforming "established models of political participation" (Arizpe 1990, iv) by adopting internal democracy, following innovative strategies of mobilization, and raising demands that change the very language of political representation, providing "a new conception of what is political" (Arizpe 1990, xviii).[20] These "changes in the definition of what is the private and public domain (in terms of the role of the state, social reproduction, marital relations, and political participation by women, which reflect women's demands) surpass by far the programs for social transformation currently presented by most political parties" (Arizpe 1990, xviii; see also Feijoó 1990, Jelin 1990b, Caldeira 1990).

Yet studies of recent developments suggest that the existence of these social movements might not challenge the organization and distribution of political power fundamentally. Furthermore, no direct relationship should be expected between macroeconomic variables or patterns of inequality and their political consequences (Acuña and Smith 1994).[21] Paradoxically, the political demands initiated by these social movements can have unexpected consequences. For example, "political struggles may propel market-oriented reform in a direction in which state capacity to induce efficient investment and allocation of resources is enhanced" (Acuña and Smith 1994, 33).

Whereas these social movements, centered around gender issues and women, do not subvert necessarily the logic of the organization of political power or the market, their primary site of (often hidden) resistance involves the organization and distribution of wealth and authority within households. This dimension has not been as emphasized as the other two. Largely, this is because analysts over the past decade often have sought to identify a new site of resistance to markets and states, and households are often represented as bounded by an alternative logic of social organization. As sites, households may be part of a logic of resistance but also can be part of a logic of accumulation or a logic of rule.[22] It is difficult enough to establish the analytical boundaries of households as sites: Seeking to identify theoretically through them an alternative logic to markets and states is an impossible task. The particular mode of interaction between the sites (states, enterprises, and households) and the logics (accumulation, rule, and resistance) discussed in this chapter is an empirical question that can only be addressed through historical inquiry.

Seeking to identify the many sites and terrains of a logic of resistance, on the other hand, might be more useful. Through this resistance, after all, social forces actively shape processes of accumulation and processes of rule. While each of these logics has its own dynamics — in the case of resistance, for example, leading to hidden or open manifestations (Scott 1990) — the analysis of their interaction provides a fruitful arena for bringing together the study of democratic transitions, economic restructuring, informality, and social movements.

Conclusion

To the extent that deepening differentiation affects social substances, challenges are likely to continue, particularly in face of the difficulties in constructing a new paradigm of economic, social, and political development. These difficulties are probably inherent in the rise of innovation as a new lodestar of development. With industrialization as a premise of models of political organization, growing political participation, income redistribution, and state regulation of conflicts could be justified easily as necessary or eventual components of development. Innovation is a more problematic theme. For example, innovation as a strategy of growth may not generate either massive employment (due to characteristics of new technologies) or a substantial redistribution of income. For these reasons, and particularly in situations lacking high rates of economic growth, it becomes more difficult to use innovation as a basis for a new political discourse.

It is hard to speculate on which type of imagined community can reconcile the social tensions resulting from this process of deepening differentiation or what uses will be made of the opportunities afforded by the creative destruction of previous institutional arrangements (for example, at the level of the state but also within enterprises or households). In many ways, as other analysts have noted, one continues in the middle of the storm and often can discern only vaguely the general outline of the new social identities that are emerging from these transformations.

It is less difficult to foresee possible dangers. In the 1920s, fascism arose as a response to the strains of a self-regulated market, and although no socialist threat remains today to provide a *raison d'être* to fascism, the politics of intolerance certainly can become appealing as all social boundaries come to be challenged. In this sense, the reconstitution of identity politics will be very much at the center of developments as the year 2000 approaches.

Notes

1. This chapter has benefitted from detailed comments by Ann E. Forsythe. A previous version of this paper also received useful comments from Liliana Goldín, Walter Goldfrank, Miguel E. Korzeniewicz, and William C. Smith, as well as from all the participants in the workshop that served as the basis of this book. Mitali Sen provided important research assistance.

2. Likewise, the World Bank (1991, 49) has come to emphasize more strongly that "there is no clear link, in either direction, between growth and changes in income distribution....But economic growth is strongly associated with a reduction in the incidence of poverty." Thus, "any notion of strictly economic progress must, at a minimum, look beyond growth in per capita incomes to the reduction of poverty and greater equity, to progress in education, health, and nutrition, and to the protection of the environment" (World Bank 1991, 4).

3. In Chile, the combination of declining unemployment and rising wages has in fact become a major issue of concern for enterprises engaged in exports.

4. Other authors also distinguish between adjustment and restructuring. For Tironi and Lagos (1991), economic adjustment has promoted social disintegration, but processes of restructuring produce new forms of identity and collective action. Naim (1993) emphasizes the difference between these two sets of policies to express his pessimism regarding the chances for rapid economic growth in the near future.

5. As indicated by the World Bank (1991, 34) itself, "the success of state planning in achieving rapid industrialization in the Soviet Union (for so it was perceived) greatly influenced policymakers in the 1950s. Its avowedly egalitarian character was also appealing. The staggering human costs of this transition became apparent only much later."

6. In the late 1980s, exports accounted for 35 percent of the gross domestic product (GDP) in South Korea, 52 percent in Taiwan, and roughly 100 percent in Hong Kong and Singapore (Gereffi 1989, 513).

7. Hence, Albert Hirschman (1970, 19) noted "both laissez-faire and interventionist doctrines have looked at market and nonmarket forces in a strictly manichean way, it being understood that the laissez-faire advocate's forces of good are the interventionist's forces of evil and vice versa." Along similar lines, Alejandro Portes (1985, 12) later observed that "in Latin America, entrepreneurs frequently blame their problems on the drain produced by bureaucratic appropriation of profits, while experts in the public sector counter with attacks on the private utilization of the surplus, which often ends up as luxury consumption rather than productive investment."

8. The initial versions of these approaches subsequently were criticized seriously. Successful strategies, and those that failed, involved a mix of outward- and inward-oriented strategies (Wade 1990, Gereffi and Fonda 1992). By the early 1990s, while continuing to call for a "market-friendly" strategy of growth, even the World Bank

(1991, 1) now suggested that "it is not a question of state or market: Each has a large and irreplaceable role." On the other hand, the East Asian models of development did not rely exclusively, or even primarily, on low wages. Regarding the alternative interpretation of the East Asian models, Gary Gereffi (1989, 515) has noted that these states "were motivated by the principle of dynamic competitive advantage rather than by their static comparative advantage in cheap, disciplined labor." Already by the mid-1980s, wages in East Asian countries were higher, and later increased at a faster rate, than in Mexico or Brazil (U.S. Department of Labor 1992, 5).

9. There is a long tradition of studies that have emphasized the active role played by states in promoting industrialization among nations of later development (Hirschman 1965, Gershenkron 1962, de Schweinitz 1964). The issue was later incorporated under the literature on dependent development (Evans 1979, Cardoso and Faletto 1979) and the Bureaucratic-Authoritarian state (O'Donnell 1973, Collier 1979). More recently, the topic has been central to the literature on the developmental state (Amsden 1979 and 1985, Wade and White 1984, Evans 1989, Wade 1990).

10. Even within countries, efforts to imitate successful strategies often will fail to produce expected results. For example, farmers in Chile in the early 1990s sought to replicate the successful experience of grape exporters by engaging in kiwi production, but the outcome was a world glut and falling prices of kiwis in subsequent years.

11. Already in the late 1950s, for example, Hirschman (1965, 56) noted that "a major difficulty for the speedy industrialization of today's underdeveloped countries consists precisely in the fact that they are not prepared to incur those social costs that were so spectacularly associated with the process during the early nineteenth century in Western Europe."

12. This is why Portes suggests that cleavages among workers in Latin America over most of the postwar period involved the extent to which labor markets and the workplace were regulated by the state. To explain the appeal of regulating processes of "creative destruction," Hirschman (1970, 9) notes that human beings "like...surplus but [are] fearful of paying its price."

13. Of course, there is also considerable debate on the extent to which states have retreated effectively from market regulation. Ambiguities around this issue are likely to continue, particularly given the new emphasis of economic policymakers and international development on the need to promote greater social equity and maintain a balance between state and market regulation. The World Bank (1991, 5) now suggests that the successful development experiences of the 1980s "refute the case for thoroughgoing dirigisme as convincingly as they refute the case for laissez-faire."

14. For organizations such as the World Bank (1991, 9), an optimal outcome would involve restrained state regulation, to target social areas and problems "where markets alone cannot be relied upon," and to promote innovative practices by providing an appropriate infrastructure, while remaining sensitive to the signals arising from market competition.

15. For example, Portes observed that urban strains were likely to intensify residentially based demands among the informal proletariat: "The fluid and temporal character of their employment...militates against organized struggles for better wages or more security....The interests around which informal workers coalesce have to do less with control over the means of production than with minimal access to the means of collective reproduction, such as transportation, water and other basic services, and shelter" (Portes 1985, 31).

16. Hirschman (1970, 30) distinguished between the two by defining voice as "any attempt at all to change, rather than to escape from, an objectionable state of affairs, whether through individual or collective petition to the management directly in charge, through appeal to a higher authority with the intention of forcing a change in management, or through various types of actions and protests, including those that are meant to mobilize public opinion."

17. The most substantial change between 1971 and 1991 took place in Mexico (where women's share of the labor force increased by 8.3 percent) and Venezuela (where it increased by 6.4 percent). In both these nations, and particularly in Mexico, most of this growth took place in the 1970s.

18. The remainder of this paragraph borrows from Korzeniewicz, Goldfrank, and Korzeniewicz 1994.

19. Other female informants emphasized that work allowed them to enhance their social life and indicated that during the off-season they missed "the affective and intimate atmosphere generated in the work space" (Medel R., Olivos M., and Riquelme G. 1989, 36). There is also some evidence that attitudes toward working conditions may be significantly related to the length of participation in the labor force.

20. Although detailed studies of these "new" forms of social mobilization and political organization have shown considerable heterogeneity along all of these dimensions. For example, clientelistic forms of internal organization have been as prevalent as democratic forms (Blondet 1990, Caldeira 1990).

21. For example, "under conditions of economic deterioration and falling income, governments can reduce the virulence of sociopolitical contestation by increasing the costs and reducing the benefits of individual participation in collective action," or deterioration can be slow enough to allow enterprises and households to adapt to new conditions (Acuña and Smith 1994, 31). On the other hand, "most rational actors (collective or individual) in a recovering economy will, if their capacity for contestation has not been curtailed, increase their demands and the level of conflict before either sustainable growth or the possibility of non-inflationary redistribution is assured" (Acuña and Smith 1994, 31).

22. Logics of accumulation and rule are explored in Arrighi 1994. The notion of a third logic, involving resistance, has been suggested by Forsythe 1994.

References

Acuña, Carlos, and William C. Smith. 1994. "The Political Economy of Structural Adjustment: The Logic of Support and Opposition to Neoliberal Reform." In *Latin American Political Economy in the Age of Neoliberal Reform*, eds. William C. Smith, Carlos H. Acuña, and Eduardo A. Gamarra. Coral Gables, Fla.: University of Miami North-South Center.

Ames, Barry. 1987. *Political Survival: Politicians and Public Policy in Latin America*. Berkeley: University of California Press.

Amsden, Alice. 1985. "The State and Taiwan's Economic Development." In *Bringing the State Back In*, eds. Peter Evans, D. Rueschmeyer, and Theda Skocpol. New York: Cambridge University Press.

Amsden, Alice. 1979. "Taiwan's Economic History: A Case of 'Etatisme' and a Challenge to Dependency Theory." *Modern China* 5: 341-380.

Appelbaum, Richard P., and Jeffrey Henderson, eds. 1992. *States and Development in the Asian Pacific Rim*. Newbury Park, Calif.: Sage.

Arizpe, Lourdes. 1990. "Foreword: Democracy for a Small Two-Gender Planet." In *Women and Social Change in Latin America*, ed. Elizabeth Jelin. London: Zed Books.

Arriagada, Irma. 1990. "Unequal Participation by Women in the Working World." *CEPAL Review* 40: 83-98.

Arrighi, Giovanni. 1994. *The Long Twentieth Century: Money, Power, and the Origins of Our Times*. London: Verso.

Arrighi, Giovanni. 1991. "World Income Inequalities and the Future of Socialism." *New Left Review* 189: 39-65.

Arrighi, Giovanni, and Jessica Drangel. 1986. "The Stratification of the World-Economy: An Exploration of the Semiperipheral Zone." *Review* 10: 9-74.

Balassa, Bela. 1981. *The Newly Industrializing Countries in the World Economy*. New York: Pergamon Press.

Baño, Rodrigo. 1993. "Socioeconomic Structure and Collective Behavior." *CEPAL Review* 50: 181-199.

Blondet, Cecilia. 1990. "Establishing an Identity: Women Settlers in a Poor Lima Neighborhood." In *Women and Social Change in Latin America*, ed. Elizabeth Jelin. London: Zed Books.

Bollen, Kenneth. 1983. "World-System Position, Dependency, and Democracy: The Cross-National Evidence." *American Sociological Review* 48: 468-479.

Bonilla, Elssy. 1990. "Working Women in Latin America." In *Economic and Social Progress in Latin America: 1990 Report*. Washington, D.C.: Inter-American Development Bank.

Bresser Pereira, Luiz Carlos. 1993. "Economic Reforms and Economic Growth: Efficiency and Politics in Latin America." In *Economic Reforms in New Democracies*, eds. Luiz Carlos Bresser Pereira, José María Maravall, and Adam Przeworski. Cambridge: Cambridge University Press.

Caldeira, Teresa Pires de Rio. 1990. "Women, Daily Life and Politics." In *Women and Social Change in Latin America*, ed. Elizabeth Jelin. London: Zed Books.

Canitrot, Adolfo. 1981. "Teoría y práctica del liberalismo: Política antiinflacionaria y apertura económica en la Argentina, 1976-1981." *Desarrollo Económico* 21: 131-189.

Canitrot, Adolfo. 1975. "La experiencia populista de redistribución de ingresos." *Desarrollo Económico* 15: 331-351.

Cardoso, Fernando H. 1979. "On the Characterization of Authoritarian Regimes in Latin America." In *The New Authoritarianism in Latin America*, ed. David Collier. Princeton, N.J.: Princeton University Press.

Cardoso, Fernando H., and Enzo Faletto. 1979. *Dependency and Development in Latin America*. Berkeley: University of California Press.

Castells, Manuel. 1983. *The City and the Grassroots*. London: Edward Arnold.

Cavarozzi, Marcelo. 1994. "Politics: A Key for the Long Term in Latin America." In *Latin American Political Economy in the Age of Neoliberal Reform*, eds. William C. Smith, Carlos H. Acuña, and Eduardo A. Gamarra. Coral Gables, Fla.: University of Miami North-South Center.

Chase-Dunn, Christopher. 1975. "The Effects of International Economic Dependence on Development and Inequality: A Cross-National Study." *American Sociological Review* 40: 720-738.

Chase-Dunn, Christopher. 1990a. *Global Formation*. Cambridge, Mass.: Basil Blackwell.

Chase-Dunn, Christopher. 1990b. "Resistance to Imperialism: Semiperipheral Actors." *Review* 13: 1-31.

Collier, David, ed. 1979. *The New Authoritarianism in Latin America*. Princeton, N.J.: Princeton University Press.

CEPAL (Comisión Económica para América Latina y el Caribe). 1992. *El perfil de la pobreza en América Latina a comienzos de los años 90*. Santiago de Chile: CEPAL.

CEPAL News (various issues).

Cumings, Bruce. 1984. "The Origins and Development of the Northeast Asian Political Economy." *International Organization* 38: 1-40.

de Schweinitz, Karl. 1964. *Industrialization and Democracy: Economic Necessities and Political Possibilities*. New York: Free Press.

Díaz, Alvaro. 1993. "Restructuring and the New Working Classes in Chile." *Discussion Paper of the United Nations Research Institute for Social Development* 47 (October).

ECLAC (Economic Commission for Latin America and the Caribbean). 1993. *Preliminary Overview of the Economy of Latin America and the Caribbean 1993*. Santiago, Chile: United Nations.

ECLAC. 1988. *The Decade for Women in Latin America and the Caribbean*. Santiago, Chile: United Nations.

ECLAC. 1995. *Social Panorama of Latin America 1995*. Santiago, Chile: United Nations.

Escobar, Arturo, and Sonia Alvárez, eds. 1992. *The Making of Social Movements in Latin America: Identity, Strategy, and Democracy*. Boulder, Colo.: Westview Press.

Evans, Peter. 1989. "Predatory, Developmental, and Other Apparatuses: A Comparative Political Economy Perspective on the Third World State." *Sociological Forum* 4: 561-587.

Evans, Peter. 1979. *Dependent Development: The Alliance of Multinationals, State and Local Capital in Brazil.* Princeton, N.J.: Princeton University Press.

Falabella, Gonzalo. 1988. "El sistema de trabajo temporal (o la institucionalización de la desconfianza, la incertidumbre y la desorganización social)." Paper presented at the Seminario Internacional Sobre la Agricultura Latinoamericana: Crisis, Transformaciones y Perspectivas, Punta de Tralca, Chile (September 1-4).

Fanelli, José María, Roberto Frenkel, and Guillermo Rozenwurcel. 1994. "Growth and Structural Reform in Latin America: Where We Stand." In *Latin American Political Economy in the Age of Neoliberal Reform,* eds. William C. Smith, Carlos H. Acuña, and Eduardo A. Gamarra. Coral Gables, Fla.: University of Miami North-South Center.

Feijoó, María del Carmen. 1990. "Women in the Transition to Democracy." In *Women and Social Change in Latin America,* ed. Elizabeth Jelin. London: Zed Books.

Felix, David. 1983. "Income Distribution and the Quality of Life in Latin America: Patterns, Trends, and Policy Implications." *Latin American Research Review* 18: 3-34.

Férez, Juan Carlos, and Arturo León. 1990. "The Magnitude of Poverty in Latin America." *CEPAL Review* 41: 133-151.

Forsythe, Ann E. 1994. "Gender and the Logic of Resistance." Unpublished manuscript.

Fröbel, F., J. Heinrichs, and O. Kreyo. 1979. *The New International Division of Labor.* New York: Cambridge University Press.

Gálvez, Thelma, and Rosalba Todaro. 1990. "Chile: Women and the Unions." In *Women and Social Change in Latin America,* ed. Elizabeth Jelin. London: Zed Books.

Gamarra, Eduardo A. 1994. "Market-Oriented Reforms and Democratization in Latin America: Challenges of the 1990s." In *Latin American Political Economy in the Age of Neoliberal Reform,* eds. William C. Smith, Carlos H. Acuña, and Eduardo A. Gamarra. Coral Gables, Fla.: University of Miami North-South Center.

Gereffi, Gary. 1989. "Rethinking Development Theory: Insights from East Asia and Latin America." *Sociological Forum* 4 (4): 505-533.

Gereffi, Gary, and Stephanie Fonda. 1992. "Regional Paths of Development." *Annual Review of Sociology* 18: 419-448.

Gereffi, Gary, and Miguel Korzeniewicz, eds. 1994. *Commodity Chains and Global Capitalism.* Westport, Conn.: Greenwood Press.

Gershenkron, Alexander. 1962. *Economic Backwardness in Historical Perspective.* Cambridge: Belknap.

Gonick, Lev S., and Robert M Rosh. 1988. "The Structural Constraints of the World-Economy on National Political Development." *Comparative Political Studies* 21: 171-199.

Hirschman, Albert O. 1970. *Exit, Voice, and Loyalty: Responses to Decline in Firms, Organizations, and States.* Cambridge, Mass.: Harvard University Press.

Hirschman, Albert O. [1958] 1965. *The Strategy of Economic Development.* New Haven, Conn.: Yale University Press.

Infante, Ricardo, and Emilio Klein. 1991. "The Latin American Labour Market, 1950-1990." *CEPAL Review* 45: 121-135.

Inter-American Development Bank. 1990. *Economic and Social Progress in Latin America: 1990 Report.* Washington, D.C.: Inter-American Development Bank.

Inter-American Development Bank. 1992. *Economic and Social Progress in Latin America: 1992 Report.* Washington, D.C.: Inter-American Development Bank.

Jelin, Elizabeth, ed. 1990a. *Women and Social Change in Latin America.* London: Zed Books.

Jelin, Elizabeth. 1990b. "Introduction." In *Women and Social Change in Latin America*, ed. Elizabeth Jelin. London: Zed Books.

Jelin, Elizabeth. 1984. *Familia y unidad doméstica: Mundo público y vida privada.* Buenos Aires: Estudios CEDES.

Jelin, Elizabeth, and María del Carmen Feijoó. 1980. *Trabajo y familia en el ciclo de vida femenino: El caso de los sectores populares de Buenos Aires.* Buenos Aires: Estudios CEDES.

Korzeniewicz, Roberto, Walter Goldfrank, and Miguel Korzeniewicz. 1994. "Vines and Wines in the World Economy." In *Food and Agricultural Systems in the World Economy*, ed. Philip McMichael. Westport, Conn.: Greenwood Press.

Krawczyk, Miriam. 1990. "The Growing Presence of Women in Development." *CEPAL Review* 40: 69-81.

Krueger, Anne. 1974. "The Political Economy of the Rent-Seeking Society." *American Economic Review* 64: 291-303.

Lechner, Norbert. 1982. *¿Qué significa hacer política?* Lima: DESCO.

Maravall, José María. 1993. "Politics and Policy: Economic Reforms in Southern Europe." In *Economic Reforms in New Democracies*, eds. Luiz Carlos Bresser Pereira, José María Maravall, and Adam Przeworski. Cambridge: Cambridge University Press.

Medel R., Julia, Soledad Olivos M., and Verónica Riquelme G. 1989. *Las temporeras y su visión del trabajo (condiciones de trabajo y participación social).* Santiago de Chile: Centro de Estudios de la Mujer.

Melucci, Alberto. 1980. "The New Social Movements: A Theoretical Approach." *Social Science Information* 19: 199-226.

Morawetz, David. 1981. *Why the Emperor's New Clothes are not Made in Colombia.* New York: Oxford University Press.

Morley, Samuel A. 1995. *Poverty and Inequality in Latin America: The Impact of Adjustment and Recovery in the 1980s.* Baltimore: The Johns Hopkins University Press.

Myrdal, Gunnar. 1957. *Economic Theory and the Underdeveloped Regions.* London: Duckworth.

Naim, Moisés. 1993. "Latin America: Post-Adjustment Blues." *Foreign Policy* 92 (Fall): 133-150.

O'Donnell, Guillermo. 1994. "The State, Democratization, and Some Conceptual Problems (A Latin American View with Glances at Some Post-Communist Countries)." In *Latin American Political Economy in the Age of Neoliberal Reform*, eds. William C. Smith, Carlos H. Acuña, and Eduardo A. Gamarra. Coral Gables, Fla.: University of Miami North-South Center.

O'Donnell, Guillermo. 1973. *Modernization and Bureaucratic-Authoritarianism: Studies in South American Politics.* Berkeley, Calif.: Institute of International Studies.

Olson, Mancur. 1982. *The Rise and Decline of Nations. Economic Growth, Stagflation and Social Rigidities.* New Haven, Conn.: Yale University Press.

Oman, Charles P., and Ganeshan Wignaraja. 1991. *The Postwar Evolution of Development Thinking.* New York: St. Martin's Press.

Porter, Michael. 1990. *The Competitive Advantage of Nations.* New York: The Free Press.

Porter, Michael. 1985. *Competitive Advantage: Creating and Sustaining Superior Performance.* New York: The Free Press.

Portes, Alejandro. 1985. "Latin American Class Structures: Their Composition and Change during the Last Decades." *Latin American Research Review* 20 (3): 7-40.

Prebisch, Raúl. 1959. "Commercial Policy in Underdeveloped Countries." *American Economic Review: Papers and Proceedings* 49 (2): 251-273.

Prebisch, Raúl. 1950. *The Economic Development of Latin America and Its Principal Problems.* New York: United Nations.

Programa de Economía del Trabajo. 1992. *Series de indicadores económico sociales. Series anuales 1960-1991.* Santiago de Chile: Programa de Economía del Trabajo.

Przeworski, Adam. 1993. "Economic Reforms, Public Opinion, and Political Institutions: Poland in the Eastern European Perspective." In *Economic Reforms in New Democracies*, eds. Luiz Carlos Bresser Pereira, José María Maravall, and Adam Przeworski. Cambridge: Cambridge University Press.

Remmer, Karen L. 1993. "The Political Economy of Elections in Latin America, 1980-1991." *American Political Science Review* 87 (2): 393-407.

Rostow, W.W. 1960. *The Stages of Economic Growth: A Non-Communist Manifesto.* Cambridge: Cambridge University Press.

Schumpeter, Joseph A. 1942. *Capitalism, Socialism and Democracy.* New York: Harper & Row.

Schumpeter, Joseph A. 1934. *The Theory of Economic Development.* Cambridge, Mass.: Harvard University Press.

Scott, James C. 1990. *Domination and the Arts of Resistance: Hidden Transcripts.* New Haven, Conn.: Yale University Press.

Singer, Hans. 1950. "Distribution of Gains Between Investing and Borrowing Countries." *American Economic Review* 40: 473-485.

Taylor, Peter J. 1985. *Political Geography: World Economy, Nation-State and Locality.* London: Longman.

Tironi, Eugenio, and Ricardo A. Lagos. 1991. "The Social Actors and Structural Adjustments." *CEPAL Review* 44: 35-50.

U.S. Department of Labor (Bureau of Labor Statistics). 1992. *International Comparisons of Hourly Compensation Costs for Production Workers in Manufacturing, 1991.* Washington, D.C.: U.S. Department of Labor.

Vacs, Aldo C. 1994. "Convergence and Dissension: Democracy, Markets, and Structural Reform in World Perspective." In *Latin American Political Economy in the Age of Neoliberal Reform*, eds. William C. Smith, Carlos H. Acuña, and Eduardo A. Gamarra. Coral Gables, Fla.: University of Miami North-South Center.

Vernon, Raymond. 1979. "The Product Cycle Hypothesis in a New International Environment." *Oxford Bulletin of Economics and Statistics* 41: 255-267.

Wade, Robert. 1990. *Governing the Market: Economic Theory and the Role of Government in East Asian Industrialization.* Princeton, N.J.: Princeton University Press.

Wade, Robert, and Gordon White. 1984. "Developmental States in East Asia: Capitalist and Socialist." *Institute of Development Studies Bulletin* 15: 1-70.

Wallerstein, Immanuel. 1983. *Historical Capitalism.* London: Verso.

Whitehead, Laurence. 1989. "Tigers in Latin America?" *The Annals* 505: 142-151.

Williamson, John. 1990. *Latin American Adjustment: How Much Has Happened?* Washington, D.C.: Institute for International Economics.

World Bank. 1987. *World Development Report 1987.* New York: Oxford University Press.

World Bank. 1991. *World Development Report 1991.* New York: Oxford University Press.

World Bank. 1993a. *Social Indicators of Development 1993.* Baltimore: The Johns Hopkins University Press.

World Bank. 1993b. *World Development Report 1993.* New York: Oxford University Press.

World Bank. 1993c. *World Tables 1993.* Baltimore: The Johns Hopkins University Press.

World Bank. 1996. *World Development Report 1996.* New York: Oxford University Press.

Zermeño, Sergio. 1993. "La derrota de la sociedad." *Revista Mexicana de Sociología* 2.

Index

G

H

R

W

Y

Z

Production
Notes

This book was printed on 60 lb. Glatfelter, Natural, text stock with a 10 point CIS cover stock.

The text and index of this volume, designed by Susan Kay Holler, were set in Garamond at the North-South Center Press, using Aldus PageMaker 6.0, on a Power Macintosh 8500/120 computer.

The cover was created by Mary M. Mapes using QuarkXpress 3.32.

The book was edited by Jayne M. Weisblatt and Kathleen A. Hamman.

This publication was printed by Edwards Brothers, Inc. of Lillington, North Carolina, USA.